THE TRANSCRIPTION SPECIALIST

A Text - Workbook

THE TRANSCRIPTION SPECIALIST

A Text - Workbook

EDITH E. ENNIS
University of Iowa

MARILYN E. PRICE
Kirkwood Community College

SHEILA K. VEDDER
University of Iowa

HARCOURT BRACE JOVANOVICH, INC.

New York   San Diego   Chicago   San Francisco   Atlanta
London   Sydney   Toronto

Requests for permission to make copies of any part of the work should
be mailed to Permissions, Harcourt Brace Jovanovich, Inc., 757 Third
Avenue, New York, NY 10017.

Printed in the United States of America

Library of Congress Catalog Card Number: 81-50524

ISBN: 0-15-592348-X

ILLUSTRATION CREDITS

Page 12:	(top left) Courtesy of QYX Division of Exxon Enterprises, Inc.
	(top right) Courtesy of IBM Office Products Division
	(bottom) Courtesy of Wang Laboratories, Inc.
Pages 14, 16:	Courtesy of Dictaphone Corporation
Page 17:	(left) Courtesy of Lanier Business Products, Inc.
Pages 17 (right), 27:	Courtesy of IBM Office Products Division
Page 53:	Courtesy of Lanier Business Products Division
Pages 66, 88:	Courtesy of Olivetti, Inc.
Page 96:	Yvonne Gerin

PREFACE

By most measures of time, word processing is a relatively new concept and machine transcription, the very heart of the modern word processing center, is a relatively new profession. From the outset, the demand for efficient, competent personnel, trained in and equipped with the essential skills, has grown steadily and impressively. Today's employment outlook for the transcription specialist is, therefore, bright with challenge and reward.

The Transcription Specialist: A Text-Workbook has been designed to provide you with the intensive skill development and extensive review needed to prepare you to step into positions in any office where written communications are processed. As you assume these positions, you will find that the business world has certain expectations. At all times, employers will demand the production of mailable documents and require that work be processed with the utmost efficiency by skilled and cooperative personnel. In keeping with these real-world requirements, we have focused throughout on the concepts of mailability, cost efficiency, professionalism, and decision making.

The Transcription Specialist uses a systems approach to machine transcription by providing background and training in the seven elements of transcription skill: knowledge of equipment, listening, professional development, proofreading, keyboarding (typing), formatting techniques, and English grammar and usage. Each of these elements is taught and practiced intensively and extensively by means of a wide variety of text and tape exercises. In order to provide immediate feedback, we have included in the Appendix complete answer keys for all the exercises, as well as self-checking supplementary practice drills designed to reinforce instruction and previous practice in a wide range of English skills.

The text-workbook is organized in phases, corresponding to the five components of the transcription process:

Phase I offers a detailed introduction to machine transcription, focusing on its role in today's office, its relationship to word processing procedures, and the equipment used in the transcription process.

Phase II emphasizes the importance of cultivating positive, professional job attitudes and awareness of cost consciousness. This phase provides the training in listening, decision making, and proofreading skills necessary to establish criteria for evaluating and producing error-free copy.

Phase III offers a comprehensive review and reinforcement of all the typing skills needed by the transcription specialist, with particular emphasis on style and formatting decisions.

Phase IV surveys and summarizes all the English skills used in machine transcription and includes a wide range of pretests, posttests, self-check exercises, and supplementary drills for skill development and ongoing proficiency evaluation.

Phase V is a real-world office simulation, in which you assume the role of a transcription specialist trainee working in a simulated word processing center at a wide variety of actual transcription tasks for a large number of firms and originators.

Each of the five phases is introduced by a Student Tally Sheet designed to guide you as you work through the activities of the phase, help you establish personal professional phase goals, and enable both you and your instructor to evaluate your progress regularly. Within the phase, each step in the learning process is explained in detail, illustrated with examples, and reinforced by practice activities that progress logically from easy to difficult and from the simple to the complex. Because precise mastery goals follow the tally sheet at the outset of the phase, you will know exactly what you are expected to do and how to do it at every step in the course.

In *The Transcription Specialist: A Text-Workbook*, a wealth of exercises, applications, and self-evaluations illustrate, supplement, and verify mastery of related yet distinct skills, culminating in the ability to work in realistic office settings. Throughout the text you will find explicit, clearly stated skill objectives, combined with numerous review and reinforcement drills, pretests, posttests, skill evaluations, and supplementary practice. All these activities are integrated and directed in such a way that the text-workbook can be used either for self-paced learning or in the traditional classroom environment.

The illustration program is yet another aid in fostering comprehension and facilitating learning. A Mailability Analysis Chart is provided to enable you to check a completed document and verify its acceptability. Other charts summarize and itemize information, and ''reminders'' appear frequently to highlight and set off key points. Photographs and schematic drawings display and differentiate transcription equipment and explain and clarify job activities. In the Phase V office simulation, office-style Job Instruction Sheets guide you in the completion of machine transcription assignments for the 18 firms for which you will work.

A special feature of *The Transcription Specialist* is the Tape Program, which offers intensive progressive machine transcription from cassette tapes for four of the phases: Phase I (transcription orientation tape); Phase II (listening tape); Phase IV (English skills tapes); and Phase V (office simulation tapes). The Phase V tape activities—the capstone of the course—integrate and incorporate all the previously mastered skills and apply them to a comprehensive range of office-style materials taken from the files of 18 actual business firms. More than 170 graded transcription items are included, representing various levels of difficulty, from simple, precisely dictated material—requiring little or no decision making—to complex, unguided dictation—which challenges you to make a substantial number of major style and formatting decisions.

We hope and expect that *The Transcription Specialist* will not only be a meaningful vocational experience but an enjoyable one as well. After you have completed the course, the book should continue to serve you and your co-workers as a ready-reference manual of acceptable transcription skills, as a means of reviewing, reinforcing, and updating previous instruction, and as a guide in on-the-job training programs.

The Transcription Specialist: A Text-Workbook is the product of the labors of many people in many places. We are especially grateful to:

•Our colleagues and students at the University of Iowa and Kirkwood Community College for their cooperation, suggestions, and support.

•Professors Rosemarie McCauley, Montclair State College; Patricia A. Parzych, Hostos Community College; Adele Stock, Normandale Community College; and Sue Trautwein, Linn-Benton Community College, for their thoroughgoing and constructive critiques of the manuscript.

•The staff at Harcourt Brace Jovanovich, Publishers: Alice F. Gallagher, Director, Division of Business and Office Education; our editors, Harold S. Pollock and Robert Henry, who refined the manuscript and made us keep to our schedule, and particularly Dennis L. Gladhill, whose faith, foresight, and determination made this book a reality; and the production team of Tracy K. Cabanis, Helen Faye, Harry W. Rinehart, Robert Winsor, and Paul Agresti, who, with care and professionalism, shepherded our typescript through all stages of design, composition, and production.

•Last—but far from least—our unfailingly patient families and friends, who have been throughout a source of unending understanding and selfless encouragement.

Edith E. Ennis
Marilyn E. Price
Sheila K. Vedder

CONTENTS

LIST OF FIGURES

PHASE III: STYLE AND FORMATTING DECISIONS

PHASE V: YOU'RE EMPLOYED!

THE TRANSCRIPTION SPECIALIST

A Text - Workbook

STUDENT'S TALLY SHEET/PHASE I

Name _____

Target Completion Date _____

STUDENT'S ACTIVITY	DATE COMPLETED	STUDENT'S QUESTIONS AND COMMENTS
STUDY **Introduction to Phase I**		
STUDY **Phase I**		
DO Exercise I.1		
DO Exercise I.2 (tape)		

PERSONAL GOALS FOR PHASE I

1. EXAMPLE: *Increase understanding of word processing concept.*
2. _____
3. _____
4. _____

INSTRUCTOR'S COMMENTS:_____

_____

_____

PHASE I

PHASE I

THE TRANSCRIPTION PROCESS

INTRODUCTION

HAVE YOU EVER THOUGHT about the vital role written communication plays in our world? Think about the ways *you* have communicated in writing both in your academic and in your personal life. During your first years in school, you wrote simple answers to questions and composed short stories. Later, you used written communication in additional ways—writing themes and responding to test questions, for example.

In your personal life, written communication has always been important. When you were born, a birth certificate was filled out recording that fact. Over the years, you've written letters to friends and relatives and jotted down notes to family and classmates. When applying for jobs, you filled out forms requesting various types of information.

Can you imagine what life would be like without written communication? How would you complete your school work? How would you communicate with that distant pen pal? How would you apply for a driver's license or fill out Social Security forms? How could you compose a poem or a jingle?

So it is in the world of business. Business simply cannot survive without written communication. The written word is vital to its every operation.

Phase I is designed to provide you with information regarding the written word and its relationship to the transcription process.

4

After completing Phase I, you will

- Recognize the reasons for the increasing importance of written communication in business.

- Understand how businesses are affected by the quality of their written communication systems.

- Know the types of internal and external documents that are part of a communication system.

- Understand the importance of word processing in the communication system of a business.

- Evaluate the various methods used by executives in originating documents.

- Appreciate the important role that transcriptionists play in the communication process and be aware of the excellent employment opportunities for skilled transcriptionists.

- Know the various types of dictating and transcribing equipment.

- Be able to use transcribing equipment.

WHAT THE TRANSCRIPTIONIST DOES

As a transcriptionist, your function in your company's written communication system will be to serve as the channel through which the dictator's spoken word is translated into written form (Figure I.1).

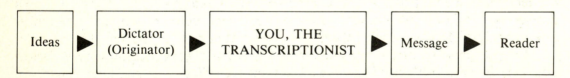

Figure I.1 Your Position in the Transcription Process

As you process written communications, your *accuracy* will determine whether a particular message is transmitted as the dictator intended. Your *transcription speed* will determine how promptly the originator (dictator) can relay the message or information to its receiver. Therefore, your transcription skill will either aid or hinder the dictator and, in turn, affect the total operation of the organization. A business functions effectively and reflects a good image to the outside world only when its documents are sent out error-free and with dispatch.

5

Office administrators and business executives recognize the importance of the transcriptionist in the communication process. Frequently, transcriptionists still find it difficult to appreciate their importance in this key role. Therefore, one of the goals of this text-workbook is to make you aware of the value of your contribution to the organization for which and in which you will work.

SEVEN SKILLS OF THE TRANSCRIPTION SPECIALIST

Machine transcription may be defined simply as the process of transforming the spoken word into usable (mailable) form. You should be familiar with the seven skills needed by the transcriptionist:

1. **Know your equipment.** A thorough knowledge of the equipment you are using requires careful study of the operator's manual. You will find a discussion of equipment in the latter part of this phase.
2. **Learn to listen.** The ability to listen and to translate what is heard into correct written form will be discussed in Phase II. Listening exercises to help you develop this skill accompany the text discussion.
3. **Develop a professional attitude.** An awareness program for dictation etiquette and techniques for developing effective transcription attitudes are found in Phase II.
4. **Proofread carefully.** Error correction—the ability to *locate* and *correct* errors in context (meaning) as well as typographical and spelling errors—is discussed in Phase II. Proofreading exercises accompany this discussion. Proofreader's marks are located on the inside front cover.
5. **Maintain superior typing (keyboarding) skills.** Good *speed* and *accuracy* in producing typewritten material is the cornerstone of the transcriptionist's success. Phase II includes a review of correct typewriting techniques.
6. **Develop good judgment in formatting.** Making decisions on such formatting problems as paragraphing, spacing, and style requires good judgment. You will find some helpful suggestions in Phase III.
7. **Utilize correct English skills.** A knowledge of spelling, punctuation, grammar, numbers, and word division rules is essential to success in your work. The exercises on English skills in Phase IV will serve as a good review in this area.

The transcription specialist must develop and maintain a high level of proficiency in each of these skills. All seven are vital to the transcription process.

WRITTEN COMMUNICATION IN BUSINESS

Both the transcriptionist and the originator must work together in producing written business communications. These communications fall into two classifications: internal and external. *Internal* communication refers to information transmitted *within* the organization—memos, reports, directives, and policy statements.

External communication refers to communications sent *outside* the company. The most common forms of external communication are letters, statistical reports, minutes of meetings, and proposals.

A business must develop an efficient communication system. Depending on its effectiveness, this system can have a positive or a negative influence, both internally and externally.

An efficient system of communication is one in which information is processed correctly, confidentially, tactfully, and promptly at MINIMUM EFFORT AND COST. Such a system builds internal efficiency, projects a good company image, and provides better service to the public.

An inefficient system of communication is one in which there is a lack of effective procedures, an absence or misuse of equipment, or poorly trained personnel. A communication system with any or all of these characteristics will produce inaccurate records of transactions or cause delay in transmitting messages. Such a system impairs internal efficiency and detracts from a good company image. In addition, wasted or ineffective communication situations can cut severely into profits and even lead to a business failure.

An example of the tremendous importance of communication in business is illustrated by this information: "At least 85 percent of business is conducted either completely or partially by mail. The more than 30 billion first-class letters mailed annually in the United States alone attest to the importance of written communication."[1]

These 30 billion-plus letters serve business in a number of ways. They

1. Provide information.
2. Serve as permanent records of a business transaction.
3. Help sell products.
4. Substitute for personal visits.
5. Substitute for telephone calls.
6. Provide services to customers.

All the evidence indicates that, for the foreseeable future, written communication will continue to be vital to the business world. We are living through nothing less than an information explosion, characterized by a need for accurate and usable information that is available within a matter of minutes.

WORD PROCESSING

The information explosion responsible for the vast increase in written communication in recent years has, in turn, been partly responsible for rising communication costs. In response, business has been forced to find faster and more efficient ways to produce documents. Many firms have done so through word processing—a concept conceived during the middle 1960's. Word processing has been defined as "The method of producing written communication at top speed, with the greatest accuracy, the least

[1]Isabelle A. Krey and Bernadette V. Metzler. *Principles and Techniques of Effective Business Communication.* New York: Harcourt Brace Jovanovich, 1976, p. 9.

effort, and the lowest possible cost through the combined use of proper procedures, automated equipment, and trained personnel."[2]

The "trained personnel" in this definition is the transcriptionist, who processes the spoken word into appropriate written form either from machine dictation or from dictation which has been recorded in written or machine shorthand.

The "automated equipment" used by the transcriptionist usually centers around text-editing typewriters capable of printing at extremely high speeds. These typewriters are commonly combined with various types of dictating and transcribing equipment at a secretarial work station.

Word processing is continually affected by changes in machine technology. Just a few short years ago, for example, a "new" piece of equipment was capable of storing one page of typed material and printing out that material at 150 words per minute. Today there are machines that are capable of storing 50 or more pages of typed material and printing out that material at over 1,500 words per minute.

Not too long ago, every person who dictated had to have access to a rather bulky dictating machine and had to deliver the recorded material directly to the transcriptionist. Today an originator (dictator) at a distant location may use a telephone wired directly to the transcriptionist's work station, where automated equipment records the material instantaneously.

Virtually all the new technology associated with transcribing affects one of three factors: (1) method and machinery used for dictating, (2) method and machinery used for transcribing, (3) method and machinery used for keyboarding (typing). The variety of available equipment is immense, both in the number of manufacturers and in machine capability. Even greater diversity can be expected in the future. As a professional transcriptionist, you should keep aware of changing technology so that you can make knowledgeable recommendations about improving efficiency or replacing out-of-date equipment.

Procedures, unlike technology, are often controlled by people in a job situation. Although procedures vary, the task of using equipment most efficiently rests with the organizational skills of the equipment operator—the dictator or the transcriptionist.

Like operating procedures, transcription skills are also under the control of individuals involved in the production of the written word. A perceptive transcriptionist will realize that mastery of English skills, good typewriting ability, good judgment, and decision-making ability form the foundation of the transcription process and, thus, are the responsibility of every person in a word processing setting.

To sum up, knowledge of the procedures and possession of the basic skills needed by the transcriptionist provide the basis of the transcription process. A person equipped with this knowledge and these skills will have little difficulty applying them to new technology.

Word Processing Centers

In many organizations, the typing and transcription functions are centralized in what are known as *word processing centers* that house modern typewriting and transcribing equipment. The degree to which time and money can be saved through the operation of a center depends to a great extent on the ability of the company to hire well-trained transcriptionists, as well as other staff members.

[2]John B. Dykeman. "Word Processing, the New Approach to Internal Profit." *Modern Office Procedures*, August, 1972, Vol. 17, No. 8, p. 36.

The manager of the center should have supervisory experience, as well as a special talent for working with personnel throughout the department or company. In addition, the manager must be cost-conscious and committed to an operation that produces quality documents in the shortest time.

A center may employ as few as 3 or as many as 100 or more transcriptionists to operate transcribing and text-editing equipment. Their titles may vary from *correspondence secretary* to *transcription specialist* or *typewriting specialist*.

To complement the word processing center, a firm may employ *administrative secretaries* who perform nontyping duties and work under supervision, using standardized procedures. Responsibilities may include reception duties, handling reprographics, mailing functions, records management, record keeping, conducting research, letter composition and dictation, and decision making. In certain situations, an administrative secretary may do emergency or confidential typing.

Employment Opportunities in Word Processing.   With the increasing number of word processing centers and the resulting growth in machine dictation, transcriptionists are very much in demand today. To attract qualified personnel, many firms are establishing career paths. Thus, an able new employee may assume an entry-level position and, with a good performance record and good interpersonal skills, may progress in time to a supervisory position. Figure I.2 shows a typical career path for a correspondence secretary. The types of duties in each position vary with the different levels of responsibilities. For a complete description of each position, turn to the Office Manual in Phase V.

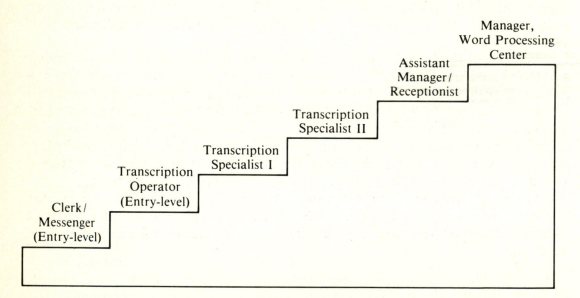

Figure I.2 Typical Career Path for a Correspondence Secretary (Transcription Specialist)

Word processing also has enlarged the employment opportunities for persons with physical disabilities—especially the blind. From employer reports, persons with impaired vision have proven to be superior transcriptionists.

One example of an employer with strong feelings about hiring the handicapped is the U.S. Army. According to Joyce Hubbs of the Academy of Health Sciences, "Handicapped operators in my word processing center have increased productivity, im-

proved morale, and been invaluable to the total operation.''[3] Supervisors cite several reasons for the expertise of handicapped employees; namely, that a blind operator will generally have better hearing than the average person—a distinct advantage in transcribing—and that deaf typists have faster keyboarding speed because of their greater powers of concentration. Dottie Carter, supervisor for the U.S. Army Surgeon General's Office, further documents the feeling about hiring the handicapped: "I'd hire the handicapped, no matter what their disability. . . . they'd be my best workers."[4]

Employment opportunities for transcriptionists are excellent. There is a great demand for transcriptionists in word processing centers, as well as a demand for persons who will use their transcribing skills in traditional secretarial positions.

HOW DOES AN EXECUTIVE ORIGINATE DOCUMENTS?

There are a number of ways in which an executive can originate a document—whether internal or external, whether dictated into a word processing center or to a secretary in a conventional office environment. Some of the methods of input you are likely to encounter on the job are: longhand, rough draft, dictation to a secretary directly at the typewriter, dictation to a secretary who takes written or machine shorthand, and dictation into a machine.

1. **Longhand.** Many originators simply write out messages by hand and give them to their secretaries for transcription. The main advantage of this method is that it is easy for the originator, who merely reaches for a pencil and a piece of paper and proceeds to write.

   Because the average person writes longhand at the rate of only 15 words a minute, one of the main disadvantages of this method is that it is slow and, therefore, costly. Another drawback lies in the difficulty the transcriptionist may have in deciphering the handwriting; the result is a slow transcription rate and still higher costs.

2. **Rough draft.** At the typewriter, the originator "roughs out" the material to be processed, with little regard to questions of format. Such material may also contain some handwritten additions or corrections.

   Although rough-draft copy is easier for the typist to read than longhand, the process is time-consuming for the person originating the document and, therefore, costly on a per-hour basis.

3. **Dictation at the typewriter.** The originator dictates to a secretary seated at a typewriter. Direct dictation provides an opportunity to give instructions, clarify content, and discuss any unresolved aspects of the document.

   Although this means of creating correspondence may be convenient for the dictator, it is inefficient for the reasons that the time of two persons is involved and that the dictator must wait for the secretary to make corrections and revisions.

[3]Paula Hantman. "Physically Handicapped Are Great Word Processors." *The Office*, November, 1977, Vol. 86, No. 5, p. 44.
[4]Ibid., p. 58.

4. **Dictation to a secretary taking shorthand.** This method provides an alternative for the originator whose secretary is skilled in either written or machine shorthand. It gives the participants the opportunity of working on a one-to-one basis and allows time for questions and consultation between the dictator and secretary.

   The main disadvantage is that, as with dictation at the typewriter, this method involves tying up the time of two persons during the dictating phase.

   Though this type of input is twice as fast as longhand, the originator still averages only about 30 words per minute.

5. **Machine dictation.** The dictator originates documents by using one of the several types of dictating equipment:
   a. A small portable unit
   b. A desk-top unit to which a microphone is attached
   c. A telephone specially wired to a centralized recording system
   d. A receiver that looks like a telephone and which is linked to an endless loop dictation system—either in the immediate office area or in a centralized recording system in a word processing center.[5]

   In terms of not only the originator's time but also the total cost of producing documents, machine dictation is the most efficient method of input. Studies show that a dictator can record at an average rate of 60 words a minute as opposed to 15–30 words a minute for the other methods. Still another advantage is the fact that the secretary transcribes from the spoken word and does not have to decipher longhand or shorthand notes.

   As with other methods of creating documents, machine dictation has its own disadvantages. Some originators tend to pronounce their words carelessly; others fail to give adequate instructions. This indifference increases transcription time and, therefore, raises the cost of producing communication. Finally, the originator must have access to equipment in order to dictate, which may require an additional purchase.

The typical executive in today's fast-moving world may use any one or all of the input methods we've discussed in this section, so it is to your advantage to develop and maintain a high level of skill in both shorthand and machine transcription.

OFFICE SETTINGS FOR MACHINE TRANSCRIPTION

In any working situation, you may be using a variety of transcribing machines in a variety of settings. Some widely used office settings for machine transcription are illustrated in Figure I.3 and are described below.

1. You may be working on a one-to-one basis with your employer, who dictates into a machine that uses magnetic belts, cassette tapes, or magnetic discs. These belts, tapes, or discs are frequently referred to as *discrete media* because the people involved in the process must physically handle the item on which the

---

[5]The endless loop system is described later in this phase.

recording was made—belt, tape, or disc. In this work situation, you will have the transcribing (or decoding) unit at your desk. The recording will be routed to you and you will transcribe from it.

Your employer may also dictate into an endless loop dictation system, in which documents are dictated onto and transcribed from a continuous magnetic tape in the form of a loop. Both the dictator's and transcriptionist's units are linked to the continuous tape (see Figure I.4).

Figure I.3   Office Settings for Machine Transcription

Working on a one-to-one basis

A mini word processing center

A large centralized word processing center

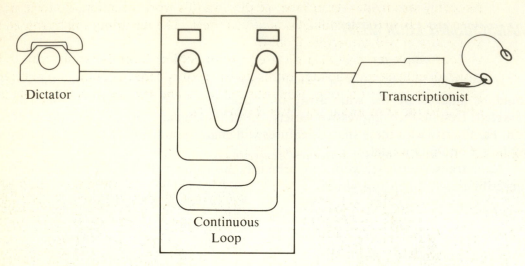

Figure I.4   A Simple Diagram of an Endless Loop System

2. You may be employed in a centralized word processing center—an installation equipped with modern text-editing typewriters and multiple recording and transcribing units. Ordinarily the word processing center is available to dictators throughout an organization.

   Dictation (input) may be submitted in one of two ways: (1) tapes, belts, or discs are delivered to the center; or (2) telephones are so wired that the originator can pick up the receiver, dial a designated number, and proceed to dictate. As he or she speaks, the dictation is recorded on the equipment in the word processing center. Special dialing instructions are provided that permit the dictator to back up and review the dictation, to make revisions, or to give special instructions.

   The transcriptionist at the word processing center removes the recorded tape, disc, or belt from the recording unit; inserts it into the transcribing unit; listens to the dictation; and transcribes the material. In the case of an endless loop system, the transcriptionist, having nothing to handle, merely connects with the system and transcribes.

   Occasionally, centralized word processing centers employ stenographers for use on those occasions when an originator prefers dictating to a "live" stenographer to talking into a machine.

3. You may be working in a "mini" word processing center located in a firm that prefers to maintain small, separate departmental word processing installations. The primary reasons for this arrangement are:

   a. Because departments may be located at some distance from each other, a centralized system might be less accessible and, therefore, cost more to maintain.

   b. The nature of the material to be transcribed may necessitate a close working relationship between the originator and the transcriptionist. For example, many highly technical reports require frequent explanations and verification as they are transcribed. Stationing the originator and the transcriptionist within easy access of each other makes possible better utilization of time and facilitates face-to-face communication.

Regardless of the office setting, you—the transcriptionist—will be responsible for developing superior communication skills.

TRANSCRIBING EQUIPMENT

If you were to visit one of today's modern office equipment showrooms, you would be amazed by the wide array of transcribing and dictating machines being marketed. Despite their impressive variety, all of these machines have features in common. Familiarity with these shared features will enable you to adapt your skill easily to any brand and any model.

As a transcriptionist, you will primarily be using two items of equipment: a transcribing unit and a typewriter.

The Transcribing Unit

The transcribing unit has three components:
1. The *central transcribing unit*, which holds the belt, cassette tape, or disc and permits the operator to regulate the tone, volume, and speed of the dictation.
2. The *headset*, which enables the transcriptionist to listen to the dictation.
3. The *foot pedal*, which allows the operator to pace the dictation and to back up for review of the dictation when necessary.

An illustration of a traditional transcribing unit is shown in Figure I.5. Your instructor will provide you with manuals or detailed instructions for operating your particular transcribing unit.

Figure I.5 Typical Transcribing Unit

In an endless loop system, the small transcribing unit contains no media, such as a tape or belt, but is wired instead to the continuous loop, which is encased in a special unit that may be located at some distance from both the dictator and transcriptionist. An indicator light on the transcribing unit signals the operator that dictation is waiting to be transcribed. (Refer to Figure I.4, the diagram of the endless loop system.)

The Text-Editing Typewriter

Both standard and text-editing typewriters are used in transcribing dictation. Here is how the text-editing typewriter is used:

1. The operator types (keyboards) a message, which is automatically recorded on a magnetic card, cassette tape, magnetic disc, or in an electronic memory. To actuate the record mode, the operator keyboards the instruction on the typewriter.
2. Depending on the type of equipment used, the message may be recorded on paper or on a visual display screen (see Figure I.6).
3. To correct an error, the operator (a) backspaces and types over the error or (b) depresses a key that will delete the copy and then retypes the material.
4. To move words, lines, or paragraphs, the operator simply keyboards the instruction.
5. On some machines, margins are automatically set and can even be justified.

Modern technology is rapidly expanding and improving many of these distinctive features.

After the copy is in final, correct form, the operator puts the machine in print mode—again, by keyboarding the instruction. The document is then printed out at a rate of 150 to 1,500 or more words per minute, depending on machine capability. The copy may be printed out either on the same machine on which it was originally typed or on a separate printer linked to the keyboarding unit.

Figure I.6 A Text-Editing Typewriter with Visual Screen

There are many advantages to using text-editing equipment, especially (1) the tremendous speed with which documents may be produced, (2) the accuracy with which copy is printed, and (3) the storage capability of the memory.

One of many instances in which text-editing equipment may be a great advantage is in the processing of form letters. Let's say that you are asked to produce a letter that is to go out to 100 customers 4 times a year. Using modern equipment, your procedure might be something like this:

1. You transcribe (keyboard) the letter on your typewriting unit. As you type, your copy appears on a visual screen and is simultaneously recorded on a magnetic disc.
2. After completing the keyboarding, proofreading, and correcting, you type instructions to file away the letter on the disc for permanent storage. Once the copy has been carefully proofread in the input stage, there is no need to proofread again.
3. You then proceed to keyboard the names and addresses of 100 customers and also store that information.
4. When the time arrives for you to type the letters, you simply "retrieve" the letter—bringing it out on your screen and keyboarding an instruction to print one copy to each of the 100 customers.

   In a highly sophisticated system, you load letterhead paper and envelopes in a separate unit that feeds automatically into the printer. Thus, having given instructions for the letter to be printed, you need not handle the paper after the initial loading.

This production sequence need take only a matter of minutes. Contrast it with a procedure requiring you to type, proofread, and correct 100 individual letters and envelopes!

Modern machine technology is full of exciting changes. Thanks to constant improvement in equipment and steady refinement in procedures, today's business world has been able to cut dramatically the cost of written communication. To take one example, while the cost of turning out a single business letter once ran as high as $6, that expense has been cut to well under $1 today. As a trained transcriptionist, you will become part of this world of change and challenge, bringing to it specialized skills and personal qualities of your own that will help cut costs even further.

Dictating Equipment

Standard dictating equipment has two components:
1. The *central dictating unit*, which holds the belt, cassette, or disc.
2. The *microphone*, which allows the originator to record the message. Many executives find it convenient to use a small portable dictating unit equipped with a built-in microphone.

During the dictation process, the originator is able to back up the tape or belt to review what has already been said. In addition, the originator can dictate any special instructions needed by the transcriptionist. A typical dictating unit is illustrated in Figure I.7.

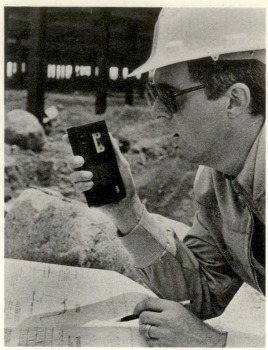

Figure I.7   Typical Dictating Units

When necessary to give special instructions to the transcriptionist, the dictator can use a visual device often referred to as an *indicator slip* (Figure I.8)—or an audio device—sometimes referred to as an *electronic cue*. These are used for two purposes:

1. To give the transcriptionist clues to the length of the letter. After dictating each item, the dictator depresses a lever or button on the microphone; this action leaves a small mark on the indicator slip or records an electronic cue on the tape.

2. To put the transcriptionist on notice that special instructions are provided for the dictation. Again, the dictator depresses a lever which leaves a mark on the indicator slip or records an electronic cue. An example of a special instruction might be: ''Transcriptionist, please add this 'PS' to the letter to Grace Hiler: 'I plan to be in Springfield the 10th of June and hope to see you.' ''

Make sure you understand all the characteristics and capabilities of your dictating equipment. Only then will you be able to produce quality documents in minimum time.

NO.	DATE	DICTATOR		FROM	ON

0 • 10 • 20 • 30 • 40 • 50 • 60 • 70 • 80 • 90 • 100 • 110 • 120 •

Figure I.8   Diagram of an Indicator Slip for a Transcribing Unit

THE TRANSCRIPTION PROCEDURE

As you take your first steps in your new profession as a transcription specialist, follow these procedures:

1. *Listen to the dictation in thought phrases.* During the first few weeks of the course, depress the foot pedal, *listen to five or six words only*, release the foot pedal, and transcribe.

    As you improve your thought-carrying ability, you will find yourself able to listen to longer phrases and to transcribe on a continuing basis, rather than in a stop-start pattern. (See Figure I.9.)

BEGINNING TRANSCRIPTION TECHNIQUE

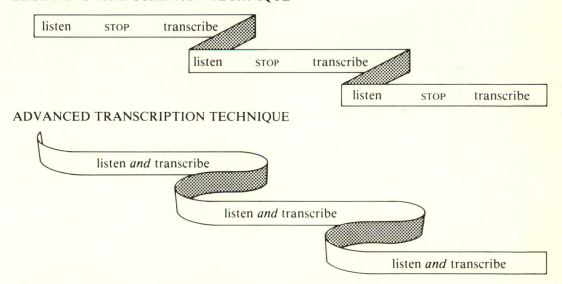

ADVANCED TRANSCRIPTION TECHNIQUE

Figure I.9   The Transcription Skill-Building Process

2. *Review all special instructions before transcribing.* The originator may give instructions by
    a. Marking them on a indicator slip or providing an electronic cue.
    b. Writing them on a separate sheet of paper.
    c. Phoning them in.
    d. Giving them verbally (face to face).
3. *Check with your supervisor or the originator if the dictation is unclear.* Indicate—in a courteous manner—that you need clarification before you can continue transcribing. A note or a telephone call may be appropriate.
4. *Ask your dictator to identify the type of document in the preliminary instructions.*

Whatever the reason for the communication, you will find your task easier if you request specific information.

The assignments that follow are designed to help you review and summarize the introduction to transcription presented in Phase I. They will also provide orientation in your use of transcribing equipment.

Name_____ Date_____

EXERCISE I.1: PHASE I WORKSHEET

INSTRUCTIONS: Write your answers to the following questions relating to the goals of Phase I. If you are in doubt about any answer, consult your text-workbook.

CHECK YOURSELF

1. Why is the transcriptionist important to the communication process?

_____

_____

_____

_____

2. Why is there an increasing need for transcriptionists today?

_____

_____

_____

3. Explain how a business is positively affected by having an efficient communication system.

_____

_____

_____

4. List two examples of internal communication and two examples of external communication.

   a. Internal: _____

   b. External: _____

5. Identify the seven skills of the transcription specialist.

   a. _____ e. _____

   b. _____ f. _____

   c. _____ g. _____

   d. _____

6. Contrast the office setting of a transcriptionist working in a word processing center with that of a transcriptionist employed in a traditional secretarial position.

_____

_____

_____

_____

_____

7. Identify one advantage and one disadvantage of each of the following three methods of originating documents:

    a. Longhand   Advantage: _____

                                   Disadvantage: _____

    b. Shorthand Dictation   Advantage: _____

                                   Disadvantage: _____

    c. Machine Dictation   Advantage: _____

                                   Disadvantage: _____

8. What are the various roles that written communication can play in business?

_____

_____

_____

9. Give your definition of an efficient communication system.

_____

_____

10. Describe the advantages for transcriptionists using the text-editing typewriter.

_____

_____

_____

11. Describe how a dictator communicates special instructions to a transcriptionist.

_____

_____

_____

_____

12. Contrast the duties of an administrative secretary and a correspondence secretary.

_____

_____

_____

_____

INSTRUCTIONS: Check your answers with the Key to Exercise I.1: Phase I Worksheet in Appendix C.

EXERCISE 1.2: TRANSCRIPTION ORIENTATION

You are now ready to listen to the Introductory Tape. The purpose of this tape is to help you become oriented to the following:

APPLY
YOUR SKILLS

1. This text-workbook
2. Your equipment
   NOTE: Before you listen to the tape, ask your instructor to demonstrate the transcribing equipment you will be using.

SUPPLIES AND EQUIPMENT YOU WILL NEED:

1. A copy of the text-workbook
2. A transcribing unit (central unit plus headset and foot pedal)
3. A typewriter
4. Typing paper
5. A pen or pencil

INSTRUCTIONS:

Listen to the tape, transcribing according to the directions given on the tape.

STUDENT'S TALLY SHEET/PHASE II

Name _____

Target Completion Date _____

STUDENT'S ACTIVITY	DATE COMPLETED	STUDENT'S QUESTIONS AND COMMENTS
STUDY **Introduction to Phase II**		
STUDY **Developing Professional Job Attitudes**		
DO Exercise II.1		
STUDY **Attitudes and Cost Efficiency**		
STUDY **Working as a Team**		
DO Exercise II.2		
STUDY **Attitudes: The Basis for Decision Making**		
DO Exercise II.3		
STUDY **Effective Listening**		
DO Exercise II.4 (tape)		
STUDY **Information Sources**		
DO Exercise II.5		
DO Exercise II.6		
STUDY **Proofreading**		
DO Exercise II.7		
DO Exercise II.8		
DO Exercise II.9		
DO Exercise II.10		
DO Exercise II.11		

STUDENT'S ACTIVITY	DATE COMPLETED	STUDENT'S QUESTIONS AND COMMENTS
STUDY **Mailability**		
STUDY **Care of Office Equipment**		

PERSONAL GOALS FOR PHASE II

1. EXAMPLE: *Sharpen my proofreading skills.* _____

2. _____

3. _____

4. _____

INSTRUCTOR'S COMMENTS: _____

_____

_____

PHASE II

PROFESSIONALISM AND TRANSCRIBING EFFICIENCY

INTRODUCTION

YOUR SUCCESS as a transcription specialist in today's office depends upon your technical knowledge, your efficiency, and your attitude toward your work. The level and quality of your professionalism will be evident each day as you interact with your supervisor and co-workers to accomplish individual and organizational goals.

As a participating member of a communications team, your primary goal will be to produce mailable units of information in a positive, efficient manner. Phase II will show you how to achieve that goal.

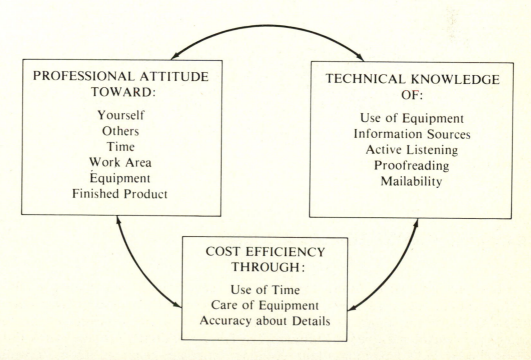

Figure II.1 Your Professional Success

After studying and completing the exercises in Phase II, you will

- Understand the importance of transcription efficiency and cost consciousness.
- See the importance of cultivating a professional attitude.
- Be aware of the originator's and transcriptionist's separate responsibilities.
- Apply positive attitudes in decision making.
- Demonstrate ability to listen effectively.
- Use information sources accurately.
- Demonstrate good proofreading techniques.
- Understand the importance of operating your office equipment with care and safety.

Figure II.2   Professional Employees

DEVELOPING PROFESSIONAL JOB ATTITUDES

Everyone who works develops conscious and unconscious ongoing job attitudes—attitudes about oneself as an employee, about one's supervisor and co-workers, about time and equipment, about the work to be produced. The true professional aims consciously to develop positive job attitudes. The Transcriptionist's Professional Attitude Chart (Figure II.3) makes important recommendations to help you become a professional.

27

As you study the Transcriptionist's Professional Attitude Chart, try to think of specific examples where and when you have been able to display positive attitudes in either a class or job. For example, in the section *My Attitudes About Myself As An Employee*, the first suggestion under *My Job Attitudes* is "Be a dependable worker." The specific example you think of might be to be consistently early for class or work. Ask yourself if you have always been on time; if so, you are displaying a positive professional attitude.

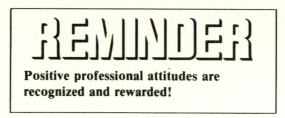

Positive professional attitudes are recognized and rewarded!

Figure II.3   The Transcriptionist's Professional Attitude Chart

---

MY ATTITUDES ABOUT MYSELF AS AN EMPLOYEE

My Personal Attitudes

- Wear appropriate business attire.
- Maintain good health.
- Get sufficient rest.
- Cultivate proper eating habits.
- Strive to eliminate nervous habits.
- Emphasize positive qualities.
- Be enthusiastic.

My Job Attitudes

- Be a dependable worker.
- Aim for accuracy in my work.
- Look for better ways of accomplishing tasks.
- Develop personal interest in my job.
- Cultivate poise in dealing with difficult situations and people.
- Be ready to admit mistakes.
- Accept praise graciously.
- Strive for a feeling of pride in work.

MY ATTITUDES ABOUT MY SUPERVISOR OR ORIGINATOR

- Show respect to everybody with whom I work.
- Adopt the degree of formality followed in the office.
- Keep confidences and confidential information to myself.
- Listen carefully to all instructions.
- Ask any questions needed to clarify.
- Be alert to nonverbal language.
- Consult before making changes.
- Avoid frequent interruptions by grouping questions together.
- Use tact when giving an opinion.
- Voice "concerns," but avoid petty "complaining."
- Accept gracefully any suggestions for change.
- Remain flexible and sensitive to company goals.

MY ATTITUDES ABOUT CO-WORKERS

- Respect co-workers' contributions.
- Be receptive to individual differences.
- Listen to opinions, but remain an independent thinker who evaluates the thinking of others but is not easily swayed.
- Keep busy—share talents by offering to help co-workers.
- Practice sincere courtesy by using "please" and "thank you."
- Eliminate a "know-it-all" impression by listening attentively to suggestions and opinions.
- Avoid unnecessary borrowing of co-workers' supplies.
- Work cooperatively—contribute to the "team" atmosphere.

MY ATTITUDES ABOUT TIME

- Contribute to an efficient, cost-conscious atmosphere by being active and productive.
- Avoid excessive social "chatter."
- Restrict personal phone calls to emergencies.
- Use written reminders to help meet deadlines.
- Set work priorities.
- Develop the ability to move quickly from task to task.
- Look for work during slow periods.
- Concentrate on work.
- Ask: "Can my firm afford my level of productivity?"

MY ATTITUDES ABOUT EQUIPMENT AND WORKPLACE

- Know the capabilities and limitations of office equipment.
- Arrange equipment for efficient use.
- Turn equipment off when not in use.
- Have equipment cleaned and serviced regularly.
- Consult manufacturers' machine operating manuals.
- Store supplies in an accessible location; check and replenish them regularly.
- Avoid wasting supplies.
- Store confidential documents when leaving the work area.
- Maintain a clean, neat workplace.

MY ATTITUDES ABOUT THE FINISHED PRODUCT

- Ask: "Does this work represent my very best effort?"
- Check completed material for "first impression" impact.
- Proofread all materials for context, grammatical accuracy, and typographical errors.
- Consult information sources regularly, as necessary.
- Work for "mailability" the first time.
- Take pride in my accomplishments!

```
┌─────────────────────────────┐
│                             │
│  REMINDER                   │
│                             │
│  Positive thinking is essential for success │
│  in both your personal life and your pro-   │
│  fessional career. Cultivate it consciously │
│  each day, and review the Transcrip-        │
│  tionist's Professional Attitude Chart      │
│  periodically.              │
│                             │
└─────────────────────────────┘
```

EXERCISE II.1: RECOGNIZING YOUR ATTITUDES

CHECK YOURSELF

INSTRUCTIONS: On the blanks provided, write specific examples of when and where you have displayed *positive attitudes* about each item.

1. About yourself as an employee
   EXAMPLE: *To be consistently early for class or work.*
   a. _____
   b. _____

2. About your supervisor or originator
   a. _____
   b. _____

3. About co-workers
   a. _____
   b. _____

4. About time
   a. _____
   b. _____

5. About equipment and work area
   a. _____
   b. _____

6. About the finished document or product
   a. _____
   b. _____

ATTITUDES AND COST EFFICIENCY

Now that you have studied the Transcriptionist's Professional Attitude Chart and made a list of examples for various attitudes, you are able to see how developing positive attitudes can contribute to the cost efficiency of the organization for which you will work. For example, under *Attitudes About Co-Workers,* sharing your talents by offering to help could contribute concretely to cost efficiency. Let's assume, for example, that one of your co-workers is struggling to set up a graph. You like this type of activity and do it well. You have a few spare moments and offer to help your co-worker with the project. The offer is accepted. The result: increased job efficiency for you both and an enhanced atmosphere of company teamwork and cooperation.

REMINDER

Become "irreplaceable" to your employer by developing a cost-conscious attitude toward organizational and individual tasks.

WORKING AS A TEAM

The dictation/transcription process should be thought of as a team effort. Each member of the team has distinct expectations and responsibilities.

The originator expects . . .	*The transcriptionist expects . . .*
. . . a neatly typed, properly formatted, and accurately proofread document, completed on time by a cooperative, professional transcriptionist.	. . . a well-organized and clearly dictated message accompanied by complete, accurate directions from a competent, appreciative originator.

Figure II.4 Expectations of the Originator and the Transcriptionist

As you become involved in the ongoing team process, you will develop distinct attitudes toward the different originators or supervisors for whom you work. Become thoroughly familiar with the responsibilities of the originator and the transcriptionist as outlined in the "Team Responsibility Chart" that follows. As you study the chart, keep in mind that these are ideal goals toward which all members of the team should strive. You will be lucky indeed if your originator achieves all of them. By the same token, if you fulfill all of the transcriptionist's responsibilities, the originator will be most fortunate to have you as a team member.

Figure II.5   Team Responsibility Chart

THE ORIGINATOR'S RESPONSIBILITIES	THE TRANSCRIPTIONIST'S RESPONSIBILITIES
Prepare for Dictation	*Prepare for Transcription*
Gather relevant materials	Gather information sources
Check equipment and supplies	Clear the work area of unnecessary
Allow reasonable time for dictation	materials
Plan for reasonable turnaround time	Check equipment and supplies
Organize Your Thoughts	*Organize Your Materials*
Identify the purpose	Adjust the sound on equipment
Itemize the main points	Insert the indicator slip (if applicable)
List thoughts by paragraph	Assemble needed materials—paper,
Establish the "tone" of a document	carbon, etc.
Visualize the reader	Gather supplementary references or
	directions
	Listen carefully to specific instructions
Dictate the Material	
Speak distinctly	*Transcribe the Material*
Enunciate each word	Concentrate while transcribing
Use indication device	Remain alert for needed punctuation
Identify yourself by name and title	Maintain a consistent typing pattern,
Identify type of document	with minimal pauses
Dictate number of carbon copies	Consult information sources as needed
required	Ask the dictator before making
Mention special format or letter	changes in context
style	Double check all names and numbers
Identify "rush" items	Type the date and enclosure notations
Dictate special mailing notations	as needed
Dictate the inside address	Proofread thoroughly
Match the tone of the salutation and	Check for consistencies of dates and
closing	amounts
Dictate paragraphs and unusual	Make neat corrections
punctuation	Type envelopes or labels for letters
Spell all names unless a source	and carbons as needed
document is available for	Analyze the typed document for
transcriptionist's reference	mailability
Spell unfamiliar technical terms	
Emphasize numbers for accuracy	*Submit Material for Approval*
Dictate enclosures	Slip the envelope flap over top or side
Repeat carbon copy distribution	of the letter
Indicate the end of the dictation	Attach enclosures or reminders for
Thank the transcriptionist	the originator
	Place checkmarks by names for
Check Completed Work for Mailability	carbon copy distribution
Read the typed transcript for accuracy	Place assembled materials in a folder
Sign the letter or initial the memo	Obtain the originator's signature if the
Compliment the transcriptionist for	document is mailable
exceptional quality	

The following example of dictation will help acquaint you with the originator's responsibilities described in the Team Responsibility Chart.

This is Ken Armstrong, Director of Internal Operations.

Transcriptionist, here is a short letter with two carbons. Please type this letter in full-block style. Address the letter to: Mr. J. W. Greene (spelled G-R-E-E-N-E), 1270 Fifth Avenue, River Falls, Wisconsin 54022.

Dear JW: We are very anxious for you to visit our new plant during the week of October 15 while you are attending the National Conference. (period and paragraph)

Enclosed is a copy of the layout as well as a copy of the annual report. (period) You should be especially interested in the information on pages 5 and 6. (period and paragraph)

Just call me at 2-3-4 (dash) 0-5-8-3 when you arrive in Los Angeles, (comma) and I will be glad to meet you at the airport. (period) Cordially, Kenneth E. Armstrong

Please send the two carbons to my assistants, Jayne (spelled J-A-Y-N-E) Motejl (spelled M-O-T-E-J-L) and Bill van Winkle. (The "v" in "van" is not capitalized.) Thank you. End of dictation.

Figure II.6 Sample of Dictated Letter

Notice that the date and enclosure notations are generally NOT dictated. It is your responsibility to add these notations automatically to the letter or memo. Although all punctuation is dictated in the example, many dictators rely on the transcriptionist to supply the necessary punctuation. Always remain alert, therefore, as you transcribe.

EXERCISE II.2: DICTATION PRACTICE

INSTRUCTIONS: To become more aware of the dictation procedures and more understanding of the originator's job, simulate a dictation session by dictating the letter and memo described below. You may wish to record your words on a dictation unit or cassette recorder. *Do not write out the letter or memo.* Simply organize your thoughts by making short notes in the space provided. Then proceed with the dictation.

APPLY YOUR SKILLS

1. Dictate a letter of congratulations to a former college friend who took and passed the Certified Professional Secretary (C.P.S.) examination administered by the National Secretaries Association. Organize your thoughts here:

_____

_____

_____

_____

2. Dictate a memo to your supervisor requesting time off with pay to attend a seminar on word processing at the local university. Also, request reimbursement of the $25 registration fee because the topic is directly related to your work as a transcriptionist. Organize your thoughts here:

_____

_____

_____

_____

ATTITUDES: THE BASIS FOR DECISION MAKING

In any job, there will be times when things do not go smoothly and when decisions have to be made as to how to solve a situation or problem. Being able to *identify* your attitude about any problem and to decide what action to take to solve it are both part of your professional development. The professional attitudes you are learning to develop as a student of transcription techniques will be transferable to such situations.

REMINDER

Develop professional attitudes about:
a. Yourself as an employee
b. Your supervisor or originator
c. Your co-workers
d. Time
e. Equipment
f. Your workplace
g. The finished product resulting from your transcription

Name _____ Date _____

EXERCISE II.3: DECISION MAKING IN JOB SITUATIONS

INSTRUCTIONS: Study the situations below and determine the persons or things requiring the display of specific attitudes; then write these attitudes in the space provided. Next, write the specific action you propose to take. You may find it helpful to refer to the Transcriptionist's Professional Attitude Chart (Figure II.3) and the Team Responsibility Chart (Figure II.5).

APPLY YOUR SKILLS

EXAMPLE: "Tuesday, April 7" is dictated; but April 7 actually falls on a Wednesday.

a. Involves attitudes about:

Yourself (aim for accuracy in work); originator (ask questions to clarify); time (be active and productive)

b. Action to be taken:

Check information sources; check with supervisor; check with originator.

1. You are unable to understand a phrase in the dictation.

   a. Involves attitudes about:

   _____

   _____

   b. Action to be taken:

   _____

   _____

2. Your originator dictates numerous outdated expressions.

   a. Involves attitudes about:

   _____

   _____

   b. Action to be taken:

   _____

   _____

3. The magnetic tape breaks in the middle of a "rush" letter.

   a. Involves attitudes about:

   _____

   _____

   b. Action to be taken:

   _____

   _____

4. Your boss compliments your efficiency in front of co-workers.

    a. Involves attitudes about:

    _____

    _____

    b. Action to be taken:

    _____

    _____

5. You question the grammatical correctness of a dictated memo.

    a. Involves attitudes about:

    _____

    _____

    b. Action to be taken:

    _____

    _____

6. Your transcribing machine stops abruptly.

    a. Involves attitudes about:

    _____

    _____

    b. Action to be taken:

    _____

    _____

7. You forget to type a "file" carbon of a letter.

    a. Involves attitudes about:

    _____

    _____

    b. Action to be taken:

    _____

    _____

8. An office friend frequently interrupts your work with unnecessary chatter.

    a. Involves attitudes about:

    _____

    _____

    b. Action to be taken:

    _____

    _____

9. Your transcribing equipment is outdated and unreliable.

   a. Involves attitudes about:

   _____

   _____

   b. Action to be taken:

   _____

   _____

10. Your dictator has dictated a sentence that does not make sense.

   a. Involves attitudes about:

   _____

   _____

   b. Action to be taken:

   _____

   _____

11. Your dictator speaks so rapidly that you need to play the tape two or three times before you can understand the dictation.

   a. Involves attitudes about:

   _____

   _____

   b. Action to be taken:

   _____

   _____

12. You are unable to find a word whose spelling you are checking in the dictionary.

   a. Involves attitudes about:

   _____

   _____

   b. Action to be taken:

   _____

   _____

13. Your dictator rambles aimlessly instead of organizing in advance the content of letters and memos.

   a. Involves attitudes about:

   _____

   _____

   b. Action to be taken:

   _____

   _____

14. After mailing an important letter, you realize that you forgot to obtain the dictator's signature.

    a. Involves attitudes about:

    _____

    _____

    b. Action to be taken:

    _____

    _____

15. You are transcribing an urgent, top-priority report. Your phone repeatedly interrupts you. Time is becoming short, and you will not be able to finish the report on time if interruptions continue.

    a. Involves attitudes about:

    _____

    _____

    b. Action to be taken:

    _____

    _____

INSTRUCTIONS: Check your answers with the Key to Exercise II.3 in Appendix C. Perhaps discussing several of the situations with classmates will add to your thoughts concerning attitudes and decision-making skills.

REMINDER
The dictation/transcription process requires teamwork and the application of positive attitudes.

EFFECTIVE LISTENING

The way in which you listen on the job will have a direct bearing on the overall effectiveness and efficiency of your work. In fact, you're probably already aware how easily misunderstandings can arise simply because someone didn't take the trouble to listen carefully. Misunderstandings resulting from poor listening can be costly to a business by taking a heavy toll in lost time, lost dollars, or both. To minimize such errors, you will want to develop and maintain the ongoing ability to listen carefully and attentively.

The purpose of this section is to help you identify your personal listening strengths and weaknesses, as well as provide exercises that will help improve your concentration and listening ability. If you train yourself to be a good listener, you will be a better transcriptionist, a more efficient employee, and a public relations "booster" to your firm.

Hearing and Listening

Have you ever thought about the difference between *hearing* and *listening*? Hearing, one of the five senses of the human body, is the activity by which we perceive sound. Listening, on the other hand, is hearing *plus* concentration; it channels our thoughts in the direction of understanding ideas or facts needed for communication.

Good listening skills in the office will be essential in meeting your responsibilities, such as transcribing correspondence, recording messages, greeting callers, and receiving important information. You can take the first step toward sharpening your listening skills by recognizing the barriers to listening that interfere with concentration.

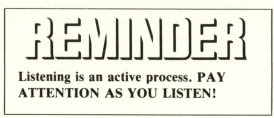

REMINDER

Listening is an active process. PAY
ATTENTION AS YOU LISTEN!

Barriers to Listening

The experts list seven barriers to listening: (1) poor physical condition, (2) "excursions," (3) "tuning out," (4) prejudice, (5) appearance, (6) background noise, and (7) facts versus ideas.

Poor Physical Condition.   Your physical condition can have a direct influence on your listening efficiency. EXAMPLE: You were out late last night "partying" and are "dead tired." In addition, it's almost noon and your stomach is growling (you slept late and didn't have time to eat breakfast). The word processing supervisor asks you to

take a file folder to the third floor right after lunch. You don't pay much attention because all you can think about is going to the canteen for a quick sandwich, a carton of milk—and taking a short nap. When you return from lunch, you forget all about your supervisor's instructions and start transcribing instead. Your supervisor returns to discover the file folder still on your desk!

"Excursions."   The average person thinks at the rate of approximately 400 words a minute but speaks at about 125 words a minute. Listeners, therefore, tend to go on mental "excursions" while waiting for more information. EXAMPLE: At a departmental meeting, you are asked to take minutes. Because one of the department members speaks slowly, your mind wanders off. You continue on your mental excursion a bit too long and have to ask that some important information be repeated.

"Tuning Out."   Some people "tune out" a speaker when convinced they know exactly what is going to be said. EXAMPLE: You have always transcribed the company quarterly report and have always been given the same instructions: "This report goes to Jones, Ryan, Barber, and Prince." However, on this particular occasion you are told, "Send a copy of this report to Jones, Ryan, Barber, Prince, *and* Moscatelli." You quit listening after the name *Ryan* because you think you know all the names. As a result, Miss Moscatelli does not receive a copy of the quarterly report. Your dictator receives a reprimand and, of course, so do you.

Prejudice.   The fourth barrier to listening is prejudice against a speaker on the basis of certain words, phrases, or ideas. EXAMPLE: You are asked to attend a demonstration of some new transcribing equipment manufactured by the EPV Company. You have specific instructions to evaluate the equipment and then report to your supervisor. As you watch the demonstration, you keep hearing the sales representative repeatedly refer to the "girls" doing the transcribing. Your blood pressure rises as you focus in on the stereotype. Before you know it, several minutes have passed, and you have missed the discussion on machine costs and features. When reporting to your supervisor, you do not recommend the equipment sold by EPV Company. Later, a friend tells you about the fine equipment made by EPV. This is confirmed by an equipment evaluation report that comes to your desk. You then become aware that you let the sales representative's use of the word "girls" prejudice you against the equipment.

Appearance.   It is all too easy to pass judgment on someone's remarks because of the speaker's appearance. EXAMPLE: A middle-aged man enters your office. He is dressed in faded, dirty jeans and a torn sweat shirt. He asks to speak to your boss, Mr. Hill, and tells you it's important that he see Mr. Hill by five o'clock. The visitor declines to identify himself. He continues talking, but you really don't give him your full attention because of his distasteful appearance. Mr. Hill suddenly walks in and greets the visitor warmly with "Hi, Tom, I thought you were on your way fishing. What are you doing here?" After the two exchange a few words, Mr. Hill turns to you and says, "Gina Adams, I'd like you to meet Tom Fisher." In an instant, you recall that Mr. Fisher is a prospective customer whose business is expected to boost company profits for years to come.

Background Noise.   In any office there is bound to be noise from many sources—both inside and outside—that may interfere with listening. EXAMPLE: Mrs. Rath is sitting beside your desk dictating a rush letter. Considerable noise is coming from the direction of the riveting machine being used in the remodeling of the office.

Later, when transcribing the letter, you sign Mrs. Rath's name as usual and put the letter in the mail. Three days later, Mrs. Rath discovers that you transcribed a price quotation incorrectly. You must now send out another letter apologizing for the error.

Facts versus Ideas.   Always listen for ideas, and sometimes for specific facts. EXAMPLE: Your supervisor asks you to listen to the tape of a speech and to draft a general outline for review. After listening to the tape, you find that your notes mention only dates and money amounts. Obviously, you didn't listen for ideas! Before you can turn in the outline, you will have to listen to the tape again, concentrating this time on ideas.

SECOND EXAMPLE: You take a long-distance call informing you of some price changes. You leave a message for Mr. Madsen, your boss, notifying him of price increases on three items. Later Mr. Madsen inquires, "What items are increasing and how much are they increasing?" You admit you didn't get this information. You realize too late that you failed to listen for specific facts.

Aids to Listening

There are specific techniques you can use to minimize—and even eliminate—barriers to effective listening and to improve your concentration. Here are some of them:
1. Try to minimize interruptions and distractions.
2. Show respect for the speaker by remaining alert.
3. Maintain eye contact with the speaker.
4. Show facial animation by nodding or gesturing.
5. Focus your attention on the message.
6. Use verbal reinforcement. (Example: "Yes, all right.")
7. Take notes to serve as a reminder.
8. Seek clarification of facts and ideas.

Most people have difficulty listening with 100 percent effectiveness. However, utilizing these aids will help you enhance job efficiency and achieve high productivity. So work at being a good listener!

> # REMINDER
> **Take notes to help eliminate listening barriers and improve listening competence.**

EXERCISE 11.4: LISTENING TAPE

APPLY
YOUR SKILLS

INSTRUCTIONS: You are now ready to check your listening ability by completing the listening exercises. The exercises and instructions are on the Listening Tape. As you progress through the exercises on the tape, take notes on a separate sheet of paper. Then organize your answers on the worksheets that follow.

SITUATION 1: Listening to directions on completing job assignments

EXAMPLE

Response to Question 1: _____ *two* _____
Response to Question 2: _____ *accounting* _____

Part A

Response to Question 1: _____
Response to Question 2: _____

Part B

Response to Question 1: _____
Response to Question 2: _____
Response to Question 3: _____
Response to Question 4: _____

Part C

Response to Question 1: _____
Response to Question 2: _____
Response to Question 3: _____
Response to Question 4: _____
Response to Question 5: _____
Response to Question 6: _____
Response to Question 7: _____

SITUATION 2: Taking telephone messages

Message A

WHILE YOU WERE OUT

To _____

Date _____ Time _____

Name _____

of _____

Phone _____

☐ telephoned	☐ please call
☐ returned your call	☐ will call again
☐ wants appointment	☐ urgent

Message _____
_____
_____
_____
_____
_____

Operator _____ ☐ *continued* ➤

Message B

WHILE YOU WERE OUT

To _____

Date _____ Time _____

Name _____

of _____

Phone _____

☐ telephoned	☐ please call
☐ returned your call	☐ will call again
☐ wants appointment	☐ urgent

Message _____
_____
_____
_____
_____
_____

Operator _____ ☐ *continued* ➤

Message C

WHILE YOU WERE OUT

To _____

Date _____ Time _____

Name _____

of _____

Phone _____

☐ telephoned	☐ please call
☐ returned your call	☐ will call again
☐ wants appointment	☐ urgent

Message _____
_____
_____
_____
_____
_____

Operator _____ ☐ *continued* ➤

Message D

WHILE YOU WERE OUT

To _____

Date _____ Time _____

Name _____

of _____

Phone _____

☐ telephoned	☐ please call
☐ returned your call	☐ will call again
☐ wants appointment	☐ urgent

Message _____
_____
_____
_____
_____
_____

Operator _____ ☐ *continued* ➤

SITUATION 3: Filling in gaps in the tape

Missing Word 1: _____

Missing Word 2: _____

Missing Word 3: _____

Missing Word 4: _____

Missing Word 5: _____

Missing Word 6: _____

Missing Word 7: _____

Missing Word 8: _____

SITUATION 4: Instructions for transcription

SPACE FOR NOTES:

SITUATION 5: Ordering equipment and supplies

SPACE FOR NOTES:

Equipment Needed	*Supplies Needed*
1. _____	_____
2. _____	_____
3. _____	_____
4. _____	_____
5. _____	_____
6. _____	_____
7. _____	_____
8. _____	_____

Additional action or information needed:

1. _____

2. _____

3. _____

4. _____

SITUATION 6: Listening without taking notes

Here's a down-to-earth situation in which you're caught by surprise and are totally unprepared to take notes. First, listen to the narration; then decide what message you would transmit. Write your answer below.

_____

_____

_____

_____

END OF LISTENING EXERCISES (Please rewind the tape!)

INSTRUCTIONS: Check your responses with the Key to Exercise II.4 in Appendix C. If you had any difficulty, you may want to play the tape a second time.

INFORMATION SOURCES

One of the attributes of the true professional is an awareness of the need to verify facts and figures. The responsible, efficient transcriptionist never guesses about such things as the spelling of a word, the correct use of the comma, or the format for a footnote. When in doubt, therefore, be sure to consult one of the many available information sources. Figure II.7 is a list of frequently used sources. Be sure to become familiar with them.

Figure II.7   Frequently Used Information Sources[1]

1. Dictionary (Includes word meanings, spelling, pronunciation, parts of speech, synonyms, antonyms)
2. Word book (Gives correct spelling and word division)
3. Secretarial handbook (Explains style, format, grammar, punctuation; gives abbreviations, forms of address, secretarial tips, and shortcuts)
4. National Zip Code and Post Office Directory (Published annually; lists available mail services, publications, Postal Service information, Zip Codes, address formats)
5. Thesaurus (Gives word alternatives)
6. Calendar (Displays dates and specific days of the week)
7. Metric converter (Itemizes weight, volume, temperature, area, distance, speed)
8. Atlas and interstate maps (Illustrates geographic location; lists distance and population)
9. Style manual (Gives specifics on format and usage, especially helpful in report writing)
10. Telephone book and city directory (Lists names, addresses, phone numbers; includes city map and product or service ads)
11. Airline schedule (Itemizes flight times and routes served)
12. Public library (Offers complete reference service)

[1]See Appendix A for a bibliography of information sources.

The exercise that follows will give you practice in deciding which sources to use when confronted with a style or usage problem.

REMINDER

The transcription specialist is always responsible for the accuracy of the finished product, so be sure to consult the appropriate information source when necessary.

EXERCISE II.5: INFORMATION SOURCES

CHECK
YOURSELF

INSTRUCTIONS: On the lines provided, write the name of the most appropriate information source in which to locate the information needed.

EXAMPLE: the date and time of a home game
for the Kansas City Royals

Call the public library reference desk.

WHEN YOU ARE UNSURE OF: CONSULT:

1. the correct spelling of <u>accommodate</u>   1. _____

2. where to divide <u>December</u>   2. _____

3. whether to use a comma or semicolon   3. _____

4. the correct format for the second-page heading on a letter   4. _____

5. the difference between <u>its</u> and <u>it's</u>   5. _____

6. whether or not to capitalize <u>spring</u>   6. _____

7. a two-letter state abbreviation   7. _____

8. the format of an unbound manuscript   8. _____

9. the Roman numeral for <u>100</u>   9. _____

10. another word for <u>procedure</u>   10. _____

11. how to type a footnote in a formal report   11. _____

12. the full name and correct address of a local company   12. _____

13. whether or not to abbreviate a title   13. _____

14. a shortcut for addressing envelopes   14. _____

15. the distance between Dallas, Texas, and Chicago, Illinois   15. _____

16. a Zip Code   16. _____

17. how to convert six quarts to liters   17. _____

18. the difference between special delivery and
    special handling

18._____

19. an airline flight number and flight arrival time

19._____

20. the difference in meaning between diverse and divert

20._____

INSTRUCTIONS: Check your answers with the Key to Exercise II.5 in Appendix C.

REMINDER

For maximum accuracy, regularly update your personal information source library.

Equal in importance to knowing *where* to look for information is being able to find information *quickly*. For example, although the correct spelling of a word is given in both a dictionary *and* a word book, you will find using a word book faster because it has no definitions and is therefore smaller and easier to handle. Try the following exercise to determine your "finding efficiency."

EXERCISE II.6: EFFICIENCY AND INFORMATION SOURCES

INSTRUCTIONS: Using a word book, look up each of the following words; then, in the space provided, write the page number on which you found the word. Time yourself as you complete the exercise.

CHECK YOURSELF

Beginning time on clock: _____

1. *knowledge,* page _____

4. *generosity,* page _____

2. *coincidence,* page _____

5. *visualize,* page _____

3. *phonetic,* page _____

6. *amalgamate,* page _____

Ending time on clock: _____   Total time elapsed: _____

INSTRUCTIONS: Check your time with the Key to Exercise II.6 in Appendix C.

REMINDER

Time is money! Streamline your use of information sources and develop cost consciousness, but never sacrifice accuracy for speed.

PROOFREADING

In today's business world, quality work at any level is noticed. The basis of all quality work is accuracy in fulfilling assigned tasks. As a transcription specialist, you will be responsible—and held accountable—for the checking and proofreading of all your work. Your ability to find and correct errors *before* returning a finished document to the originator is crucial if work is to flow smoothly, free of unexpected and irritating interruptions. Therefore, include among your top professional goals the need to develop a keen proofreading skill and a sharp eye. Keep in mind as you refine this skill that you are checking for *content* as well as for *typographical errors*.

Accuracy in proofing and correcting will earn you your dictator's professional confidence and, at the same time, greatly enhance your sense of personal pride in your own accomplishments. Keep these rewards in mind as you study the Guidelines for Proofreading in Figure II.8, page 50.

The transcriptionist, as well as the originator, should be familiar with standard proofreader's marks. Some of them are illustrated on the inside back cover of this book.

If a copy is being sent to a publisher, the transcriptionist may want to add symbols in the margin, as well as make proofreader's marks within the copy.[2]

REMINDER

Good proofreading habits contribute to cost efficiency by reducing the number of errors and time-consuming corrections.

EXERCISE II.7 PROOFREADING FOR CONTENT

APPLY YOUR SKILLS

INSTRUCTIONS: The following sentences contain errors in the transcription of simple words. In order to spot the errors, as you read, concentrate on CONTENT. Circle each error you find and write the correct word directly above the incorrect word. Try to find the error on the FIRST reading. NOTE: There may be more than one error in a sentence.

1. You new typewriter should arrive in a month or six weaks, according to the representative you send to my office.

2. When you have the next opportunity, by sure to stay it the downtown location.

3. Let Ms. Perez no as soon as you have finished the travel itinerary.

4. Please introduce my bother, Marv, to Coni when she arrived.

5. Katy was changed too much for the item at the cashier's desk.

[2]Consult a secretarial reference book for a complete list of marginal symbols and examples of their use.

6. Are department works vary will together.

7. If you complete the from before Tuesday, you'll receive a gift form the bank.

8. I wanted to think you, Daniel, for helping my last week.

9. Did you here about the precedent that was set by the unit members?

10. The Southland Cooperation in South Yale Boulevard is the best locale source for the product.

INSTRUCTIONS: After completing the exercise, check your answers with the Key to Exercise II.7 in Appendix C.

EXERCISE II.8: PROOFREADING SENTENCES

INSTRUCTIONS: Proofread the following five sentences and identify the 12 errors in them. Circle the errors. You may refer to any reference book you wish.

APPLY YOUR SKILLS

1. Show enthusiasm for your jab *each* day.
2. Display good buisness manners as your work with colleagues and clients?
3. From the habit of looking for the good qualities an others.
4. Decid today too get along with everyone in your offfice.
5. Build your self-confidince—it is an integrall quality of sucess.

INSTRUCTIONS: Check your work with the Key to Exercise II.8 in Appendix C.

EXERCISE II.9: PROOFREADING A PARAGRAPH

INSTRUCTIONS: Proofread the following paragraph and circle the 12 errors. Do not count spacing between sentences as errors.

APPLY YOUR SKILLS

Learn to spot your typing errors. Proofreading skills canbe imporved, but you must want to improve. perhaps if you recognise that uncorrected errors can result in in extra expense, you will develope sharper proofreading skills. Just decide today that you want to develop a positive atitude toward ''finding and correcting' those error. Your improved job performance will be noticed. and rewarded!

INSTRUCTIONS: Check your work with the Key to Exercise II.9 in Appendix C.

Figure II.8   Guidelines for Proofreading

---

1. **PROOFREAD EVERY WORD**
   - Don't look just for the errors you "think" you made.
   - Watch for letter transpositions.
   - Pay special attention to words that recur.

2. **READ SLOWLY**
   - Develop a sensitivity to errors.
   - Allow enough time to read an entire document without feeling rushed.
   - Say each punctuation mark to yourself as you read.
   - Read forward for *content* and, on crucial documents, reread *backwards* to slow eye movement and identify additional errors.

3. **CONCENTRATE**
   - Block out distracting noises.
   - Avoid excessive interruptions, but take a short break in the middle of a lengthy project.
   - Regularly ask yourself: "Does this sentence make sense?"

4. **RECOGNIZE INCONSISTENCIES**
   - Check headings, subheadings, titles.
   - Verify proper format.
   - Check the number sequence in enumerations.
   - Double-check amounts by recalculating.
   - Compare days of the week with dates.

5. **IDENTIFY MISSPELLINGS**
   - Consult information sources when necessary.
   - Verify spellings of proper names.
   - Know when to trust your own spelling expertise.

6. **CHECK GRAMMATICAL DETAILS**
   - Verify correct usage of punctuation, capitalization, grammar, word division.

7. **DOUBLE-CHECK NUMBERS AND SYMBOLS**
   - Locate the original source or consult your supervisor if you question dictated figures.
   - Watch for transposed numbers.
   - Use the two-person method (one person reads aloud while the other person proofs the retype).
   - Count and compare numbers with the dictation.

8. **PROOFREAD BEFORE REMOVING MATERIAL FROM TYPEWRITER**
   - Use the paper bail as a line guide.

9. **CHECK COMPLETENESS AND PLACEMENT**
   - Verify that all material is included.
   - Adjust placement by shortening or lengthening the final lines on the letter.

10. **DEVELOP A SENSE OF ACCOUNTABILITY**
    - Make careful proofreading a point of personal pride.
    - Keep sharpening and improving your proofreading skills.

EXERCISE II.10: PROOFREADING A MEMO

INSTRUCTIONS: Assume that the following memo was typed in rough-draft form. Using proofreader's marks, edit the memo. Then—if time permits—retype the memo to reinforce your mastery of proofreader's marks.

APPLY YOUR SKILLS

To: Dave Dixon

FROM: Arlene Jordon

dATE: March 27, 1981

SUBJECT: Secreterial Seminar

As your requested, i have selected four secretaries form our staff too particpate in the seminar on Friday April 14. All of the secretaries listed below have been released ~~for~~ theday.

       Bev Taylor, Personnell

       Betty Wilson, Bookkeepping

       Colleen McNamara-Sales

       Shirley Wyrick, Marketting

The registrations fee is $25 per participant, Please send the Check for $75 to my office and I will forward the payment before the Apr. 10 dead line.

I believe this seminar will be an excellant activity for our staff. Thankyou for this opportunity to participate.

mk

INSTRUCTIONS: Check your proofreading accuracy with the Key to Exercise II.10 in Appendix C.

EXERCISE II.11: PROOFREADING A LETTER

**APPLY
YOUR SKILLS**

INSTRUCTIONS: Let's assume that the following letter was typed in rough-draft form. Using proofreader's marks, edit the letter. If time permits, retype the letter to reinforce your mastery of proofreader's marks.

```
Feburary 5,


Mis Mae J. Albers
  1455 West Alps Road
Athens, GA30604

Dear Miss Mae:

CONGRADULATIONS!  We just read in The Alumnus magzine that you

have passed you C.P.S, examination.  You must  be vrey proud of

your accomplishmnets.


If you can get away from your job, the college would like

like to honor you at the anual graduate lunchen no Thursday,

February 16 1 p.m.  The luncheon will be held in the Governer's

Room in Memorial Hall.


Inclosed is a reply card for your convience in in responding.

We realy hope you will be able to join us the 12th.

Cordially


Donna Browning    chairperson

Graduate Lunchen Committe

tn
```

INSTRUCTIONS: Check your proofreading accuracy with the Key to Exercise II.11 in Appendix C.

MAILABILITY

Today's organizations are concerned with creating a positive public image. The transcription specialist produces letters, reports, and other documents which can either improve or impair this image. For example, if you mail a letter with an unconventional format that makes an unfavorable first impression, the quality of the message is weakened and the company image is adversely affected. Therefore, it is vital to master the elements of mailability so that you send only copy considered "mailable." Illustrated below are the three major qualities of mailability.

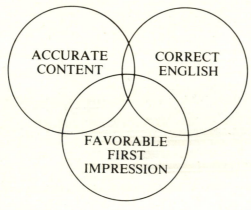

Figure II.9 Qualities of Mailability

The Mailability Analysis Chart (Figure II.11) will help you identify the specific characteristics that make your work acceptable. Use this chart as a "check" to insure the mailability of a document.

Notice that at the bottom of the chart you will indicate the number of minutes it took to type your document. The purpose of this record is to develop a balance between speed and accuracy. Your goal will be to transcribe at a rate that minimizes needless errors and reduces correcting or retyping time.

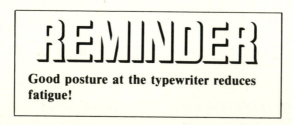

REMINDER

Good posture at the typewriter reduces fatigue!

Figure II.10 Proofreading Documents

Figure II.11   Mailability Analysis Chart

Name _____   Starting Time _____

Date _____   Ending Time _____

(Note: Complete this chart after typing each document.)

	YES	NO
FIRST IMPRESSION		
Is your document		
In the proper format and style?	____	____
Free of spacing or alignment errors?	____	____
Centered horizontally and vertically with even margins?	____	____
Typed on appropriate stationery?	____	____
Typed with a clear, dark ribbon?	____	____
Free of obvious corrections and strikeovers?	____	____
Neat, crisp, and free of smudges?	____	____

	YES	NO
CORRECT ENGLISH		
Is your document		
Free of punctuation errors?	____	____
Free of spelling errors?	____	____
Free of grammar errors?	____	____
Free of capitalization errors?	____	____
Free of inappropriate abbreviations?	____	____
Free of incorrectly divided words?	____	____
Free of incorrect number usage?	____	____

	YES	NO
CONTENT		
Is your document		
Free of uncorrected typing errors?	____	____
Equipped with complete, accurate information?	____	____
Clear, with each sentence making sense?	____	____
Free of omissions or alterations that change meaning?	____	____
Free of inconsistencies?	____	____
Current, with today's date?	____	____
Complete with appropriate titles and ending notations?	____	____

- IF YOU ARE ABLE TO ANSWER "YES" TO EACH OF
  THE ABOVE QUESTIONS, YOUR DOCUMENT IS MAILABLE.

- IF YOUR ANSWER WAS "NO" TO ANY OF THE ABOVE
  QUESTIONS, TAKE ACTION TO CORRECT THE ERROR.

How long did it take you to type and proof your work?   _____ minutes

CARE OF OFFICE EQUIPMENT

Both your ability to perform effectively on the job and your attitude toward your work are influenced by the office machines you will use each day. Among the transcription specialist's top priorities are the need (1) to understand the capabilities of transcription equipment and (2) to care for the equipment properly. Figure II.12 makes important recommendations to insure both your safety and the proper care and maintenance of machines you use.

Figure II.12 Suggestions for the Transcriptionist's Safety and Care of Equipment

1. Read and study the operator's manual accompanying the machine.
2. Refer to the manual before calling in a service representative in case of a problem or malfunction.
3. Clean equipment regularly, following the instructions in the manual.
4. Review the maintenance service agreement, if still in force.
5. Avoid leaning over the equipment and letting hair or jewelry tangle up machine parts.
6. Don't hold small objects, such as paper clips, near open areas in the machine. If objects lodge in machine parts, damage may result.
7. To avoid spills which can cause expensive repair bills, avoid eating or drinking near equipment.
8. Store machine attachments and typing elements in a safe place.
9. Close desk and filing cabinet drawers each time to avoid tripping over them.
10. Let correction fluid dry completely before continuing to type to prevent fluid build-up on typing element or paper bail.
11. Turn equipment off after each use.
    (Caution: On some automatic typewriters, material is automatically erased in the machine "memory" when the motor is turned off. Therefore, be careful to consult your operator's manual *before* using such equipment.)
12. Cover all equipment to minimize collection of dust and to extend equipment life.

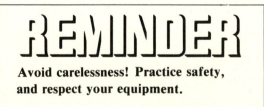

REMINDER
Avoid carelessness! Practice safety,
and respect your equipment.

STUDENT'S TALLY SHEET/PHASE III

Name _____

Target Completion Date_____

STUDENT'S ACTIVITY	DATE COMPLETED	STUDENT'S QUESTIONS AND COMMENTS
STUDY **Introduction to Phase III**		
STUDY **Selecting Supplies**		
DO Exercise III.1		
STUDY **Correcting Errors**		
DO Exercise III.2		
DO Exercise III.3		
STUDY **Crowding and Spreading Typewritten Copy**		
DO Exercise III.4		
STUDY **Spacing After Punctuation**		
DO Exercise III.5		
STUDY **Abbreviations**		
DO Exercise III.6		
STUDY **Letter Style Review**		
DO Exercise III.7		
STUDY **Interoffice Memos**		
STUDY **Envelopes**		
DO Exercise III.8		

STUDENT'S ACTIVITY	DATE COMPLETED	STUDENT'S QUESTIONS AND COMMENTS
STUDY **Placement of Copy on the Page**		
DO Exercise III.9		
STUDY **Final Steps Before Mailing**		
STUDY **Tips for the Transcriptionist**		
STUDY **Manuscripts**		
STUDY **Rough Drafts**		
STUDY **Tables**		
STUDY **Graphs**		
STUDY **Minutes of Meetings**		
STUDY **Outlines**		
STUDY **Making Formatting Decisions**		
DO Exercise III.10		
DO Exercise III.11		
STUDY **Working With "Odd" Size Paper**		
DO Exercise III.12		
DO Exercise III.13		

PERSONAL GOALS FOR PHASE III

1. EXAMPLE: *Become familiar with simplified letter style.*

2. _____

3. _____

INSTRUCTOR'S COMMENTS: _____

_____

_____

PHASE III

PHASE III

STYLE AND
FORMATTING DECISIONS

INTRODUCTION

IT WILL COME AS NO SURPRISE to you to learn that typewriting skills play a crucial role in determining the transcription specialist's success. A large part of these skills consist of the ability to make decisions about the design, format, and style of the documents you will type. Phase III has been designed to "polish" your keyboarding skills and, by so doing, to equip you to take giant steps down the road to becoming a skilled transcription specialist.

After completing Phase III, you will

- Be able to choose the right supplies for the right job.

- Know how to make neat, accurate corrections.

- Be able to use good judgment in spacing and alignment.

- Be aware of acceptable letter and memo styles.

- Be able to crowd and spread when making corrections.

- Understand when and how to use tables and graphs.

- Be competent in the techniques of rough-draft typing.

- Be aware of correct address styles.

- Recognize what final preparations are necessary before letters and memos are mailed.

- Know the proper typed format for a manuscript and for minutes of a meeting.

Because there are many acceptable document formats, only the more popular styles are illustrated in Phase III. If, for any reason, you think it desirable to deviate from those you are about to learn, be sure to check for correctness with an authoritative secretarial style manual.

SELECTING SUPPLIES

Before transcribing a document, it will be necessary for you to make decisions about the supplies needed. Choosing supplies carefully is important for three reasons—appearance, correctness, and cost efficiency.

The physical appearance of a document should enhance the readability of the message rather than distract from it. For example, if you use old, worn carbon paper, the person receiving the copy may have difficulty reading it.

Use of the correct form denotes the transcriptionist's competence. For instance, a memo is an internal communication and should not, therefore, be typed on letterhead stationery. The dictator expects you to know which stationery to use and when to use it.

Finally, proper selection of supplies is an important element in cost efficiency. You would not be using good judgment, if, for example, you typed a rough draft on good bond paper. Use a low-quality paper for rough drafts to keep costs down.

Study the following tips for selecting and using stationery, carbon paper, and typewriter ribbons, illustrated in Figures II.1, III.2, and III.3. Become familiar with their most appropriate uses.

Figure III.1   Stationery

BOND PAPER
- Good erasing quality. Available in 15 to 100 percent rag content. Most common rag content is 25 to 50 percent. Twenty-pound bond is the most common weight.
- Watermarks are sometimes noticeable when the paper is held up to a light. They denote rag content, design, trademark, or brand name.
- Use plain bond for final copies of manuscripts or other straight-copy documents; use letterhead bond for letters.

SULPHITE PAPER
- Poor erasing quality. Lower quality bond made from wood pulp. Most common weights are 16 pound and 20 pound.
- Use sulphite paper for rough drafts and less important documents.

ONIONSKIN PAPER
- Thin paper with either smooth or cockle finish. Generally purchased in 8- to 13-pound weights.
- Use onionskin for file copies in order to reduce bulk.

REMINDER

To reduce the cost of file copies, consider using manifold or copy paper in place of onionskin.

Tips for Selecting and Using Stationery

1. Paper has a "right" and "wrong" side. For best results in making corrections, always type on the "right" side of a sheet of paper. To determine the "right" side, do one of two things: (a) hold the paper so that you can read the watermark right-side-up; (b) notice how the paper is packaged. Generally the right side is face-up in the package.
2. Weight of paper is determined by weighing 500 sheets of paper measuring 17 inches by 22 inches. If, for example, 500 sheets weigh 20 pounds, the paper is called 20-pound paper. The manufacturer then cuts the sheets into four equal parts to obtain the standard size of $8\frac{1}{2}$ by 11 inches.
3. Letterhead stationery is used in typing the first page of a letter. Plain bond paper that matches the size and quality of the letterhead is used in typing all other pages.
4. Store paper flat and in a dry area.
5. Help reduce costs by recycling paper for rough-draft typing or as scratch paper.

Figure III.2 Carbon Paper Supplies

CARBON PAPER	CARBONSETS
• Available in various weights, finishes, and qualities. The harder the finish, the higher the quality.	• Carbon paper and lightweight plain sheets assembled in sets. More efficient to use since supplies are already assembled, but initial cost is higher than for carbon paper.
• Generally used for making carbon copies for filing and distribution. Makes up to three or four clear copies.	• Usually cleaner to handle than carbon paper.
• Can be messy to handle.	

Tips for Selecting and Using Carbon Paper

1. Use carbonsets only once; use carbon paper repeatedly until the type becomes illegible.
2. Take advantage of the color-coding capabilities of carbonsets and assembled carbon packs.
3. NCR paper (No Carbon Required—sometimes referred to as "carbon sensitive paper") is preferred when working with forms; however, NCR paper is more expensive than carbonsets.
4. Store carbon paper in its original box to prevent curling of edges.
5. Eliminate "treeing" or wrinkling of carbon paper by pulling the paper release lever forward and then pushing it back in order to "relax" the carbon pack after inserting it into the typewriter.
6. Keep in mind that production tends to slow down when carbon copies are being prepared.
7. Correct errors on carbon copies by placing a card IN FRONT OF—RATHER THAN BEHIND—the carbon paper to eliminate uneven wear on the carbon. This technique also prolongs the life of carbon paper.

Figure III.3 Typewriter Ribbons

FABRIC RIBBON	CARBON (FILM) RIBBON
• Generally made of cotton, silk, or nylon.	• Higher quality but more expensive.
• Produces lower quality print. Effectiveness decreases and color fades with use and age.	• Consistent, dark print, giving a professional look. Used on self-correcting typewriter. Must be used when typing offset masters and preferred when original will be run with offset press.
• Cannot be used when typing offset masters.	• Can be used only once.

Tips for Selecting and Using Typewriter Ribbons

1. Replace fabric ribbons when they produce light impressions which are difficult to read.
2. Carbon and fabric ribbons are not generally interchangeable on typewriters. Therefore, your decision as to which ribbon to use will have to be made at the time you purchase your typewriter.
3. Select the appropriate carbon ribbon to match the correcting tape for the typewriter. Some manufacturers color code both the typewriter ribbon and the correcting tape.

As a transcriptionist, you will be making recommendations and decisions about supplies to be bought for your use. To be cost efficient, consider both the dollar cost of the supplies and the resulting labor cost of their use. Study the following chart to help put labor and dollar costs in perspective.

Figure III.4   Cost Efficiency of Supplies Utilization

	DOLLAR COST	LABOR COST	QUALITY
PAPER			
Bond	HIGH	low	HIGH
Sulphite	low	medium	low
Onionskin	medium	low	medium
CARBON PAPER			
Carbon Sheets	low	HIGH	medium
Carbonsets	HIGH	medium	HIGH
RIBBON			
Fabric (nylon)	medium	low	medium
Fabric (cotton)	low	low	low
Carbon (film)	HIGH	HIGH	HIGH

Local variation in prices may affect these relative dollar and labor cost estimates.

Exercise III.1 will give you experience in selecting the appropriate supplies for transcribing tasks.

EXERCISE III.1: PAPER AND RIBBON SELECTION

INSTRUCTIONS: In the blanks to the right, show the type of paper and ribbon you would use and the number of carbon copies you would make. Remember to include a file copy in your count, and assume you have access to typewriters that use both carbon and fabric ribbons.

CHECK YOURSELF

	PAPER	RIBBON	NUMBER OF CARBONS
EXAMPLE: A letter confirming an appointment	*bond-letterhead*	*carbon*	*1*
1. A memo to a co-worker			
2. A letter to a United States Senator			
3. A rough draft of a five-page report			
4. A form letter to be photo-copied and then printed on offset copier			
5. A letter to a competitor			
6. A letter and three interoffice carbons			
7. An outline to be photocopied followed by reproduction of 500 copies by offset process			
8. A set of minutes for a committee of four			
9. A table to be enclosed with a letter to a customer			
10. A draft of a speech which will be revised and retyped			

INSTRUCTIONS: Check your responses with the Key to Exercise III.1 in Appendix C.

CORRECTING ERRORS

When preparing a final copy of a document, you will, of course, be aware that uncorrected errors and strikeovers are *not acceptable* since they reflect on both the organization and the transcriptionist. A strikeover, for example, tells the person reading the document that you saw the error but were too unconcerned to correct it.

REMINDER

Leave a positive impression by correcting each typing error neatly.

Figure III.5 illustrates the various types of correction materials and the most effective ways to use them.

Figure III.5   Correction Techniques

HARD ERASER
- Use for erasing on original copy. Removes an error permanently.
- Stroke only with the grain of the paper. Avoid touching the print with your fingers to avoid smudges.
- Use special correction shields to protect the characters or words next to the error.

SOFT ERASER
- Use for erasing on onionskin and carbon copies. Removes an error permanently.
- Use for erasing smudges or roller marks.

CORRECTION TAPE
- Use *with care* on originals.
- Deposits chalk-like substance over stroking error. Correction substance wears off with age.
- Does *not* remove errors permanently. Errors can be visible when light shows through the paper.
- Available in sheets or rolls and in colors to match paper.

CUT AND TAPE
- Use on documents to be photo-copied.
- Allows sections on a page to be moved by cutting, rearranging, and taping. (Transparent tape preferred)
- Use to correct errors or delete words and lines by applying an adhesive white cover-up tape. Type or write directly on the tape when necessary.

FLUID
- Use on documents to be photo-copied.
- Brush fluid thinly over the error and allow to dry completely.
- DO NOT USE ON ORIGINAL DOCUMENTS TO BE MAILED.
- Available in colors to match paper.

LIFT-OFF TAPE
- Use for original documents. Correct carbons separately, using other methods.
- Adhesive tape lifts errors from paper. Most effective manual correction method.
- Available only on typewriters with the correction feature.

TEXT-EDITING
- Correction is accomplished by electronic or magnetic devices. Most sophisticated correction method.
- Words, lines, and paragraphs are easily corrected and rearranged.

Figure III.6

Text-Editing Typewriter

ALIGNING TYPEWRITTEN COPY

By this time you've learned that the best time to make corrections is while your paper is still in the machine. Occasionally, despite your best efforts, you will discover an error only *after* the paper has been removed from the typewriter. When that happens, you will have no choice but to reinsert the paper, realign the copy, and make the correction. Neat realignment takes practice.

To realign, use the paper release lever to adjust your copy horizontally and the variable line spacer to adjust your copy vertically. Some transcriptionists hold a piece of onionskin paper or some cellophane taken from a window envelope over the space and then strike the proper keys to test alignment. When the copy is aligned, remove the onionskin or cellophane and make the correction.

Another method to test alignment of characters is to place the typewriter in "stencil" position.

EXERCISE III.2: ALIGNMENT

INSTRUCTIONS: Insert a sheet of typing paper; then follow the directions for each of these five drills in order to practice aligning copy.

APPLY YOUR SKILLS

1. TYPE   **I will strive f r mailability.**

   REMOVE your paper from the typewriter. Next, REINSERT your paper and ALIGN your copy. Then TYPE the missing **o** in the word **for.**

   REPEAT this exercise until you have mastered perfect alignment.

2. TYPE   **I will strive for ma lability.**

   REMOVE your paper from the typewriter. Then REINSERT your paper and TYPE the missing **i** in the word **mailability.**

3. TYPE   **I will stri e for mailability.**

   REMOVE your paper from the typewriter. Then REINSERT your paper and TYPE the missing **v** in the word **strive.**

4. TYPE   **I ill strive for mailability.**

   REMOVE your paper from the typewriter. Then REINSERT your paper and TYPE the missing **w** in the word **will.**

5. Repeat one of the above exercises on a different make, model, or pitch of typewriter.

INSTRUCTIONS: Evaluate each assignment critically. Your next goal is to learn to make these alignments QUICKLY. If time permits, try the exercises again to improve your efficiency.

If you are having difficulty with this exercise, be sure to ask your instructor to demonstrate the correct technique.

When typing on a form, allow a little extra time to properly align the copy with the printed lines on the form. Your finished document will be easier to read if the type and the printed lines do not overlap.

Contrast an example of poor placement on a form (Figure III.7) with an example of correct placement on a form (Figure III.8). Which makes a favorable impression? Which makes a poor impression? Whom would you hire?

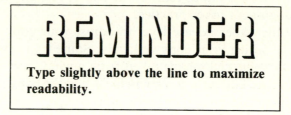

REMINDER
Type slightly above the line to maximize readability.

Figure III.7   Poor Placement on a Form

Name ——— MRS. MAE LAATSCH ———————————

Phone ——— 273-0294 ———————————————

Number ———— Sx-3927-12 ———————————

Graduation Date—— June 1, 1982 ——————————

Check one: Associate of Arts Degree

Associate of Applied Science Degree

Certificate

Diploma

X	

Figure III.8   Correct Placement on a Form

Name ————— MR. STUART GLASS ——————————

Phone ————— 273-5873 ——————————————

Number ————— Sx-3924-41 —————————————

Graduation Date————— June 1, 1982 ————————

Check one: Associate of Arts Degree

Associate of Applied Science Degree

Certificate

Diploma

X

Name_____ Date_____

EXERCISE III.3: PLACEMENT OF TYPING ON A FORM

INSTRUCTIONS: Insert this form in your typewriter and complete the requested information about yourself. Pay special attention to proper line placement.

NAME _____

ADDRESS _____

PHONE_____ SOCIAL SECURITY NO._____

Will you graduate this year? [   ]   [   ]

                                                      YES   NO

INSTRUCTIONS: Analyze your line placement. If you need additional practice, use the forms below and repeat the exercise.

NAME _____

ADDRESS _____

PHONE_____ SOCIAL SECURITY NO._____

Will you graduate this year? [   ]   [   ]

                                                      YES   NO

NAME _____

ADDRESS _____

PHONE_____ SOCIAL SECURITY NO._____

Will you graduate this year? [   ]   [   ]

                                                      YES   NO

CROWDING AND SPREADING TYPEWRITTEN COPY

Occasionally, you may have to "crowd" or "spread" typewritten copy to avoid retyping an entire page. For example, if you typed the word *rise* but the word should have been *raise*, you would need to "crowd" an extra letter into the space. To do this, simply erase the incorrect word, realign your copy (if the paper is already out of the machine), and use the half-backspace lever[1] to permit the crowding of the word. When the situation is reversed (you typed *raise* when you should have typed *rise*), it will be necessary for you to "spread" the type evenly over the space. (See Figures III.9 and III.10.)

Figure III.9   "Spreading" on the Typewriter

ORIGINAL INCORRECT COPY:

Please raise when the judge enters the courtroom.

ERASE THE ERROR:

Please   when the judge enters the courtroom.

SPREAD THE CORRECT WORD IN THE SPACE:

Please r i s e when the judge enters the courtroom.

Figure III.10   "Crowding" on the Typewriter

ORIGINAL INCORRECT COPY:

Our goal is to rise $1,000 for the benefit fund.

ERASE THE ERROR:

Our goal is to $1,000 for the benefit fund.

CROWD THE CORRECT WORD IN THE SPACE:

Our goal is to raise $1,000 for the benefit fund.

REMINDER

When crowding or spreading typewritten copy, take special care to leave the same space between characters.

[1]If your machine does not have a half-backspace lever, ask your instructor to demonstrate this procedure on your typewriter.

EXERCISE III.4: CROWDING AND SPREADING

APPLY YOUR SKILLS

INSTRUCTIONS: Insert a sheet of typing paper; then follow the directions for each of the three drills on crowding and three drills on spreading.

1. TYPE   **I will strive to be succesful each day.**

   You need to "crowd" the missing **s** in the word **successful.**

   ERASE   **ful**
   CROWD   **sful**

2. TYPE   **I will stive to be successful each day.**

   You need to "crowd" the missing **r** in **strive.**

   ERASE   **st** or **stive**
   CROWD   **str** or **strive**

3. TYPE   **I will strive to be successful ach day.**

   You need to "crowd" the missing **e** in **each.**

   ERASE   **ach**
   CROWD   **each**

4. TYPE   **Today is important--I will learn annd improve.**

   ERASE   **annd**
   SPREAD   **and** between **learn** and **improve**

5. TYPE   **Today is iimportant--I will learn and improve.**

   ERASE   **iimpo**
   SPREAD   **impo** between **is** and **rtant**

6. TYPE   **Today is important--I I will learn and improve.**

   ERASE   The second **I** and **will**
   SPREAD   **will** between the first **I** and **learn**

INSTRUCTIONS: Look at your work. Evaluate each correction critically. If you need additional practice, be sure to make the time necessary to master this skill.

REMINDER

A 10-pitch (pica) typewriter has 10 spaces to the inch (2.5 centimeters).

A 12-pitch (elite) typewriter has 12 spaces to the inch (2.5 centimeters).

SPACING AFTER PUNCTUATION

When transcribing a dictated document, you will be striving for a mailable product, one that shows proper spacing following punctuation. In order to be certain that your work is properly arranged and consistent in spacing, review the following rules in Figure III.11; then complete Exercise III.5.

Figure III.11   Spacing Rules

AFTER A . . .		SPACE . . .	Example:
,	Comma	once	Therefore, will
;	Semicolon	once	in June; however,
.	Period (Abbreviations)	once	K. L. Lantz
.	Period (End of Sentence)	twice	today. Will Marva Kae
!	Exclamation Point	twice	Don't forget! We
?	Question Mark	twice	Hawaii? Or would
:	Colon	twice	following: two reams

DO NOT SPACE BEFORE OR AFTER A . . .		Example:
,	Comma (In Numbers)	Bring 5,000 copies
-	Hyphen	A two-page report
--	Dash	That is great--I really
'	Apostrophe (Within a Word)	Won't you try harder?

DO NOT SPACE AFTER A . . .		Example:
"	Beginning quotation mark	She said, "Hi, Shellee
(	Left parenthesis	Send me fifteen (15) sets
$	Dollar sign	He needs $100 before

DO NOT SPACE BEFORE AN . . .		Example:
"	Ending quotation mark	can't wait."
)	Right parenthesis	five dollars ($5)

REMINDER

A dash is expressed by typing two consecutive hyphens without a space before or after.

REMINDER

Whenever you have questions about correct spacing, consult a typing textbook or a secretarial reference book.

EXERCISE III.5: SPACING AFTER PUNCTUATION

CHECK YOURSELF

INSTRUCTIONS: Complete the following exercises by identifying the spacing errors.

A. Circle each spacing error in the following sentences.

1. Please give the information to Mr. S.Q. Ortiz.

2. Did you see a Broadway musical when you were on your two - week vacation?

3. The policy implies that a $15 deposit is required.

4. Are the members ready? I hope so .

5. If possible, try to produce 2, 400 parts before March 30,1982.

6. It ' s important -- very important.

7. Yesterday, Mr. Avis said, "Jim's contract requires that $50 (fifty dollars) be deposited by noon on Friday."

B. Circle each spacing error in the following paragraph.

Enclosed is a check for $ 3,500. 65 and

a supply of request-for-payment forms. I want

to remind you of the necessity for quarterly

financial progress reports. Send five(5) copies

of the report to: Archdiocese of Detroit, 305 Michigan

Avenue,Detroit, Michigan 48226. Also enclosed is a copy

of the memorandum outlining what should be contained

in the quarterly report ending June,1982.

INSTRUCTIONS: Check your answers with the Key to Exercise III.5 in Appendix C.

ABBREVIATIONS

Abbreviations are meant to aid—not confuse—the reader. Avoid using excessive abbreviations in typed documents unless they are approved technical terms or are recommended by an agency such as the United States Postal Service. Following are some tips to help you make abbreviating decisions.

Figure III.12   Abbreviating Guidelines

1. Use the approved two-letter state abbreviations in addresses, but do not use them in the context of a paragraph.
2. Use abbreviations, such as *Inc.* for *Incorporated* and *Ltd.* for *Limited*, only if the abbreviation is used in a company letterhead.
3. Don't abbreviate words like *street, boulevard,* and *avenue* unless you are following official postal guidelines. The *National Zip Code and Post Office Directory* has a complete list of recommended abbreviations designed to expedite computer sorting of mail.
4. Generally, spell out titles (*Captain, Senator, Professor*). Exceptions: *Mr., Mrs., Ms., Dr., M.D.,* or *Ph.D.*

REMINDER

Ms. is used when the marital status of a woman is unknown.

    Miss is **NOT** an abbreviation and, therefore, does not need a period.

5. Don't abbreviate proper names. (Use *William*, not *Wm.*) However, *Jr.* and *Sr.* are acceptable when they follow the name.
6. Don't abbreviate locations. (Use *Los Angeles*, not *L.A.*)
7. Don't abbreviate measurements in the context of a paragraph. (Use *feet*, not *ft.*)
8. Use *No.* for *number* when followed by figures. (My first choice is Model No. 315.)
9. Don't abbreviate months of the year, days of the week, or years. (Use 1982, not '82.) However, use *a.m.* and *p.m.*
10. Use a symbol only if it is part of the company name (Russell & Sons, Inc.).

REMINDER

Use abbreviations and acronyms only if you are sure the meaning will be understood by the reader. An acronym is a word formed from the initial letters of words; for example, UNICEF is formed from *United Nations International Children's Emergency Fund.*

    Consult an unabridged dictionary for a complete listing of abbreviations.

EXERCISE III.6: ABBREVIATIONS

CHECK YOURSELF

INSTRUCTIONS: Read the following sentences and circle any misuse of the Abbreviating Guidelines (Figure III.12). Directly above the circle, write the correct word or abbreviation. If the sentence is correct, place a C next to the number.

1. Bradley is a recent graduate of the University of AL.

2. On Jan. 5 the Collins Co. will merge with Rockwell, International.

3. Did Doctor Ben Mahachek give you that advice about Model #16, or did Prof. Erica Kane give it to you?

4. N. Y. City has the largest population of any city in the United States.

5. The steak weighed 2.2 lbs. or 1 kilogram.

6. Our national speed limit is 55 mph or 88 km.

7. Will you be working next Sat., Oct. 21?

8. She has lived in L.A., Calif., for 11 yr. because she moved there in '70.

9. Mr. and Mrs. B. F. Maytag will be hosting the party from 6 p.m. to 8 p.m.

10. Wm. and Sue's new address is 14537 N. Girard Blvd., Columbus, Ohio.

INSTRUCTIONS: Check your accuracy by consulting the Key to Exercise III.6 in Appendix C.

LETTER STYLE REVIEW

According to the prestigious Dartnell Corporation,[2] the cost of the "average" business letter for 1980 was $6.07. Over half of that cost went to pay for labor costs of the dictator's and transcriptionist's time. One very important way in which a transcriptionist can contribute to the cost efficiency of a company is by being thoroughly knowledgeable about proper letter format.

The letter styles shown in Figures III.13 through III.16 are examples of the four most common letter styles: full-block, block (or modified block), simplified, and social/business. In each example, the formatting rules and specific letter characteristics are highlighted. Since you will be using all of these letter styles in Phase V, be sure to study each figure carefully.

REMINDER

You make an important contribution to the cost efficiency of your firm when you type mailable documents on your *first* attempt.

---

[2]The Annual Dartnell Letter Costs Survey, Dartnell Corporation, 4660 North Ravenwood, Chicago, Illinois 60640.

You will notice in the examples that two different styles of punctuation are illustrated—mixed punctuation and open punctuation. In *mixed punctuation*, a colon (:) follows the salutation and a comma (,) follows the complimentary close. In *open punctuation*, no punctuation is used after the salutation and the complimentary close. Although the more popular style is mixed punctuation, the open style seems to be growing in popularity because it presents a modern, clean appearance and because it saves time.

Figure III.13 Full-Block Letter, Mixed Punctuation

Dateline

May 23, 19--

Mailing Notation (centered vertically)

REGISTERED

REMINDER
- **All lines begin at the left margin. Well balanced when letterhead design extends to right side.**
- **Easy to type.**
- **Considered the most popular style.**

Inside address
Orlando Office Supply, Inc.
1022 Central Boulevard, South
Orlando, FL 32800
one blank line

Attention Line (optional)

ATTENTION: SHIPPING DEPARTMENT
one blank line

Salutation

Gentlemen or Ladies:
one blank line

Subject line (optional)

SUBJECT: OUR ORDER NO. 239-475R
one blank line

On April 2, we ordered from you 75 reams of white bond paper (No. 364). On April 7, you wrote us that your supply of this paper was short but that you were shipping 50 reams on that day and that the remaining 25 reams would be sent on the 20th.
one blank line

Body of Letter

The shipment of 50 reams arrived on April 14; however, we have not yet received the remaining 25 reams nor have we had any word about them.
one blank line

We have been especially pleased with your service in the past and feel there must be some explanation for the delay in getting this shipment to us. When should we expect to receive the remaining part of our order?
one blank line

Complimentary Close

Sincerely,

three to five blank lines for signature

Dictator's Name & Title

Mrs. Kathleen J. Young
Purchasing Agent

Your Reference Initials

xx

Enclosures: Purchase Order
             Shipping Invoice

Vertical spacing adjustable to center the letter.

Copy Notation

c: Steven Stokes

Postscript

If you wish, I will be glad to send you copies of our previous correspondence.

Figure III.14   Block or Modified Block Letter, Open Punctuation

Start typing at center.
No punctuation is needed when day precedes month. (23 May 19--

REMINDER

- **May be typed with or without indented paragraphs. Recent trend is toward blocked paragraphs, as illustrated.**
- **Date may be backspaced from right margin, typed beginning at center, or centered.**
- **Considered the second most popular letter style.**

REGISTERED

Orlando Office Supply, Inc.
1022 Central Boulevard, South
Orlando, FL 32800

ATTENTION: Shipping Department   ) *Can be centered.*

Gentlemen or Ladies

SUBJECT: Our Order No. 239-475R   ) *Can be centered.*

The first line of each paragraph may be indented 5 spaces.

On April 2, we ordered from you 75 reams of white bond paper (No. 364). On April 7, you wrote us that your supply of this paper was short but that you were shipping 50 reams on that day and that the remaining 25 reams would be sent on the 20th.

The shipment of 50 reams arrived on April 14; however, we have not yet received the remaining 25 reams nor have we had any word about them.

We have been especially pleased with your service in the past and feel that there must be some explanation for the delay in getting this shipment to us. When should we expect to receive the remaining part of our order?

Start typing at center. (Sincerely

Mrs. Kathleen J. Young
Purchasing Agent

xx

Enclosures: Purchase Order   ) *Enclosure notation reminds*
             Shipping Invoice   *the writer to enclose an item,*
                                      and the reader to look for it.

c: Steven Stokes

"PS" initials may be omitted.

PS: If you wish, I will be glad to send you copies of our previous correspondence.

Figure III.15 Simplified Letter

May 23, 19--

REGISTERED

Orlando Office Supply, Inc.
1022 Central Boulevard, South
Orlando, FL 32800

two blank lines

OUR ORDER NO. 239-475R *) All caps! Subject replaces salutation.*

two blank lines

On April 2, we ordered from you 75 reams of white
bond paper (No. 364). On April 7, you wrote us
that your supply of this paper was short but that
you were shipping 50 reams on that day and that
the remaining 25 reams would be sent on the 20th.

The shipment of 50 reams arrived on April 14; however, we have not yet
received the remaining 25 reams nor have we had any word about them.

We have been especially pleased with your service in the past and feel
that there must be some explanation for the delay in getting this
shipment to us. When should we expect to receive the remaining part
of our order?

(Omit complimentary close.)

MRS. KATHLEEN J. YOUNG, PURCHASING AGENT *) All caps!*

xx

Enclosures: Purchase Order
            Shipping Invoice

c: Steven Stokes

If you wish, I will be glad to send you copies of our previous correspondence.

REMINDER

- A time-saving style because it has no salutation, no complimentary close, no paragraph indentions, and a standard line length for all letters.
- Requires a subject line, but the word *Subject* is omitted.
- If possible, use name of receiver in opening sentence.
- Introduced by Administrative Management Society. Increasing in popularity.

Figure III.16   Social/Business or Personal/Business

Return address needed because no letterhead is used.

63948 Westland Drive, SE
Cedar Falls, IA 50613
December 5, 19--

Dear Julie:) *A comma is sometimes used instead of the colon.*

Paragraphs may be indented.

I just read in this morning's paper about your national
award. You must be very proud. It is quite an honor
for someone so young to be recognized by a national organization.

Perhaps you can use the two extra clippings that I have
enclosed.

You must be especially busy now; but if you can find the
time, I'd love to have lunch with you. We can talk about
those good old college days.

CONGRATULATIONS, JULIE!

                                    Cordially,

                                    Kari DeMaria) *Signature may be only a first name.*
) *Typed identification line here is optional.*

Inside address may also be typed above salutation.

Ms. Julie Ann McDermott
3972 Willow Road
Brigham Canyon, UT 84006

REMINDER

- Informal letter style. Can be typed on company letterhead or on special-size stationery.
- Inside address may be typed above salutation or below signature. Include a return address if none is provided on the stationery.
- Generally has no enclosure notation or reference initials.

Typing Additional Pages

When a letter or memo continues beyond the first page, the transcriptionist should identify that page by typing the name of the addressee (always first), the date, and the page number, as illustrated in Figure III.17. This will make it possible to identify the second page should it become detached and separated from the first page.

Figure III.17   Second-Page Letter Headings

Style A

) approximately six blank lines

Jose Garcia
July 19, 19--   *) single spacing.*
Page 3

) two blank lines

Therefore, I recommend that we begin work on the project
without delay.

Would it be possible for you to fly to Portland with us
next week? This would give us an opportunity to discuss
our plans in detail.

Style B

*Date is backspaced
from right margin.*

Jose Garcia   3   July 19, 19--

) two blank lines

Therefore, I recommend that we begin work on the project
without delay.

Would it be possible for you to fly to Portland with us
next week? This would give us an opportunity to discuss
our plans in detail.

Sizes of Stationery

The four major sizes of stationery are: (1) standard, (2) legal, (3) monarch, and (4) baronial. (See Figure III.18.) The *standard* size is the most popular type used for business letters and memos. The *legal* size is used for official legal documents. *Monarch* and *baronial* are used for personal business correspondence; occasionally, organizations may decide to use the baronial size for memos.

Figure III.18   Stationery Sizes

Standard	8½ by 11 inches (21.25 by 27.5 centimeters)
Legal	8½ by 14 or 8½ by 13 inches (21.25 by 35 or 32.5 centimeters)
Monarch	7¼ by 10½ inches (18.13 by 26.25 centimeters)
Baronial (Half-sheet)	5½ by 8½ inches (13.75 by 21.25 centimeters)

In 1979 the United States Government converted to the standard-size paper. This change from the previously used size (8 by 10½) was made in an attempt to reduce stationery costs.

Letterhead and other paper are usually packaged by the ream, which consists of 500 sheets. (See Figure III.19.)

Figure III.19   Package Label for Paper

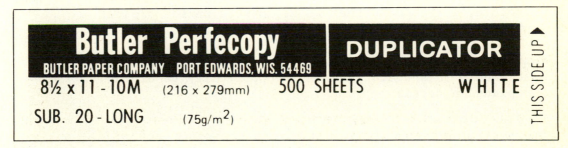

Folding and Inserting Letters

Fold letters neatly to make a good impression on the reader. Illustrated in Figure III.20 are examples of techniques for folding and inserting letters to fit the No. 10 (large) and No. 6 3/4 (small) envelopes. Be sure the crease is straight and sharp. Avoid refolding and creasing several times because the appearance would suffer.

Figure III.20   Methods of Folding and Inserting Letters

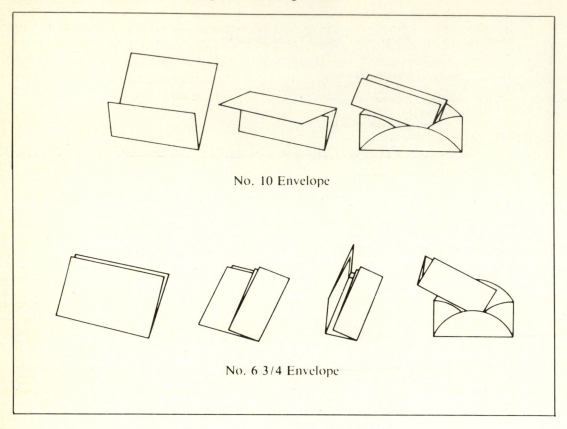

No. 10 Envelope

No. 6 3/4 Envelope

EXERCISE III.7: FOLDING A LETTER

INSTRUCTIONS: Take two sheets of standard-size stationery and demonstrate to your instructor how you fold letters quickly and accurately. Fold one sheet for the No. 10 envelope and one for the No. 6 3/4 envelope. Use the technique illustrated in Figure III.20 or another technique shown in a secretarial reference manual.

*APPLY
YOUR SKILLS*

INTEROFFICE MEMOS

While letters are most commonly used for external communication, memos are generally used for internal communication. Some companies prefer memo forms with the guide words *To, From, Date,* and *Subject* printed on them. If forms of this kind are not used by your firm, type these four words at the top of either a standard-size sheet or a half-sheet of bond paper.

There are many possible variations of correct memo style. Several of the more popular styles are illustrated in Figures III.21, III.22, and III.23. For the sake of efficiency, only one standard memo style is generally used in a firm.

Figure III.21   Memo

Use a one— or two-inch top margin.

```
TO:        All Employees
                     one blank line
FROM:      Keith Andersen, Personnel Administrator
                     one blank line
DATE:      December 15, 19--
                     one blank line
SUBJECT:   Payroll Checks
              Align here by setting a tab 11 spaces from left margin.
two or more blank lines
Effective January 1, all employees will be eligible for
family coverage through our health insurance program.  Details
of the plan are described on the enclosed brochure.
                     one blank line
We are indeed pleased to offer our staff this additional benefit.
If you have any questions regarding the coverage, don't hesitate
to call me.
                     one blank line
sl

Enclosure:  Brochure) Spacing is variable.
```

Memos are usually single spaced with a double space between paragraphs. If a memo is short, however, you may prefer to type it double spaced.

Here are two additional styles for the memo guide words:

Figure III.22   Memo

```
Date:       February 12, 19--

To:         Ross DeLong

From:       James Miller
            LaDonna Sejkora

Subject:    Sales Campaign
```

Figure III.23   Memo

```
September 25, 19--

TO:   Sue Berg, Director

FROM:  Barney Phillips,
       Sales Manager

SUBJECT:  Equipment request
```

REMINDER

If you type a job title after the name of the receiver, for the sake of consistency also type a job title after the name of the sender. Titles such as *Mr.* and *Mrs.* are generally omitted in memos unless a more formal tone is desired.

REMINDER

The use of the word *subject* in letters and memos is preferred over the abbreviation *re* (originally from the Latin, meaning *regarding*), except in some legal offices.

ENVELOPES

Two styles of envelope addresses—the *traditional* and the *modern*—are illustrated in Figures III.24 and III.25. The traditional style may soon become obsolete because of mail handling changes now being considered by the U.S. Postal Service. The modern address style is designed to be read by the computerized sorting equipment. Whichever style you use, strive for a well-placed, neatly typed envelope in order to make the best possible first impression. Equally important is the need for you to double check the accuracy of the numbers typed on the envelope. An incorrect Zip Code, for example, will cause delay in the handling and delivery of a letter.

Figure III.24   Traditional Style of Envelope Address

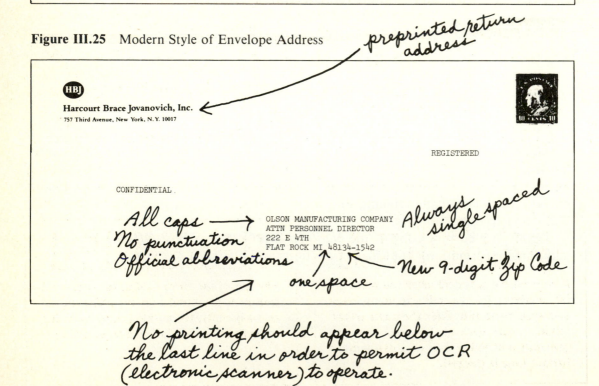

Figure III.25   Modern Style of Envelope Address

REMINDER

By 1983, the U.S. Postal Service plans to adopt a nine-digit Zip Code, expanded from the present five-digit Zip Code. This change would permit machines called *optical character readers* (OCRs) to sort mail after "reading" only one line.

Whether you use the traditional address or the modern address, you will need to know and use the U.S. and Canadian two-letter postal abbreviations that appear here and on the inside front cover of this book. (See Figure III.26 and Figure III.27.) Many transcriptionists memorize the two lists to improve their efficiency.

Figure III.28 is a list of street designator abbreviations used in the modern style of envelope address. These abbreviations also appear on the inside front cover.

If the dictator should forget to give the complete address, you will need to locate it on your own. Should you fail to find it in the files, check the local telephone directory; or, in the case of an out-of-town address, inquire at the reference desk of the public library.

REMINDER

When typing an address, use the full name of a foreign country and type it in all caps on a separate line. (Exception: *U.S.S.R.*)

Postal Regulations

In addition to being well-versed on address styles, you should be acquainted with postal regulations for envelopes. The Postal Service will not handle mail that measures less than $3^{1}/_{2}$ inches wide or 5 inches long. In addition, mail measuring more than $6^{1}/_{8}$ inches wide or $11^{1}/_{4}$ inches long will be subject to a surcharge. This surcharge applies only to first-class mail weighing one ounce or less or single-piece, third-class mail weighing two ounces or less.

Consult a current copy of the *National Zip Code and Post Office Directory* for additional information about mail restrictions and limits.

Figure III.26   U.S. Postal Abbreviations

Alabama	AL	Kansas	KS	Ohio	OH
Alaska	AK	Kentucky	KY	Oklahoma	OK
Arizona	AZ	Louisiana	LA	Oregon	OR
Arkansas	AR	Maine	ME	Pennsylvania	PA
California	CA	Maryland	MD	Puerto Rico	PR
Canal Zone	CZ	Massachusetts	MA	Rhode Island	RI
Colorado	CO	Michigan	MI	South Carolina	SC
Connecticut	CT	Minnesota	MN	South Dakota	SD
Delaware	DE	Mississippi	MS	Tennessee	TN
District of		Missouri	MO	Texas	TX
Columbia	DC	Montana	MT	Utah	UT
Florida	FL	Nebraska	NE	Vermont	VT
Georgia	GA	Nevada	NV	Virginia	VA
Guam	GU	New Hampshire	NH	Virgin Islands	VI
Hawaii	HI	New Jersey	NJ	Washington	WA
Idaho	ID	New Mexico	NM	West Virginia	WV
Illinois	IL	New York	NY	Wisconsin	WI
Indiana	IN	North Carolina	NC	Wyoming	WY
Iowa	IA	North Dakota	ND		

Figure III.27   Canadian Postal Abbreviations

Alberta	AB	Newfoundland	NF	Prince Edward	
British Columbia	BC	Northwest		Island	PE
Labrador	LB	Territories	NT	Quebec	PQ
Manitoba	MB	Nova Scotia	NS	Saskatchewan	SK
New Brunswick	NB	Ontario	ON	Yukon Territory	YT

Figure III.28   Abbreviations for Street Designators

Avenue	AVE	Harbor	HBR	Rural	R
Boulevard	BLVD	Heights	HTS	Saint	ST
Causeway	CSWY	Island	IS	South	S
Center	CTR	Lane	LN	Square	SQ
Circle	CIR	Mount	MT	State	ST
College	CLG	National	NAT	Street	ST
Crossing	XING	North	N	Town	TWN
Drive	DR	Plaza	PLZ	Upper	UPR
East	E	Prairie	PR	Village	VLG
Expressway	EXPY	Road	RD	West	W

A more complete list appears in the *National Zip Code and Post Office Directory*.

Mailing Labels

Mailing labels are an alternative to typing an address directly on the envelope; they can be typed, computer-prepared, or photocopied. The use of computer-prepared or photocopied mailing labels is an effective way of saving the transcriptionist's time when the same addresses are used frequently.

Some labels are peeled from a pre-moistened or adhesive backing before being applied to the envelope. Be careful to attach the label so that the print is parallel with the long edge of the envelope.

REMINDER

When affixing a label on a manila envelope, be sure that the flap is to your *right*.

Figure III.29 A Transcriptionist Preparing Mailing Labels

EXERCISE III.8: CONVERTING ADDRESSES

INSTRUCTIONS: The addresses at the left appear in traditional styles. Using the *National Zip Code and Post Office Directory*, convert these addresses to the modern style recommended by the U.S. Postal Service and type them on the mailing labels at the right.

APPLY YOUR SKILLS

ADDRESSES   MAILING LABELS

EXAMPLE: E. P. V. Originals, Inc.
Suite 2560
Ambassador Building
68 East 66 Street
New York, New York 10022

```
EPV ORIGINALS INC
SUITE 2560
AMBASSADOR 68 E 66 ST
NEW YORK NY 10022
```

1. Mrs. Arlene Miksch-Benton
Claims Service Representative
Grinnell Reinsurance Company
Interstate 94 at Highway 150
Ashby, Massachusetts 01431

2. Dr. Herman Sillman
15211 Ashdale Boulevard South
Portland, OR 97223

3. Turner Corporation
Attention: Mr. Robert Turner
4302 Alvin Street
Houston, TX 77051

4. Ms. Marjorie Yellow Cloud
Apartment 418
6233 South Rhodes
Chicago, IL 60637

5. Mr. Terry K. Thibedeau, Jr.
   13975 La Plaisance
   Captain Cook, HI 96704

INSTRUCTIONS: Check your addresses with the Key to Exercise III.8 in Appendix C.

PLACEMENT OF COPY ON THE PAGE

The "white space" on a page gives balance and organization to the type or print. On typewritten documents, white space "frames" the message, enhancing readability, communication, and general appearance. Exercise III.9 gives practice in typing an appealing, well-balanced document.

EXERCISE III.9: VERTICAL AND HORIZONTAL PLACEMENT

INSTRUCTIONS: Critically evaluate the following letter, memo, and envelope. On the lines to the right of each drawing, write your critique, listing any inconsistencies or inaccuracies in vertical and horizontal placement.

CHECK YOURSELF

1.

FULL-BLOCK LETTER

Your Critique:

_____

_____

_____

_____

_____

2.

MEMO

Your Critique:

_____

_____

_____

_____

_____

3.

```
┌─────────────────────────────────┐
│  ═══                            │
│  ═══        ENVELOPE            │
│  ═══                            │
│                                 │
│          _____    │
│            _____          │
│            _____            │
│                                 │
│       _____                 │
│                                 │
└─────────────────────────────────┘
```

Your Critique:

_____

_____

_____

_____

_____

INSTRUCTIONS: Check your comments with those in the Key to Exercise III.9 in Appendix C.

FINAL STEPS BEFORE MAILING

There are six final steps a transcriptionist must take before mailing a letter or sending a memo. They are:

1. ADDRESS ENVELOPES for the original and all copies. If the addresses for the copies were not dictated, check the files or ask the dictator for them. Place the flap of the envelope over the appropriate original or copy.
2. ASSEMBLE ALL ENCLOSURES and attach them to the document. If you do not have an enclosure and you are expecting the dictator to attach it, write a reminder, address it to the dictator, and attach it to the document.
3. PLACE THE DOCUMENTS in a folder to prevent loss, preserve neatness, and insure confidentiality. Present the folder personally to the dictator or place it on the dictator's desk.
4. OBTAIN A SIGNATURE for letters and authorization initials for memos. If you are authorized to sign the dictator's name or initials to the documents, be sure to place your single initial below the dictator's signature.

Example: **Cordially,**

James R. Leberman

s.   (your initial)

James R. Leberman

5. FOLD THE LETTER and insert the letter plus enclosures into the envelope. Make a quick "double check" to be sure that the envelope and letter match.
6. WEIGH letters with heavy enclosures and determine appropriate postage, or SEND LETTERS to the company mail room for processing.

REMINDER

Four sheets of standard-size paper plus one No. 10 envelope weigh under one ounce.

TIPS FOR THE TRANSCRIPTIONIST

Letters and Memos

1. *Letter style*: Become familiar with all letter styles if you transcribe for many originators.
2. *Line length*: Use a standard line length when typing letters and memos in preference to adjusting the line for different letter lengths. Standard line length is 60 spaces for pica type and 70 spaces for elite type.
3. *Date line*: Express the date in either of the following ways:
    April 7, 1982   or   *7 April 1982*
4. *Title*: Include a title (*Mr., Mrs., Miss,* or *Ms.*) in the inside address and on the corresponding envelope address. Include job titles also.
5. *Two-letter state abbreviations*: These are always typed on the envelope *and* in the inside address. Modern computer addresses are generally not used in the inside address.
6. *Attention line*: The inside address determines the form of the salutation. If the letter is addressed to a company and the attention line is addressed to an individual, the salutation should be directed to the company.
7. *Salutation*: Avoid sexist salutations like *Gentlemen*; use *Ladies and Gentlemen* instead. If you are unsure of the appropriate salutation or if you cannot find one that seems appropriate, use the Simplified letter style, in which no salutation is necessary. Choose the salutation on the basis of the first line of the inside address and the level of formality between the dictator and addressee.
8. *Company name*: Unless you are told to do otherwise, do not type the company name below the complimentary close.
9. *Complimentary close*: Capitalize only the first word in the complimentary close. Match the tone of the complimentary close with the tone of the salutation; for example, use *Cordially* or *Sincerely* with *Dear Bob*. Generally, the longer the complimentary close, the higher the level of formality.
10. *Reference initials*: If the dictator's name appears below the complimentary close, do not type his or her initials on the reference line. The transcriptionist's own initials should always be typed, however.
11. *Enclosure*: The dictator may or may not dictate the word *Enclosure* at the end of the letter. Be alert to the content of the letter and type the appropriate enclosure notation when necessary. Do not staple enclosures to a letter.

12. *Copy distribution*: Place a small check next to the name listed in the notation to facilitate distribution of each copy. Note in Figure III.30 the use of ONE *c* to denote *copy* or *copies*; this eliminates the need to distinguish between a carbon copy (cc) and a photocopy (pc).

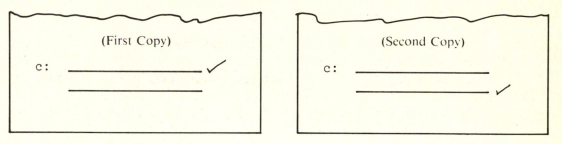

Figure III.30   Copy Distribution

13. *Blind copy*: Do not type a blind copy notation (*bc*) on the original. Type *bc* in the upper left-hand corner of the copies only.
14. *Two-page letters*: Remember to label the second and following pages of a letter or memo with the name of the addressee, the date, and the page number. Carry at least three or four lines of the body of a letter or memo over to the next page. Never begin a second or following page with fewer than two lines from a paragraph.
15. *Letter format*: Use single spacing when typing a letter of average length; use double spacing between paragraphs. If you double space a short letter, be sure to indent paragraphs.

Envelopes

1. *Addresses*: Always single space an address.
2. *Two-letter state abbreviations*: Never guess at the correct two-letter abbreviation; always double-check when you're uncertain.
3. *Window envelopes*: Check to make sure that the address is visible through the window on the envelope.

Making Changes in Content or Format

1. *Content changes*: Get your dictator's approval to make changes in content or format.
2. *Using photocopiers*: You may be able to eliminate retyping a document that will be photocopied by cutting and taping the salvageable parts of the original.
3. *Pencil-and-ink corrections*: Never "pencil in" or "ink in" a correction on final copy. Take the time either to correct the error or to retype if necessary.
4. *Substituting a word or phrase*: If you are having trouble finding the correct usage for something dictated, try substituting another word or phrase. Be careful not to alter meanings as you rewrite.
5. *Adjustments while typing*: To avoid having to retype, learn to make design adjustments on the first try. For example, if a letter seems too high on the page, spread the closing lines to give the letter better balance.

6. *Versatility of postscript*: If you have typed a document and the originator remembers something that should have been added, include it in the postscript instead of retyping the letter.

Some Final Tips

1. *Set priorities*: Transcribe URGENT documents first.
2. *Center properly*: Learn to do simple centering by estimating.
3. *Verify numbers*: Always check additions, percentages, and other figures. If there appears to be an error or a discrepancy, see your dictator.
4. *Check paragraphing*: Although most dictators dictate paragraphs, remain alert to any oversights.
5. *Listen for punctuation*: Listen to the dictator's voice changes for clues to punctuation.
6. *Evaluate memo size*: Although half-page memos save paper, they are harder to file and find.
7. *Use paper clips with care*: When attaching material to an original with a paper clip, place a small protective sheet under the clip to avoid tearing the original or making unsightly crease marks on it.

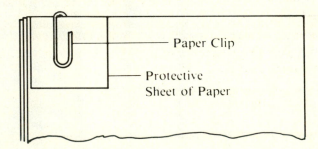

Figure III.31   Protecting the Original

8. *Staple selectively*: Never staple a two-page letter; however, two-page memos are frequently stapled. Staple diagonally across the corner of a page rather than parallel to the top edge of the paper. This technique prevents tearing of the top sheet.

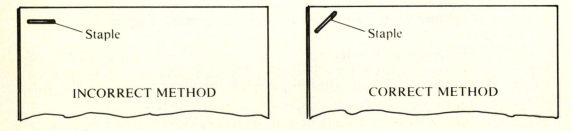

Figure III.32   Using Staples

9. *Safeguard confidential materials*: Cover confidential materials when you leave your work area.

MANUSCRIPTS

Depending upon the organization, you may find yourself typing manuscripts and reports as frequently as letters or memos. Therefore, you will want to review the specific format for manuscript typing. Manuscript style is used for organizational reports and should be typed on good-quality bond paper measuring 8½ by 11 inches.

Figure III.33   Reports

A sample of the first page of an unbound manuscript[3] is illustrated in Figure III.34.

---

[3]Leonard J. West. *Modern College Typewriting: A Basic Course*. New York: Harcourt Brace Jovanovich, 1977, p. xiii.

Figure III.34 Manuscript

Use a 1½ inch top margin.
(Start typing on line 10.)

Do not number first page. Number all other pages at top.

Center the title. ⟶ HOW TO TYPE A TERM PAPER

2 blank lines

There are several different report writing procedures. All

Use 1- or 1½-inch margins. Allow additional ½ inch if bound.

deal with the features that are common to all report writing, but

Use 1- or 1½-inch margins. Double space the body.

vary on how some of those features are treated. The style

used in many professional journals and advocated in a college

typewriting textbook[1] is explained and illustrated here.

2 blank lines

Center the heading. ⟶ Unbound Reports

2 blank lines

As is evident from this page, an unbound report has equal

side margins: either 1 or 1½ inches on each side. Whether bound

or unbound, the title of a report or term paper is centered 1½

inches from the top of the first page. All pages use a 1-inch

bottom margin. Triple space after the report title.

2 blank lines

Side heading ⟶ Headings

1 blank line

Again, as shown on this page, major divisions of a report are

typed as centered headings,[2] always preceded and followed by a

triple space. Subsections of a major division are shown by side

headings, also preceded by a triple space.

1 blank line

Paragraph Headings. The final level of heading is the

paragraph head, as illustrated in this paragraph. Note the solid

underscoring of both side and paragraph heads, as well as the

initial capitals in those heads. Notice also that there is no

extra spacing above a paragraph head.

2 blank lines

Leave a 1-inch bottom margin (6 blank lines).

[1]Leonard J. West. Modern College Typewriting: A Basic Course.

single space

New York: Harcourt Brace Jovanovich, 1977.

1 blank line

[2]It is permissible to underline centered heads, but it is not

single space

desirable to do so.

ROUGH DRAFTS

Whenever additional work remains to be done on the content of a document, you may be asked to type the document in rough-draft form. Here are several rough-draft typing tips:

1. Type the document with wide margins to provide "white" space for changes, additions, or instructions.
2. Double space or, better, triple space on the page.
3. Always correct errors; however, you can "x" out a word or line if making a major correction would be time-consuming.
4. In order to avoid confusing the reader, do not strike over incorrect letters.
5. When you are proofing a rough draft, occasional handwritten corrections are acceptable.

Consult with your dictator to arrive at an acceptable rough-draft style. When typing final copy from a rough draft, you will be able to transcribe faster and more accurately if your dictator has used proofreader's marks. Figure III.35 is an example of a rough draft typed by a transcriptionist.

Figure III.35   Rough Draft

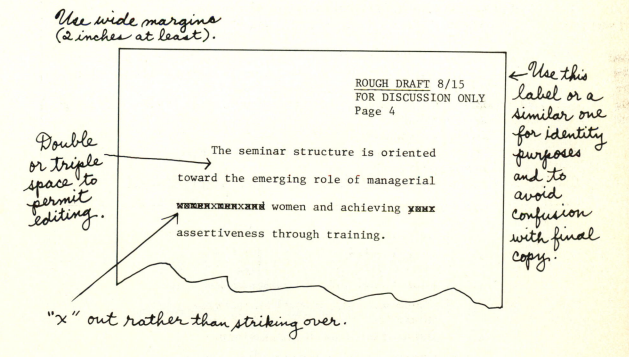

TABLES

Typed tables range all the way from simple to very complex. A table may form part of a letter, memo, or manuscript. After you develop a "feel" for the contents of a particular table, you will need to make some formatting decisions prior to typing, such as:

- Shall I type the table ruled or unruled?
- Shall I single or double space the table?
- Shall I type the table across the length or the width of a page?

When typing tables, your goals are readability and attractiveness. Figure III.36 itemizes some basic guidelines that will help you develop judgment in setting up tables.

Figure III.36   Guidelines for Typing Tables

1. Center all tables horizontally and vertically on the page or within the available space of a letter, memo, or manuscript.
2. Single or double space the body of the table.
3. Type the table title in all caps.
4. Double space between the lines of a table title and subtitles.
5. a. In an *unruled table*, triple space below the table title or subtitle and type the column headings.
   b. In a *ruled table*, double space below the table title or subtitle and type an underscore for the horizontal line. Then double space and type the column headings. Finally, single space and type another underscore.
6. Center each column heading above the longest line in the column. (Column headings usually are underscored.)
7. Double space before typing the body of the table.
8. Allow a minimum of six spaces between columns, if possible.
9. Align column numbers on the right.
10. Use a ruler and a pen with black ink when you must insert lines by hand.

REMINDER

Tables are usually given to the transcriptionist as "rough" handwritten copy rather than verbally in dictated form.

You will find an example of an unruled table in Figure III.37 and an example of a ruled table in Figure III.38.

Figure III.37   Unruled Table

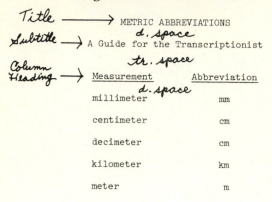

Title ⟶ METRIC ABBREVIATIONS
d. space
Subtitle ⟶ A Guide for the Transcriptionist
tr. space
Column Heading ⟶ Measurement   Abbreviation
d. space
millimeter   mm

centimeter   cm

decimeter   cm

kilometer   km

meter   m

Figure III.38   Ruled Table

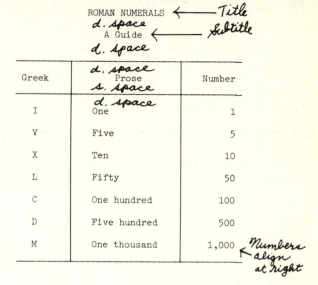

ROMAN NUMERALS ⟵ *Title*
d. space
A Guide ⟵ *Subtitle*
d. space

Greek	*d. space* Prose *s. space*	Number
	d. space	
I	One	1
V	Five	5
X	Ten	10
L	Fifty	50
C	One hundred	100
D	Five hundred	500
M	One thousand	1,000

Numbers align at right

GRAPHS

Graphs—like tables—are sometimes used to illustrate and highlight features of a report. Figures III.39, III.40, and III.41 show three types of graphs: a bar graph, a line graph, and a circle graph.

Normally, a dictator will give you a rough draft of what is wanted in the graph, rather than dictate the information. Consult a secretarial reference manual for further information.

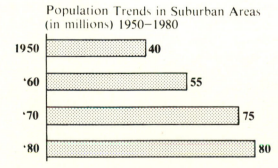

Population Trends in Suburban Areas (in millions) 1950–1980

1950 — 40
'60 — 55
'70 — 75
'80 — 80

Figure III.39   Bar Graph

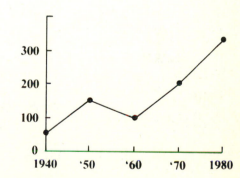

Figure III.40   Line Graph

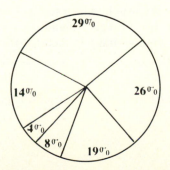

29% 26% 19% 8% 4% 14%

Figure III.41   Circle Graph

MINUTES OF MEETINGS

Many companies use a standard format for minutes of meetings. Figure III.42 illustrates a typical layout for the first and second pages of a typed set of minutes.

Figure III.42   Minutes of a Meeting

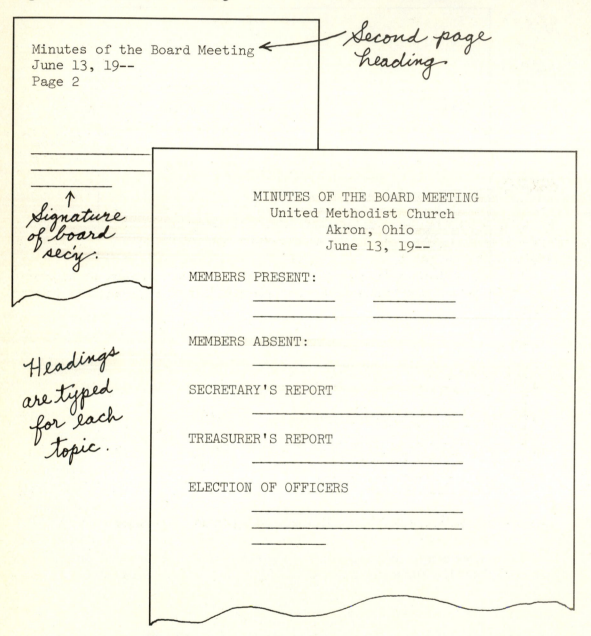

OUTLINES

Occasionally you will need to type an outline. Notice the number, letter, and spacing format in Figure III.43.

Figure III.43   Outline

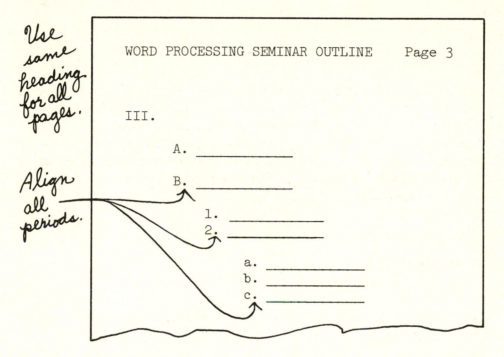

MAKING FORMATTING DECISIONS

When a dictator requests that you follow a fixed format or adhere to a specific style when typing a document, you should, of course, comply. There will be occasions, however, when no directions are given. It will then be up to you to exercise your own judgment and to use ingenuity and imagination in choosing or innovating an appropriate style. Being able to express your individuality in this way—by injecting something of yourself into a project—is a highly satisfying experience, especially when designing such flexible projects as sales fliers and conference programs. No matter what the task, be careful to follow a format that will enhance the message, not detract from it.

Figure III.44 is a list of suggestions about how to highlight and add variety to a typed document. Use these techniques only within the limits of correct style.

Figure III.44   How to Highlight in Formatting

- Indent from both margins
- Underscore a word or words
- Type words in ALL CAPS
- Change typing element
  (Orator, Script, Italic, Olde English)
- Change the pitch
- Use special keyboard characters
- Draw lines, circles, or boxes
- Backspace from the right margin
- Justify the right margin
- Center a word or line

When you type paragraphs, keep them short—in any event, not more than seven or eight lines. Also, vary the length of paragraphs in a letter or memo, making the first and last the shortest. A letter or memo with several paragraphs will look better and be easier to read than one with just one long paragraph.

You can also organize material in the following formats to add variety and to review information.

- Lists
- Tables
- Outlines
- Graphs

Use these alternatives flexibly and creatively. As time goes by, you may be given even greater responsibility for making formatting decisions or suggestions, so remain constantly alert to different ways of organizing and presenting information.

It is possible—even likely—that during your early days on the job, you will not be given the opportunity to use any of these suggestions. However, as you gain in expertise and experience, you can look forward to the time when you will have earned the right to make your own changes and set your own style.

EXERCISE III.10: PARAGRAPHING

INSTRUCTIONS: In the following exercise, locate the three logical paragraphs by inserting the paragraph symbol (¶) where each new paragraph begins.

CHECK YOURSELF

> With the spiraling cost of gasoline, transportation costs have risen sharply. One way to reduce these expenses is to take the bus. Starting the first week of July, all employees will be able to purchase monthly bus passes at the cashier's desk on the third floor. Bus schedules will also be available there. The cost of the pass is $15. The pass is good for UNLIMITED city travel for one month. In case you don't live in the immediate metropolitan area or you can't take advantage of the bus service, you may be interested in some information on car pooling that will be available in September.

INSTRUCTIONS: Check your selection with the Key to Exercise III.10 in Appendix C.

EXERCISE III.11: SELECTING A FORMAT

INSTRUCTIONS: Although the following information is accurate and complete, the reader may have difficulty assimilating it in its present format. How would you reorganize this information to make it more readable? Create your draft in the space provided, putting the cities in alphabetical order.

ATTENDANCE AT THE NATIONAL CONFERENCE

In 1980 Detroit had 2,367 participants and 3,922 in 1981.
Chicago had 5,490 participants in 1980 and 6,322 in 1981.
Minneapolis had 4,852 participants in 1980 and 7,364 in 1981.
In 1980 Kansas City had 2,893 participants and only 2,066 in 1981.
Des Moines had 1,495 participants in 1980 and 1,940 in 1981.

Draft your revision in the space provided below:

INSTRUCTIONS: Compare your draft with another student's and with the Key to Exercise III.11 in Appendix C.

WORKING WITH "ODD" SIZE PAPER

As a transcription specialist, you cannot count on always using standard 8½ x 11 inch paper. It may be necessary at times to arrange information or center a title on an "odd" size paper or on cards. Exercise III.12 provides drill in working with "odd" size stationery.

EXERCISE III.12: WORKING WITH "ODD" SIZE PAPER

INSTRUCTIONS: Complete the following exercise by calculating the vertical center and the horizontal center of each size listed. Write your answers in the spaces provided.   **CHECK YOURSELF**

If your paper size is . . .	THE VERTICAL CENTER is . . .	THE HORIZONTAL CENTER is . . .	
		PICA	ELITE
1. 3 inches long by 5 inches wide	_____	_____	_____
2. 10 inches long by 8 inches wide	_____	_____	_____
3. 11½ inches long by 7½ inches wide	_____	_____	_____
4. 8½ inches long by 5½ inches wide	_____	_____	_____
5. 14 inches long by 11½ inches wide	_____	_____	_____

INSTRUCTIONS: Check your answers with the Key to Exercise III.12 in Appendix C.

EXERCISE III.13: CREATIVITY

**APPLY
YOUR SKILLS**

INSTRUCTIONS: Let's assume your employer has asked you to prepare an "eye-catching" notice to send to all employees, announcing a company picnic at a local park. You immediately eliminate the idea of sending out a simple memo and decide to concentrate instead on developing a creative flier, giving all the necessary information such as date, time, location, and activities planned.

    In the space provided, draft your ideas, using some of the formatting techniques discussed in Phase III. Then type the final document from your draft and submit it to your instructor for evaluation and suggestions.

ORGANIZE YOUR IDEAS . . .

INSTRUCTIONS: Check your design with the list of essentials in the Key to Exercise III.13 in Appendix C.

STUDENT'S TALLY SHEET/PHASE IV: SPELLING

Name_____

Target Completion Date_____

STUDENT'S ACTIVITY	DATE COMPLETED	STUDENT'S QUESTIONS AND COMMENTS
STUDY **Introduction to Phase IV**		
STUDY **Definitions**		
STUDY **Basic Rules of Grammar**		
TAKE Pretest IV.1 and SUBMIT to instructor		
TRANSCRIBE Exercise IV.1 (tape)		
DO Exercise IV.2		
STUDY **Basic Spelling Points**		
STUDY **Spelling Rule 1** and examples		
DO Exercise IV.3		
STUDY **Spelling Rule 2.a** and examples		
DO Exercise IV.4a		
STUDY **Spelling Rule 2.b** and examples		
DO Exercise IV.4b		
STUDY **Spelling Rule 2.c** and example		
DO Exercise IV.4c		

STUDENT'S ACTIVITY	DATE COMPLETED	STUDENT'S QUESTIONS AND COMMENTS
STUDY **Spelling Rule 3** and examples		
DO Exercise IV.5		
STUDY **Spelling Rule 4** and examples		
DO Exercise IV.6		
STUDY **Spelling Rule 5** and examples		
DO Exercise IV.7		
STUDY **Spelling Rule 6** and examples		
DO Exercise IV.8		
STUDY **Spelling Rule 7** and examples		
DO Exercise IV.9		
STUDY **Spelling Rule 8** and examples		
DO Exercise IV.10		
STUDY **Spelling Rule 9** and examples		
DO Exercise IV.11		
STUDY **Spelling Rule 10** and examples		
DO Exercise IV.12		
STUDY **Summary of Spelling Rules**		
STUDY **Homonyms and Words Similar in Sound**		
DO Exercise IV.13		
DO Practice Exercises		

STUDENT'S ACTIVITY	DATE COMPLETED	STUDENT'S QUESTIONS AND COMMENTS
STUDY **One or Two Words**		
DO Exercise IV.14		
DO Practice Exercises		
TRANSCRIBE Posttest IV.1 (tape)		
STUDY **Making a List of Spelling Errors**		
BEGIN Exercise IV.15		

PERSONAL GOALS FOR IMPROVEMENT IN SPELLING

1. _____

2. _____

INSTRUCTOR'S COMMENTS: _____

_____

_____

STUDENT'S TALLY SHEET/PHASE IV: WORD DIVISION

Name_____

Target Completion Date_____

STUDENT'S ACTIVITY	DATE COMPLETED	STUDENT'S QUESTIONS AND COMMENTS
STUDY **Word Division** rules and examples		
DO Exercise IV.16		
DO Practice Exercises		

PERSONAL GOALS FOR IMPROVEMENT IN WORD DIVISION

1. _____

2. _____

INSTRUCTOR'S COMMENTS: _____

_____

_____

STUDENT'S TALLY SHEET/PHASE IV: CAPITALIZATION

Name_____

Target Completion Date_____

STUDENT'S ACTIVITY	DATE COMPLETED	STUDENT'S QUESTIONS AND COMMENTS
TAKE Pretest IV.2 and SUBMIT to instructor		
STUDY **Capitalization** rules and examples		
DO Exercise IV.17		
TRANSCRIBE Achievement Survey Tape IV.1 and SUBMIT to instructor (tape)		
DO Practice Exercises		
TRANSCRIBE Posttest IV.2 (tape)		

PERSONAL GOALS FOR IMPROVEMENT IN CAPITALIZATION

1. _____

2. _____

INSTRUCTOR'S COMMENTS: _____

_____

_____

STUDENT'S TALLY SHEET/PHASE IV: NUMBERS

Name_____

Target Completion Date_____

STUDENT'S ACTIVITY	DATE COMPLETED	STUDENT'S QUESTIONS AND COMMENTS
TAKE Pretest IV.3 and SUBMIT to instructor		
STUDY **Numbers as Figures** rules and examples		
DO Exercise IV.18		
STUDY **Numbers as Words** rules and examples		
DO Exercise IV.19		
TRANSCRIBE Achievement Survey Tape IV.2 and SUBMIT to instructor (tape)		
DO Practice Exercises		
TRANSCRIBE Posttest IV.3 (tape)		

PERSONAL GOALS FOR IMPROVEMENT IN EXPRESSING NUMBERS

1. _____

2. _____

INSTRUCTOR'S COMMENTS: _____

_____

_____

STUDENT'S TALLY SHEET/PHASE IV: COMMA

Name_____

Target Completion Date_____

STUDENT'S ACTIVITY	DATE COMPLETED	STUDENT'S QUESTIONS AND COMMENTS
READ **Introduction to Punctuation**		
TAKE Pretest IV.4 and SUBMIT to instructor		
STUDY **Series Comma** rule and examples		
DO Exercise IV.20		
STUDY **Introductory Comma** rule and examples		
DO Exercise IV.21		
STUDY **Explanatory Comma** rule and examples		
DO Exercise IV.22		
TRANSCRIBE Achievement Survey Tape IV.3 and SUBMIT to instructor (tape)		
DO Practice Exercises		
STUDY **Parenthetical Comma** rule and examples		
DO Exercise IV.23		
STUDY **Direct Address Comma** rule and examples		
DO Exercise IV.24		
STUDY **Modifier Comma** rule and examples		
DO Exercise IV.25		

STUDENT'S ACTIVITY	DATE COMPLETED	STUDENT'S QUESTIONS AND COMMENTS
TRANSCRIBE Achievement Survey Tape IV.4 and SUBMIT to instructor (tape)		
DO Practice Exercises		
STUDY **Nonrestrictive Comma** rule and example		
DO Exercise IV.26		
STUDY **Independent Clauses Comma** rule and example		
DO Exercise IV.27		
STUDY **Dates and States Commas** rules and examples		
DO Exercise IV.28		
TRANSCRIBE Achievement Survey Tape IV.5 and SUBMIT to instructor (tape)		
DO Practice Exercises		
TRANSCRIBE Posttest IV.4		

PERSONAL GOALS FOR IMPROVEMENT IN USING COMMAS

1. _____

2. _____

INSTRUCTOR'S COMMENTS: _____

_____

_____

STUDENT'S TALLY SHEET/PHASE IV: APOSTROPHE

Name_____

Target Completion Date_____

STUDENT'S ACTIVITY	DATE COMPLETED	STUDENT'S QUESTIONS AND COMMENTS
TAKE Pretest IV.5 and SUBMIT to instructor		
STUDY **Singular Noun Possessives** rule and example		
DO Exercise IV.29		
STUDY **Compound Noun Possessives** rule and example		
DO Exercise IV.30		
STUDY **Proper Name Possessives** rules and examples		
DO Exercise IV.31		
STUDY **Inanimate Object Possessives** rule and example		
DO Exercise IV.32		
TRANSCRIBE Achievement Survey Tape IV.6 and SUBMIT to instructor (tape)		
DO Practice Exercises		
STUDY **Plural Noun Possessives** rules and examples		
DO Exercise IV.33		
STUDY **Noun Understood Possessives** rule and example		
DO Exercise IV.34		

STUDENT'S ACTIVITY	DATE COMPLETED	STUDENT'S QUESTIONS AND COMMENTS
STUDY **Personal Pronoun and Indefinite Pronoun Possessives** rules and examples		
DO Exercise IV.35		
STUDY **Time and Measurement Possessives** rule and examples		
DO Exercise IV.36		
TRANSCRIBE Achievement Survey Tape IV.7 and SUBMIT to instructor (tape)		
DO Practice Exercises		
TRANSCRIBE Posttest IV.5 (tape)		

PERSONAL GOALS FOR IMPROVEMENT IN USING APOSTROPHES

1. _____

2. _____

INSTRUCTOR'S COMMENTS: _____

_____

_____

STUDENT'S TALLY SHEET/PHASE IV: COLON

Name_____

Target Completion Date_____

STUDENT'S ACTIVITY	DATE COMPLETED	STUDENT'S QUESTIONS AND COMMENTS
TAKE Pretest IV.6 and SUBMIT to instructor		
STUDY **Colon** rules and examples		
DO Exercise IV.37		
TRANSCRIBE Achievement Survey Tape IV.8 and SUBMIT to instructor (tape)		
DO Practice Exercises		
TRANSCRIBE Posttest IV.6 (tape)		

PERSONAL GOALS FOR IMPROVEMENT IN USING COLONS

1. _____

2. _____

INSTRUCTOR'S COMMENTS: _____

_____

_____

STUDENT'S TALLY SHEET/PHASE IV: SEMICOLON

Name_____

Target Completion Date _____

STUDENT'S ACTIVITY	DATE COMPLETED	STUDENT'S QUESTIONS AND COMMENTS
TAKE Pretest IV.7 and SUBMIT to instructor		
STUDY **Semicolon** rules and examples		
DO Exercise IV.38		
TRANSCRIBE Achievement Survey Tape IV.9 and SUBMIT to instructor (tape)		
DO Practice Exercises		
TRANSCRIBE Posttest IV.7 (tape)		

PERSONAL GOALS FOR IMPROVEMENT IN USING SEMICOLONS

1. _____

2. _____

INSTRUCTOR'S COMMENTS: _____

_____

_____

STUDENT'S TALLY SHEET/PHASE IV: HYPHEN

Name_____

Target Completion Date_____

STUDENT'S ACTIVITY	DATE COMPLETED	STUDENT'S QUESTIONS AND COMMENTS
TAKE Pretest IV.8 and SUBMIT to instructor		
STUDY **Hyphen with Numbers** rules and examples		
DO Exercise IV.39		
STUDY **Hyphen with Prefixes and Suffixes** rules and examples		
DO Exercise IV.40		
STUDY **Hyphen with Compound Adjectives Preceding and Following Nouns** rules and examples		
DO Exercise IV.41		
TRANSCRIBE Achievement Survey Tape IV.10 and SUBMIT to instructor (tape)		
DO Practice Exercises		
TRANSCRIBE Posttest IV.8 (tape)		

PERSONAL GOALS FOR IMPROVEMENT IN USING HYPHENS

1. _____

2. _____

INSTRUCTOR'S COMMENTS: _____

_____

_____

STUDENT'S TALLY SHEET/PHASE IV: DASH

Name_____

Target Completion Date _____

STUDENT'S ACTIVITY	DATE COMPLETED	STUDENT'S QUESTIONS AND COMMENTS
TAKE Pretest IV.9 and SUBMIT to instructor		
STUDY **Dash** rules and examples		
DO Exercise IV.42		
TRANSCRIBE Achievement Survey Tape IV.11 and SUBMIT to instructor (tape)		
DO Practice Exercises		
TRANSCRIBE Posttest IV.9 (tape)		

PERSONAL GOALS FOR IMPROVEMENT IN USING DASHES

1. _____

2. _____

INSTRUCTOR'S COMMENTS: _____

_____

_____

STUDENT'S TALLY SHEET/PHASE IV: QUOTATION MARKS

Name_____

Target Completion Date_____

STUDENT'S ACTIVITY	DATE COMPLETED	STUDENT'S QUESTIONS AND COMMENTS
TAKE Pretest IV.10 and SUBMIT to instructor		
STUDY **Quotation Marks** rules and examples		
DO Exercise IV.43		
TRANSCRIBE Achievement Survey Tape IV.12 and SUBMIT to instructor (tape)		
DO Practice Exercises		
TRANSCRIBE Posttest IV.10 (tape)		

PERSONAL GOALS FOR IMPROVEMENT IN USING QUOTATION MARKS

1. _____

2. _____

INSTRUCTOR'S COMMENTS: _____

_____

_____

PHASE IV

PHASE IV

ENGLISH SKILLS

INTRODUCTION

ONE OF THE MOST IMPORTANT RESOURCES in the transcription specialist's inventory of working skills is a proficiency in English grammar, spelling, punctuation, and usage. The importance of such competence was demonstrated in a recent U.S. Government survey which revealed that a high level of proficiency in English skills constitutes one of the most significant hallmarks of superior job performance.[1]

To help you review, reinforce, and refine your language skills, a number of different activities are provided in Phase IV. They include:

1. **Pretests.** Before you begin work on any section of this phase, you will take a pretest. Your instructor will evaluate each completed pretest and determine how much, if any, additional study you need to do in a particular section.
2. **Section Exercises.** After reading the rules and studying the examples, you will check your mastery of the material by completing the short exercises in each section.
3. **Achievement Survey Tapes.** Some sections in Phase IV provide you with the opportunity to transcribe documents from tape, applying several of the rules covered.
4. **Practice Exercises.** Additional exercises are provided in Appendix B for further review and practice.
5. **Posttest Tapes.** A taped posttest will help you and your instructor evaluate your expertise in specific English skills.

[1]*Management Introduction to Word Processing*, U.S. Department of the Army, April 1, 1975, p. 10-3.

After completing Phase IV, you will

- Know the rules for spelling, capitalization, word division, and expressing numbers.
- Understand how the comma, apostrophe, colon, semicolon, hyphen, dash, and quotation marks are used.
- Be able to do actual machine transcription.
- Be ready to produce mailable documents.

DEFINITIONS

We begin our English skills coverage with a review of the definitions of the descriptive terms you will need to know as you work through Phase IV.

Adjective
A word that describes a noun; it may tell how many, what kind, or which one.
EXAMPLES: happy, known, new, remote

Antecedent
The word, phrase, or clause to which a pronoun refers.
EXAMPLE: The directors are holding their yearly meeting today.

          antecedent   pronoun

Compound adjective
Two or more words that act as a single modifier.
EXAMPLES: air-conditioned, five-year-old,
          head-on, jet-propelled

Conjunction
A word that connects words, phrases, and clauses.
EXAMPLES: and, but, for, nor

Contraction
A word group shortened by omitting a letter.
EXAMPLES: it is = it's; could not = couldn't;
          should not = shouldn't; was not = wasn't

Dependent clause
A group of words containing a subject and a verb and that cannot stand alone.
EXAMPLE: If you have any further questions about it, please write again.

          dependent clause

125

Direct address

Use of a person's name or title.

Direct quotation

Exact words written or spoken.

Enumeration

A list of numbered items.

Inanimate object

Something that does not possess life.
EXAMPLES: book, pencil, typewriter

Independent clause

A group of words containing a subject and a verb and that can stand alone as a complete thought.
EXAMPLE: I will be here today, *but* I won't be here tomorrow.

            independent clause   independent clause

Noun

The name of a person, place, thing, quality, idea, or action.
EXAMPLES: Hector, St. Louis, footprint, knock

Nonrestrictive material

A phrase or clause that may be omitted without changing the meaning of a sentence.
EXAMPLE: Automatic typing equipment, which we use,

                             nonrestrictive
can be a great time-saver in the office.

Parenthetical material

A word, phrase, or clause that is not necessary to the rest of the sentence.
EXAMPLE: We will all be at the meeting, of course.

                         parenthetical

Personification

Act of making an inanimate object or abstract idea have the qualities of a person.
EXAMPLE: The sun smiled on us.

Phrase

A group of two or more words without a subject and verb but expressing a thought.
EXAMPLE: On the other hand, our costs have been reduced considerably.

              phrase

Pronoun

A word used to take the place of a noun.
EXAMPLE: I saw her yesterday.

            pronoun

Subject

In a sentence, one or more words about which something is said and which serves as the starting point of the action. Subjects are usually nouns or pronouns.
EXAMPLE: <u>She</u> called yesterday.

       subject

Verb

A word expressing an action or condition of the subject of a sentence.
EXAMPLE: She <u>called</u> yesterday.

          verb

BASIC RULES OF GRAMMAR

RULE: A verb agrees in number with the subject of a sentence.

EXAMPLES:

The   <u>box</u>   <u>was</u>   big.

      singular singular
      subject   verb

The   <u>boxes</u>   <u>were</u>   big.

      plural   plural
      subject   verb

RULE: Disregard intervening phrases and clauses in a sentence when establishing subject and verb agreement.

EXAMPLES:

The   <u>box</u>   of   photo   supplies   <u>was</u>   big.

    singular   intervening phrase   singular
    subject   verb

The   <u>boxes</u>   of   photo   supplies   <u>were</u>   big.

    plural   intervening phrase   plural
    subject   verb

RULE: If there are singular subjects in a sentence joined by *and*, a plural verb is required.

EXAMPLE:

The   tackle   <u>box</u>   and   fishing   <u>rod</u>   <u>are</u>   in

              singular   singular   plural
              subject   subject   verb

the car trunk.

RULE: If the subjects in a sentence are joined by *and* and refer to one person or a singular unit, a singular verb is required.

EXAMPLE:

My   math   instructor   and   football   coach   is   Mr.

subjects referring to one person   singular verb

Hartung.

RULE: If the subjects in a sentence joined by *and* are preceded by *every* or *each*, a singular verb is required.

EXAMPLE:

Each   officer   and   *every*   member-at-large   is   expected

singular verb

to be at the executive committee meeting.

RULE: If words such as *each, either, neither, everybody, anyone,* or *one* are used as the subject, a singular verb is required.

EXAMPLES:

Each   transcriptionist   is   required   to   keep

subject   singular verb

production   records.

Neither   of   the   employees   is   absent.

subject   singular verb

RULE: Compound nouns require a singular verb because the group or quantity is considered a single unit.

EXAMPLE:

The Board of Directors   is   here today.

compound noun   singular verb

RULE: Nouns plural in form but singular in meaning usually take singular verbs.

EXAMPLE:

The   local   news   is   on   television   at   6 p.m.

plural noun, singular in meaning   singular verb

RULE: Avoid changes in verb tense in a sentence.

EXAMPLES:

> **Wrong:** She approach<u>ed</u> the customer and tr<u>ies</u> to help her.

> **Right:** She approach<u>ed</u> the customer and tr<u>ied</u> to help her.

RULE: A pronoun agrees with its antecedent in number, gender, and person.

EXAMPLES:

> <u>Robin</u>   wants   to   know   whether   <u>her</u>   typewriter
>
> antecedent   pronoun
>
> has been repaired.

> The   <u>Wilsons</u>   are   hosting   the   reception   on
>
>   antecedent
>
> <u>their</u>   yacht.
>
> pronoun

RULE: When a pronoun is the subject of a verb, use the nominative form of the personal pronoun (I, we, he, she, they).

EXAMPLE:

> Helen or I can work on the project.

> > **Hint:** If you omit *Helen or* from the sentence, the nominative form *I* appears as the correct pronoun to use.

> > *I can work on the project.* Not *Me can work on the project.*

RULE: When a pronoun is the object of a verb, use the objective form of the personal pronoun (me, us, him, her, them).

EXAMPLE:

> Susie asked my friend and me over for dinner.

> > **Hint:** If you omit *my friend and* from the sentence, the objective form *me* appears as the correct pronoun to use.

> > *Susie asked me over for dinner.* Not *Susie asked I over for dinner.*

SPELLING

In the hierarchy of transcription skills, the ability to turn out a correctly spelled document ranks close to the top. The professional transcription specialist is ever conscious of the need to verify correct spelling because of the negative impact just one error can make.

Keep a dictionary or ready-reference word book near you so that you can refer to it quickly and easily. *Never* guess at the correct spelling of even a single word. The return of a document for reason of incorrect spelling can do more to downgrade a transcriptionist's professional reputation than almost any other single failing.

This section is designed to help you improve your personal spelling skills. The section opens with a pretest which checks your present skill level; this is followed by intensive and extensive drill in four different categories of spelling exercises. The section closes with a posttest that verifies, reviews, and reinforces your upgraded spelling skills.

Name _____ Date _____

PRETEST IV.1: SPELLING

INSTRUCTIONS: Circle the misspelled words in the memo in Part A and in the letter in Part B. Write the correct spelling of the misspelled words in the blank spaces.

    Some lines may have more than one misspelled word; in others, there may be none at all. Misspelled words may occur in proper names in the headings of the memo as well as in the inside address of the letter. *Do not use a dictionary or word book for the pretest.*

PART A

1. TO:	John C. Accomodate	1. _____
2. FROM:	Ronald M. Enviroment	2. _____
3. SUBJECT:	Renewal of your Subscripion	3. _____

4.   As is apparant from the enclosed notice,   4. _____

5. your subscripion will expire on February 10.   5. _____

6. Don't be embarassed; its alright. Many people   6. _____

7. forget to renew there subscripion. However,   7. _____

8. it is our belief that you definitly should   8. _____

9. take this oppurtunity to continue to recieve   9. _____

10. this fine publication. Make a concious   10. _____

11. effort to fill out the enclosed form, and you   11. _____

12. will once again have the privlege of recieving   12. _____

13. 12 more wonderful issues of PERSONAL OPPINION.   13. _____

14.   We think that your entire family will be   14. _____

15. facinated by the content of this magazine and   15. _____

16. derive alot of pleasure from it. Many people   16. _____

17. have benefitted from the valueable information   17. _____

18. in PERSONAL OPPINION. Their are reading   18. _____

19. experinces of intrest for every member of the   19. _____

20. family--for your children who are busy studing,   20. _____

21. for your daughter who is thinking about   21. _____

22. marrage, and for the man of the house who is   22. _____

23. busy with his profesion and may be coping with 23. _____

24. being transfered or finding it necesary to 24. _____

25. take over more household duties. For the wife 25. _____

26. and mother of the family, there will be arti- 26. _____

27. cles of signficance by prominant authors that 27. _____

28. she will throughly enjoy. She also will find 28. _____

29. it a convient means of keeping informed. 29. _____

30.   Don't delay. Start your copies of this 30. _____

31. practicel publication comeing your way at once. 31. _____

32. You may want to surprize a member of your 32. _____

33. family by quitly ordering a subscripion for 33. _____

34. some special occassion. Send your order today! 34. _____

35. PS: Its posible for you to renew now and be 35. _____

36. billed later. Just check the apropriate box 36. _____

37. on the enclosed card and mail it immediatly. 37. _____

38. You will recieve an acknowledgement of your 38. _____

39. renewal. 39. _____

PART B

40. Mr. Ralph O. Oppinion 40. _____

41. 2415 Occurence Boulevard 41. _____

42. Pittsburgh, PA 19105 42. _____

43. Dear Ralph: 43. _____

44.   It has occured to me that, as a teacher, you 44. _____

45. would enjoy the experinces of being amoung 45. _____

46. those who will have the privlege of seeing a 46. _____

47. fine musical preformance next month. In my 47. _____

48. judgement, the Westport Young People's Chorus 48. _____

49. can provide such an excellant experince. 49. _____

50.   This group has an interesting history, 50. _____

51. and it's reputation as a prominant musical 51. _____

52. group is a shining example of fine talent. 52. _____

53. Giving a preformance before the public can 53. _____

54. result in a great sence of satisfaction and   54. _____

55. achievment for these young musicians. That is   55. _____

56. why its perticularly important that they have   56. _____

57. a good audience for their comeing concert on   57. _____

58. Thursday evening, November 13, at 8 p.m. The   58. _____

59. concert will be preceeded by an ice cream   59. _____

60. social beginning at 6:30 p.m. in the high   60. _____

61. school cafeteria. The cost for both is merly   61. _____

62. $2. All the preceeds go to the Needy Children's   62. _____

63. Fund. This expendature is tax-deductable.   63. _____

64.   We reccomend you buy your tickets write   64. _____

65. now. Many parents have already purchased   65. _____

66. there tickets.   66. _____

67.   Enjoy the good sence of rythm and the   67. _____

68. enthusasm of this group as well as their fine   68. _____

69. tone quality. Mail your order to Westport   69. _____

70. High School Music Department. Tickets should   70. _____

71. be paid for by check or money order. Make   71. _____

72. checks payable to Westport High School. I   72. _____

73. will be greatful for your assistence and for   73. _____

74. your refering others to me.   74. _____

75. Sincerely,   75. _____

76. John A. Russell, Chairman   76. _____

77. Needy Children's Fund   77. _____

78. PS: We will apreciate your completing and   78. _____

79. returning the questionaire on the second page   79. _____

80. of the pamplet that is being sent under   80. _____

81. seperate cover. It concerns our financail   81. _____

82. drive. Your responses will be confidental.   82. _____

INSTRUCTIONS: After you have completed Pretest IV.1, submit your paper to your instructor. Your instructor will evaluate the pretest and will let you know if you need to proceed further with the Spelling section of Phase IV.

EXERCISE IV.1: SPELLING LIST TAPE

INSTRUCTIONS: Transcribe the Spelling List tape of 100 words frequently misspelled in business. The tape provides a separate sentence for each spelling word. *Transcribe only the spelling words, not the complete sentences.*

APPLY
YOUR SKILLS

After transcribing the Spelling List tape, check your dictionary or word book for any words you believe you may have misspelled. Then check your transcript with the Key to Exercise IV.1 in Appendix C. If you find any errors, complete Exercise IV.2. (You may also want to complete the exercise for those words you looked up in your dictionary or word book.)

Note: Some words may have more than one correct spelling; for example, *judgment* can also be spelled *judgement*. If you look up a word in the dictionary and find that it has two spellings, you'll find that the preferred spelling usually comes first. When completing exercises in this text-workbook, always use the preferred spelling. (Occasionally a dictator may express a strong personal preference for another spelling. In such situations, follow the dictator's preference.)

EXERCISE IV.2: SPELLING LIST

INSTRUCTIONS:
1. On the form provided, write the words you misspelled on the pretest.
2. Look up in the dictionary the pronunciation and meaning of the misspelled words.
3. Pronounce each word out loud several times.
4. Write the word as rapidly as you can until you can spell it correctly without hesitation.
5. Make up a sentence for each word.

CHECK
YOURSELF

EXAMPLE:

WORD *forty*
    Pronunciation *fôrt'-ē*
    Meaning *the number 40*
    Spelling Practice *forty forty forty forty*
    Sentence *Forty years ago, this didn't exist.*

WORD _____
    Pronunciation _____
    Meaning _____
    Spelling Practice _____
    Sentence _____

WORD   _____

    Pronunciation   _____

    Meaning   _____

    Spelling Practice _____

    Sentence   _____

WORD   _____

    Pronunciation   _____

    Meaning   _____

    Spelling Practice _____

    Sentence   _____

WORD   _____

    Pronunciation   _____

    Meaning   _____

    Spelling Practice _____

    Sentence   _____

If you have additional spelling words you need to practice, use a blank piece of paper.

BASIC SPELLING POINTS

Before proceeding further with the Spelling section of Phase IV, let's review a few basic points:

The VOWELS are *a, e, i, o, u,* and sometimes *y*. All other letters in the alphabet are consonants.

The ROOT of a word refers to the part that can stand on its own and which can be altered by adding a prefix or a suffix.

A PREFIX is placed in front of a root word. (Examples: *in, mis, non, pre, re,* and *un*.)

A SUFFIX is added at the end of a root word. Suffixes can cause spelling problems since they sometimes require spelling changes before the suffix can be added. (Examples: *ed, ful, ing, ly,* and *ment*.)

ROOT WORD	PREFIX WITH ROOT	ROOT WITH SUFFIX	ROOT WITH PREFIX AND SUFFIX
patient	*im*patient	patient*ly*	*im*patient*ly*

Be careful to pronounce words correctly. Adding or deleting sounds or syllables can cause misspellings. (Example: *ath-lete*, not *ath-a-lete*.) Use a dictionary to determine correct pronunciation.

In some cases, spelling rules do not explain why a word is spelled a certain way. It may be necessary to memorize the correct spelling of these exceptions to the rules.

Keep these points in mind as you study the spelling rules that follow.

Spelling Rules

Regardless of whether you have or haven't considered yourself a particularly good speller in the past, a review of the basic rules should greatly expand your competence and improve your spelling skill. Ten basic spelling rules are presented in this section. Study each carefully; then complete the exercise for it.

EXERCISE IV.3: SPELLING RULE 1

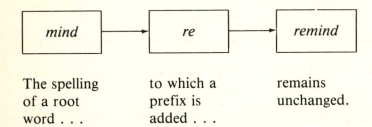

| mind | → | re | → | remind |

The spelling of a root word . . .   to which a prefix is added . . .   remains unchanged.

INSTRUCTIONS: Applying Spelling Rule 1, add the prefixes to the words indicated and write the correctly spelled word in the blank space.

CHECK YOURSELF

	ROOT WORD		PREFIX		CORRECT SPELLING
EXAMPLE:	*satisfied*	+	*dis*	=	*dissatisfied*
	agree	+	dis	=	_____
	approve	+	dis	=	_____
	qualify	+	dis	=	_____
	similar	+	dis	=	_____
	legal	+	il	=	_____
	legible	+	il	=	_____
	legitimacy	+	il	=	_____
	logical	+	il	=	_____
	balance	+	im	=	_____
	patient	+	im	=	_____
	practical	+	im	=	_____
	prudent	+	im	=	_____
	conclusive	+	in	=	_____
	directly	+	in	=	_____
	effective	+	in	=	_____
	formal	+	in	=	_____

file	+	mis	= _____
trial	+	mis	= _____
spell	+	mis	= _____
state	+	mis	= _____
competitive	+	non	= _____
compliance	+	non	= _____
inflationary	+	non	= _____
taxable	+	non	= _____
conceive	+	pre	= _____
determine	+	pre	= _____
occupied	+	pre	= _____
payment	+	pre	= _____
equal	+	un	= _____
necessary	+	un	= _____
qualified	+	un	= _____
written	+	un	= _____

INSTRUCTIONS: Check your answers with the Key to Exercise IV.3 in Appendix C.

EXERCISE 1V.4a: SPELLING RULE 2.a

Put _i_ before _e_. | _belie̲ve_ |

There are exceptions to this rule. Examples:

fore̲ign   lei̲sure   sei̲ze
he̲ight   nei̲ther   we̲ird

CHECK YOURSELF   INSTRUCTIONS: Applying Spelling Rule 2.a, insert the missing letters and write the correct spelling in the blank space.

EXAMPLE: ach __ __ ve   _achieve_ _____   f __ __ ld   _____

p __ __ ce   _____   var __ __ ty   _____

retr __ __ ve   _____   hyg __ __ ne   _____

y __ __ ld   _____   rel __ __ ve   _____

EXERCISE IV.4b: SPELLING RULE 2.b

Put *i* before *e* except after *c*.

rec__eive

There are exceptions to this rule. Examples:
anc__ient   *sc__ience*   *effic__iency*
financ__ier   *spec__ies*

INSTRUCTIONS: Applying Spelling Rule 2.b, insert the missing letters and write the correct spelling in the blank space.

CHECK YOURSELF

EXAMPLE: c __ __ ling   *ceiling* _____   dec __ __ ve   _____

conc __ __ ve   _____   rec __ __ ve   _____

perc __ __ ve   _____   conc __ __ t   _____

rec __ __ pt   _____   dec __ __ t   _____

EXERCISE IV.4c: SPELLING RULE 2.c

Put *i* before *e* except after *c* or when sounded like *a*.

__eighth

INSTRUCTIONS: Applying Spelling Rule 2.c, insert the missing letters and write the correct spelling in the blank space.

CHECK YOURSELF

EXAMPLE: e __ ght   *eight* _____   v __ __ n   _____

fr __ __ ght   _____   n __ __ ghbor   _____

th __ __ r   _____   n __ __ ghed   _____

w __ __ gh   _____   sl __ __ gh   _____

INSTRUCTIONS: Check your answers with the Keys to Exercise IV.4a, b, and c in Appendix C.

EXERCISE IV.5: SPELLING RULE 3

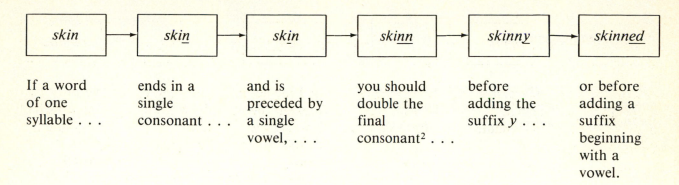

| If a word of one syllable . . . | ends in a single consonant . . . | and is preceded by a single vowel, . . . | you should double the final consonant[2] . . . | before adding the suffix *y* . . . | or before adding a suffix beginning with a vowel. |

[2]The letters *w*, *x*, and *y* are never doubled.

There are exceptions to this rule. Examples:

fix + ed   = fixed   *tax + ed   = taxed*
saw + ing = sawing   *tow + ing = towing*

CHECK YOURSELF   INSTRUCTIONS: Applying Spelling Rule 3, add the suffixes to the words as indicated; then write the correctly spelled words in the blank spaces.

	ROOT WORD		SUFFIX		CORRECT SPELLING
EXAMPLE:	*big*	+	*est*	=	*biggest*
	drop	+	ed	=	_____
	plan	+	ing	=	_____
	job	+	er	=	_____
	stop	+	ing	=	_____
	wit	+	y	=	_____
	bag	+	age	=	_____
	quiz	+	ed	=	_____
	tax	+	ing	=	_____
	clan	+	ish	=	_____
	ship	+	er	=	_____
	sit	+	ing	=	_____

INSTRUCTIONS: Check your answers with the Key to Exercise IV.5 in Appendix C.

EXERCISE IV.6: SPELLING RULE 4

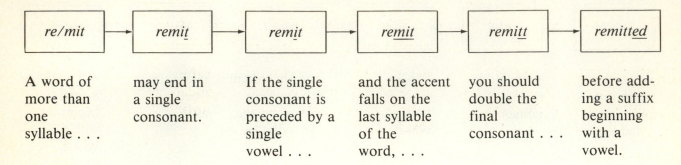

| re/mit | → | remi_t | → | rem_it | → | rem_it | → | remit_t | → | remit_ted |

| A word of more than one syllable . . . | may end in a single consonant. | If the single consonant is preceded by a single vowel . . . | and the accent falls on the last syllable of the word, . . . | you should double the final consonant . . . | before adding a suffix beginning with a vowel. |

There are exceptions to this rule. Examples:

contain + ed = contained
forbear + ance = forbearance
overflow + ing = overflowing

INSTRUCTIONS: Applying Spelling Rule 4, add the suffixes to the words as indicated and write the correctly spelled words in the blank spaces.   **CHECK YOURSELF**

	WORD		SUFFIX		CORRECT SPELLING
EXAMPLE:	*commit*	+	*ed*	=	*committed*
	prefer	+	ed	=	_____
	omit	+	ing	=	_____
	control	+	ing	=	_____
	allot	+	ed	=	_____
	begin	+	ing	=	_____
	forgot	+	en	=	_____
	occur	+	ence	=	_____
	refer	+	ed	=	_____
	excel	+	ed	=	_____
	equip	+	ing	=	_____
	transfer	+	ed	=	_____

INSTRUCTIONS: Check your answers with the Key to Exercise IV.6 in Appendix C.

EXERCISE IV.7: SPELLING RULE 5

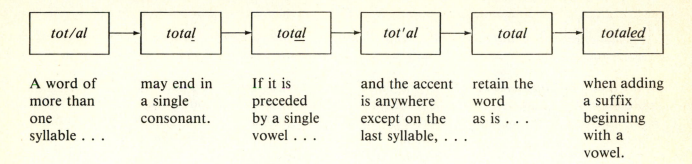

tot/al	*total*	*total*	*tot'al*	*total*	*totaled*

A word of more than one syllable . . .

may end in a single consonant.

If it is preceded by a single vowel . . .

and the accent is anywhere except on the last syllable, . . .

retain the word as is . . .

when adding a suffix beginning with a vowel.

There are exceptions to this rule. Examples:
handicap + ed = handicapped
program + er = programmer

CHECK YOURSELF   INSTRUCTIONS: Applying Spelling Rule 5, add the suffixes to the words as indicated and write the correctly spelled words in the blank spaces.

	WORD		SUFFIX		CORRECT SPELLING
EXAMPLE:	*benefit*	+	*ing*	=	*benefiting*
	credit	+	ed	=	_____
	differ	+	ence	=	_____
	diagram	+	ing	=	_____
	travel	+	ing	=	_____
	profit	+	ed	=	_____
	budget	+	ing	=	_____
	visit	+	or	=	_____
	offer	+	ing	=	_____
	label	+	ed	=	_____
	develop	+	ing	=	_____
	catalog	+	ed	=	_____

INSTRUCTIONS: Check your answers with the Key to Exercise IV.7 in Appendix C.

EXERCISE IV.8: SPELLING RULE 6

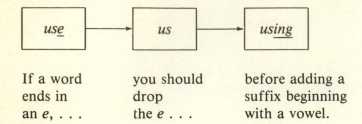

If a word ends in an *e*, . . .	you should drop the *e* . . .	before adding a suffix beginning with a vowel.

There are exceptions to this rule. Examples:

advantage + ous = advantageous   *notice + able = noticeable*
courage + ous   = courageous   *outrage + ous = outrageous*
mile + age   = mileage

INSTRUCTIONS: Applying Spelling Rule 6, add the suffixes to the words as indicated and write the correctly spelled words in the blank spaces.

CHECK YOURSELF

	WORD		SUFFIX		CORRECT SPELLING
EXAMPLE:	arrange	+	ing	=	*arranging*
	arrive	+	al	=	_____
	come	+	ing	=	_____
	continue	+	al	=	_____
	desire	+	ability	=	_____
	excite	+	able	=	_____
	excuse	+	able	=	_____
	fame	+	ous	=	_____
	guide	+	ance	=	_____
	notice	+	ing	=	_____
	simple	+	y	=	_____
	write	+	er	=	_____

INSTRUCTIONS: Check your answers with the Key to Exercise IV.8 in Appendix C.

EXERCISE IV.9: SPELLING RULE 7

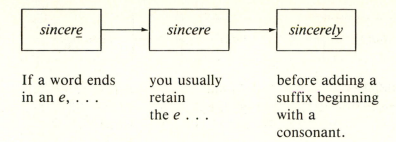

If a word ends in an *e*, . . .	you usually retain the *e* . . .	before adding a suffix beginning with a consonant.

There are exceptions to this rule. Examples:

acknowledge + *ment* = *acknowledgment*   *nine* + *th* = *ninth*
argue + *ment*   = *argument*   *true* + *ly* = *truly*
judge + *ment*   = *judgment*

CHECK YOURSELF   INSTRUCTIONS: Applying Spelling Rule 7, add the suffixes to the words as indicated and write the correctly spelled words in the blank spaces.

	WORD		SUFFIX		CORRECT SPELLING
EXAMPLE:	*achieve*	+	*ment*	=	*achievement*
	extreme	+	ly	=	_____
	care	+	less	=	_____
	excite	+	ment	=	_____
	nine	+	teen	=	_____
	absolute	+	ly	=	_____
	complete	+	ly	=	_____
	like	+	ness	=	_____
	manage	+	ment	=	_____
	nine	+	ty	=	_____
	resource	+	ful	=	_____
	definite	+	ly	=	_____

INSTRUCTIONS: Check your answers with the Key to Exercise IV.9 in Appendix C.

EXERCISE IV.10: SPELLING RULE 8

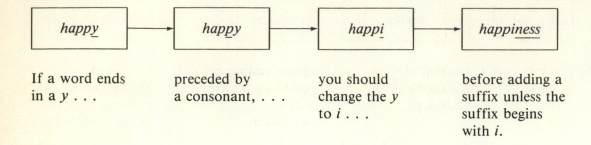

| happy | happy | happi | happiness |

If a word ends in a *y* . . .   preceded by a consonant, . . .   you should change the *y* to *i* . . .   before adding a suffix unless the suffix begins with *i*.

INSTRUCTIONS: Applying Spelling Rule 8, add the suffixes to the words as indicated and write the correctly spelled words in the blank spaces.

CHECK
YOURSELF

	WORD		SUFFIX		CORRECT SPELLING
EXAMPLES:	*copy*	+	*ist*	=	*copyist*
	ordinary	+	*ly*	=	*ordinarily*
	husky	+	ness	=	_____
	heavy	+	est	=	_____
	beauty	+	ful	=	_____
	accompany	+	ment	=	_____
	rely	+	ability	=	_____
	vary	+	able	=	_____
	empty	+	ness	=	_____
	easy	+	er	=	_____
	bury	+	ing	=	_____
	lucky	+	ly	=	_____
	rely	+	able	=	_____

INSTRUCTIONS: Check your answers with the Key to Exercise IV.10 in Appendix C.

EXERCISE IV.11: SPELLING RULE 9

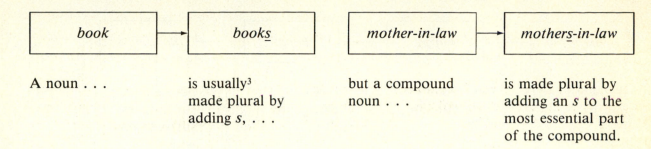

| book | → | book*s* | | mother-in-law | → | mother*s*-in-law |

A noun . . .   is usually[3]   but a compound   is made plural by
                      made plural by   noun . . .   adding an *s* to the
                      adding *s*, . . .   most essential part
                                                                        of the compound.

[3]See Rule 10 for exceptions.

**CHECK
YOURSELF**

INSTRUCTIONS: Applying Spelling Rule 9, make the following words plural.

	WORD				CORRECT SPELLING
EXAMPLES:	*neighbor*	+	s	=	*neighbors*
	son-in-law	+	s	=	*sons-in-law*
	technician	+	s	=	_____
	chamber of commerce	+	s	=	_____
	manufacturer	+	s	=	_____
	brother-in-law	+	s	=	_____
	account	+	s	=	_____
	shopper	+	s	=	_____
	tourist	+	s	=	_____
	newsstand	+	s	=	_____
	standard	+	s	=	_____
	template	+	s	=	_____
	typewriter	+	s	=	_____

INSTRUCTIONS: Check your answers with the Key to Exercise IV.11 in Appendix C.

EXERCISE IV.12: SPELLING RULE 10

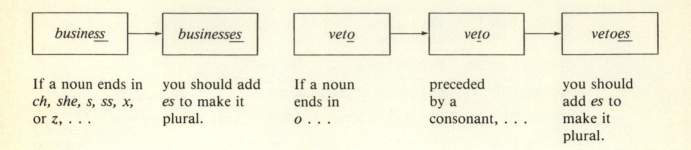

| business | → | businesses |

| veto | → | veto | → | vetoes |

If a noun ends in *ch, she, s, ss, x,* or *z,* . . . you should add *es* to make it plural.

If a noun ends in *o* . . . preceded by a consonant, . . . you should add *es* to make it plural.

INSTRUCTIONS: Applying Spelling Rule 10, make the following words plural.   ***CHECK YOURSELF***

	WORD				CORRECT SPELLING
EXAMPLES:	*bush*	+	*s*	=	*bushes*
	tomato	+	*s*	=	*tomatoes*
	address	+	s	=	_____
	potato	+	s	=	_____
	speech	+	s	=	_____
	echo	+	s	=	_____
	genius	+	s	=	_____
	hero	+	s	=	_____
	scratch	+	s	=	_____
	fox	+	s	=	_____
	lunch	+	s	=	_____
	Jones	+	s	=	_____
	waitress	+	s	=	_____

INSTRUCTIONS: Check your answers with the Key to Exercise IV.12 in Appendix C.

SUMMARY OF SPELLING RULES

Spelling Rule 1:   The spelling of a root word to which a prefix is added remains unchanged.

Spelling Rule 2a: Put *i* before *e*.

Spelling Rule 2b: Put *i* before *e* except after *c*.

Spelling Rule 2c: Put *i* before *e* except after *c* or when sounded like *a*.

Spelling Rule 3:   If a word of one syllable ends in a single consonant and is preceded by a single vowel, you should double the final consonant before adding the suffix *y* or before adding a suffix beginning with a vowel.

Spelling Rule 4:   A word of more than one syllable may end in a single consonant. If the single consonant is preceded by a single vowel and the accent falls on the last syllable of the word, you should double the final consonant before adding a suffix beginning with a vowel.

Spelling Rule 5:   A word of more than one syllable may end in a single consonant. If it is preceded by a single vowel and the accent is anywhere except on the last syllable, retain the word as is when adding a suffix beginning with a vowel.

Spelling Rule 6:   If a word ends in an *e*, you should drop the *e* before adding a suffix beginning with a vowel.

Spelling Rule 7:   If a word ends in an *e*, you usually retain the *e* before adding a suffix beginning with a consonant.

Spelling Rule 8:   If a word ends in a *y* preceded by a consonant, you should change the *y* to *i* before adding a suffix unless the suffix begins with *i*.

Spelling Rule 9:   A noun is usually made plural by adding *s*, but a compound noun is made plural by adding an *s* to the most essential part of the compound.

Spelling Rule 10:   If a noun ends in *ch, she, s, ss, x,* or *z,* you should add *es* to make it plural. If a noun ends in *o* preceded by a consonant, you should add *es* to make it plural.

HOMONYMS AND WORDS SIMILAR IN SOUND

Some words can be confusing because they sound exactly alike but mean different things. These words are called *homonyms*. Some other words can be confusing because they sound approximately alike. You will frequently be able to tell which word to use by the context (meaning) of the sentence.

EXERCISE IV.13: HOMONYMS AND WORDS SIMILAR IN SOUND

INSTRUCTIONS: The following are sets of words that sound either exactly alike or very similar. A short definition is provided for each word. Study the spellings and definitions in each set; then do the exercise sentence by writing the correct word or words in the blank space.

CHECK YOURSELF

accept (verb) to take, to receive, to admit

except (verb) to exclude
(preposition) excluding

1. Everyone was at the luncheon _____ Aaron.

ad (noun) the abbreviation for advertisement

add (verb) to join, attach, sum up

2. Please _____ the column and type the total at the bottom of the page.

addition (noun) the act of adding, something added

edition (noun) one version of a printed work

3. The new _____ was just released for sale.

adapt (verb) to adjust, make suitable

adept (adjective) proficient, skillful

adopt (verb) to choose, employ, utilize

4. Which textbook should we _____ for the course?

advice (noun) information; a recommendation; guidance

advise (verb) to recommend, give counsel, suggest

5. I need your _____ on this point.

affect (verb) to influence; to change; to assume; to pretend

effect (noun) result, outcome
(verb) to fulfill; to bring about; to cause

6. The _____ of the unionization vote will _____ all of us in the office.

allusion   (noun) an indirect reference

illusion   (noun) a misleading image or idea

 7. I was under the _____ that the restaurant would be expensive.

assistance   (noun) help

assistants   (noun) helpers, subordinates

 8. The lab _____ are paid $5 per hour.

attendance   (noun) presence

attendants   (noun) escorts, followers, companions, associates

 9. Staff meeting _____ is mandatory.

beside   (adverb) by the side of; separate from; alongside

besides   (adverb) in addition to, also

 10. _____ his regular duties, John is committee chairperson.

biennial   (adjective) occurring every other year

biannual   (adjective) occurring twice a year

 11. We have _____ meetings; this year they will be in September and June.

capital   (noun) a seat of government; a sum of money. (adjective) an upper-case letter

capitol   (noun) a building in which a legislature meets

 12. Begin each item in an outline with a _____ letter.

choose   (verb) to select, to decide on

chose   (verb) the past tense of *choose*

 13. When do you plan to _____ your new transcribing equipment?

cite   (verb) to quote, recite; to summon

sight   (noun) a view, vision

site   (noun) a place, spot, locality

 14. He asked me to _____ my sources in the report.

complement   (noun) that which completes (verb) to make complete

compliment   (noun) a flattering comment (verb) to praise

 15. _____ in public; punish in private.

conscience (noun) the sense of right and wrong

conscious (adjective) aware; sensible

16. My _____ will not allow me to be late for work.

continual (adjective) occurring in rapid and steady succession or at intervals

continuous (adjective) uninterrupted, unbroken, steady

17. Endless loop dictation equipment means the same as

_____ loop dictation equipment.

correspondence (noun) letters, writings

correspondents (noun) letter writers, distant news reporters

18. Internal company _____ is generally typed on memo paper.

council (noun) an assembly of people

counsel (noun) an attorney; a suggestion
(verb) to give advice, to suggest

consul (noun) a foreign representative or official

19. Part of an attorney's responsibility is to _____ clients.

decent (adjective) proper; moderate

descent (noun) a downward step; one's derivation from an ancestor

dissent (verb) to differ in opinion
(noun) difference of opinion

20. There was _____ among the staff members at the meeting.

device (noun) instrument; plan

devise (verb) to contrive

21. We will _____ a new system to gather the data.

disapprove (verb) to withhold approval, to find fault with

disprove (verb) to prove something to be false

22. We will attempt to _____ his theory.

do (verb) to perform, carry out

due (adjective) owing, unpaid

23. _____ you have the past-_____ notices ready to be mailed?

entrance   (noun) entry

entrants   (noun) entries, as in a contest; newcomers

24. The construction workers had the _____ blocked.

farther   (adjective) at a greater distance (refers to space)

further   (adverb) moreover, in addition (refers to time, degree, or quantity)
                              (verb) to promote or advance

25. Who do you think will move _____ up the word processing career ladder?

forth   (adverb) forward

fourth   (adjective) number

26. I was the _____ person to be interviewed.

forward   (adverb) ahead
                              (verb) to advance

foreword   (noun) preface

27. Will the accused please step _____.

formally   (adverb) in a formal manner

formerly   (adverb) before, previously

28. Mary had _____ worked for me.

hear   (verb) to perceive by ear, to listen

here   (noun) in this place; present

29. I came _____ to _____ Anna Deusinger's speech.

illicit   (adjective) unlawful

elicit   (verb) to draw forth

30. The attorney tried to _____ the facts from the witness.

its   possessive form of *it*

it's   (contraction) it is

31. _____ possible that the committee will make _____ report today.

later   (adverb) after a particular time; at another time

latter   (adjective) relating to the second of two items

32. Do you want to distribute the minutes now or

_____?

lay   (verb) to place, put

lie   (noun) a falsehood, an untruth
                               (verb) to recline; to tell an untruth

33. Please _____ the letters on my desk.

lead   (verb) to guide, conduct
                               (noun) a metal

led   (verb) the past tense of *lead*

34. John _____ the discussion at Tuesday's
     meeting.

lessee   (noun) a tenant

lesser   (adjective) smaller

lessor   (noun) one who gives a lease

35. The _____ left the lease for the

     _____ to sign.

loose   (adjective) free, not bound, separate
                               (verb) to release, to loosen

lose   (verb) to suffer the loss of, to misplace, to be defeated

loss   (noun) something lost

36. The lock on the cabinet was _____.

passed   (verb) moved along, transferred; the past tense of *pass*

past   (noun) time gone by
                               (adjective, adverb, or preposition) gone by

37. The _____-due accounts were

     _____ on to the collection agency.

patience   (noun) composure; endurance

patients   (noun) sick persons, invalids

38. The _____ must have a great deal of

     _____ to wait so long to see the doctor.

peace   (noun) calmness, quiet

piece   (noun) a portion

39. Please hand me a _____ of bond paper.

persecute   (verb) to oppress, harass

prosecute   (verb) to sue; to put on trial

40. The district attorney decided not to _____.

personal

(adjective) private; individual

personnel

(noun) the staff, office, or company work force

41. Don't let your _____ problems affect your school work.

physical

(adjective) relating to the body; material

fiscal

(adjective) pertaining to finances

42. Our _____ year begins on July 1, not January 1.

precede

(verb) to come first, go before

proceed

(verb) to advance, go on

43. I will _____ to type the manuscript.

principal

(adjective) chief, leading, main
(noun) a capital sum of money; the head of a school

principle

(noun) a rule; a general truth; a law

44. His _____ objection seemed petty to me.

quite

(adverb) entirely, totally

quiet

(adjective) calm, restful, not noisy

quit

(verb) to stop, cease

45. John was _____ upset when he heard the news.

respectfully

(adverb) in a courteous manner

respectively

(adverb) in the order indicated

46. Mary and Jane, _____, received first- and second-place awards.

stationary

(adjective) fixed, not movable

stationery

(noun) writing materials (paper, pens, pencils)

47. We need to order more letterhead _____.

than

(preposition) in comparison with
(conjunction) used with the second member of a comparison

then

(adverb) at that time; as a necessary consequence
(noun) that time

48. I would prefer meeting at 2 p.m. if you are available _____.

there   (noun) that point
                        (adverb) in that place

their   (pronoun) belonging to them

they're   (contraction) they are

49. _____ appears to be no reasoning behind
    _____ decision.

to   (preposition) toward

too   (adverb) more than enough, also

two   (adjective) number, one plus one

50. When you come _____ the meeting, bring
    _____ representatives from payroll.

weak   (adjective) lack of skill or strength

week   (noun) period of seven days

51. I will be in Pittsburgh next _____.

weather   (noun) climate or atmosphere

whether   (conjunction) if

52. What is the Midwest _____ like in February?

whose   (pronoun) possessive of *who*

who's   (contraction) who is

53. _____ book is on my desk?

your   (pronoun) possessive of *you*

you're   (contraction) you are

54. When _____ transcribing, listen to
    _____ tape carefully.

INSTRUCTIONS: Check your answers with the Key to Exercise IV.13 in Appendix C.
For additional practice in using homonyms and words similar in sound, complete the
Practice Exercises for Homonyms and Words Similar in Sound in Appendix B.

ONE OR TWO WORDS

Some pairs of words are pronounced the same way but are written as one or two words, depending on meaning. You will be able to tell from the context (meaning) of the sentence whether to use one or two words.

EXERCISE IV.14: ONE OR TWO WORDS

CHECK YOURSELF   INSTRUCTIONS: The following sets of words are frequently confused. Study the definitions; then, in the blanks provided, write the correct word or words that belong in each sentence.

a lot   a collection of items

allot   (verb) to distribute, allocate

1. We will _____ divisional budgets in July.

> # REMINDER
>
> *A lot* is always written as two words (never *alot*).

all ready   all prepared

already   (adverb) previously

2. The letters were _____ to be signed.

all right   all correct

alright   This spelling is not accepted by most authorities, although some dictionaries list it as a colloquial, variant spelling

3. Your answers are _____.

all together   all in a group

altogether   (adverb) wholly, thoroughly, entirely

4. Your response is not _____ correct.

all ways   all means or methods

always   (adverb) at all times, without exception

5. Her correspondence production records met the standards in _____.

any one   any one person in a group (any one is followed by an *of* phrase)

anyone   (pronoun) anybody

     6. _____ of you could be appointed to the position.

any way   any method

anyway   (adverb) in any case, nevertheless

     7. _____, that's the final decision.

every day   each day

everyday   (adjective) daily; ordinary

     8. The mail arrives at 10 a.m. and 3 p.m. _____.

may be   (verb) can

maybe   (adverb) perhaps

     9. _____ I'll be on time for our meeting.

no body   no group (no body is followed by an *of* phrase)

nobody   (pronoun) no one, no person

     10. _____ can use the cafeteria from 2 to 4 p.m.

some one   some person in a group (some one is followed by an *of* phrase)

someone   (pronoun) somebody

     11. _____ from our office will deliver the package.

some time   a period of time

sometime   (adverb) at some unspecified time

sometimes   (adverb) now and then

     12. It will take us _____ to learn to operate the new equipment.

INSTRUCTIONS: Check your answers with the Key to Exercise IV.14 in Appendix C. For additional practice in using one or two words, complete the Practice Exercises for One or Two Words in Appendix B.

INSTRUCTIONS: Under supervision, transcribe Posttest IV.1 in mailable form. Submit your transcript to your instructor.

MAKING A LIST OF SPELLING ERRORS

Frequently making the same spelling error seems to be a very common problem for some people; yet, it needn't be. The solution can lie in starting—and keeping up—a personal list of any words you misspell or are unsure of. Exercise IV.15 will help you design a list to meet your personal spelling skill needs.

EXERCISE IV.15: MY SPECIAL SPELLING LIST

APPLY YOUR SKILLS

INSTRUCTIONS: At the top of a separate sheet of paper, type the words, "My Special Spelling List." Record on the sheet any words you misspell. Be sure to keep this list handy throughout the rest of the course—and on the job, if still necessary. As time goes by, simply cross out each word whose spelling you are sure you have mastered. It might be helpful to use a sheet of colored paper to make it easier to refer to the list.

WORD DIVISION

Some transcriptionists habitually go out of their way to avoid dividing a word at the end of a line. Word division, however, cannot be wished away that easily. The danger of an unsightly, ragged right margin is a threat that makes periodic word division unavoidable.

Since correct division is as important as correct spelling, approach them both in the same way: When in doubt, *never* guess; instead, consult your dictionary or ready-reference word book.

REMINDER

1. Don't divide at the end of the first or last line of a paragraph or page.
2. To avoid the distraction of multiple word division, don't divide more than one line in succession.

RULE: Divide after prefixes.

> *this*: intro-duce
> *not this*: in-troduce

RULE: Divide before suffixes.

> *this*: convert-ible
> *not this*: con-vertible

RULE: Divide between double letters when the final consonant is doubled before adding a suffix.

this: concur-ring
not this: concurr-ing
(**Note:** Do not divide between double letters when adding a suffix to a root word that ends in a double letter. EXAMPLE: helpless-ness)

RULE: Whenever possible, avoid dividing parts of a person's name.

preferred:	(on one line)	Franklin Jones
all right if necessary:	(on first line)	Franklin
	(on second line)	Jones
not this:	(on first line)	Frank-
	(on second line)	lin Jones

RULE: Whenever possible, avoid dividing numbers or dates. If necessary, divide at the comma.

preferred:	(on one line)	November 22, 1985	456,789,234
all right if necessary:	(on first line)	November 22,	456,789,-
	(on second line)	1985	234
not this:	(on first line)	November	456,78-
	(on second line)	22, 1985	9,234

RULE: Whenever possible, divide compound words only at the hyphen.

preferred:	(on first line)	self-
	(on second line)	expression
all right if necessary:	(on first line)	self-expres-
	(on second line)	sion
not this:	(on first line)	self-ex-
	(on second line)	pression

RULE: Avoid dividing before a two-letter syllable word ending.

preferred: head-waiter
all right if necessary: headwait-er

RULE: Try to avoid dividing between consecutive one-letter syllables.

preferred: grad-uation or gradua-tion
all right if necessary: gradu-ation

RULE: Try to avoid dividing two-syllable word endings.

preferred: compat-ible
all right if necessary: compati-ble

RULE: Don't divide words of one syllable or words pronounced as one syllable.

this: strength   shipped
not this: streng-th   ship-ped

RULE: Don't divide contractions.

> *this*: couldn't
> *not this*: could-n't

RULE: Don't divide abbreviations.

> *this*: U.S.M.C.
> *not this*: U.S.-M.C.

RULE: Don't divide after a beginning one-letter syllable or before an ending one-letter syllable.

> *this*:   around   leaky
> *not this*: a-round   leak-y

REMINDER

1. **When dividing words at the end of a line, type as much of the word on the first line as possible within the guidelines of these word division rules.**
2. **When typing a divided word at the end of a line, don't leave a space before the hyphen.**

EXERCISE IV.16: WORD DIVISION

CHECK YOURSELF

INSTRUCTIONS: The following examples are correctly hyphenated or unhyphenated. In the space at the right, state the hyphen rule you just learned that applies to each example.

1. trans-mit _____

2. run-ning _____

3. other-wise _____

4. 7,648,749 _____

5. couldn't _____

6. November 1, 19— _____

7. chained _____

8. U.S.A. _____

9. self-confidence _____

10. Erin Foster _____

11. ahead _____

12. control-ling _____

13. $52,000 _____

14. doesn't _____

15. arrange-ment _____

16. hope-less _____

17. situa-tion _____

18. ball-player _____

19. honor-able _____

20. habitu-ally _____

INSTRUCTIONS: Check your answers with the Key to Exercise IV.16 in Appendix C. If you need additional practice on word division, turn to the Practice Exercises in Appendix B.

PRETEST IV.2: CAPITALIZATION

INSTRUCTIONS: Read the following letter and circle the 12 letters that should be capitalized. Then type the letter in mailable form.

The letter goes to: Professor Edwina Miller/Dartmouth College/Hanover, New Hampshire 03755

The letter is from: Louise Brodie/1237 Augustine Court/Los Angeles, California 90031

Dear Edwina:

    How have you been? It has been exciting living in the west and working at ucla. I'm ready to return to school and plan to enroll in the college of business at Memphis State university after january of this year.

    Will you please write a letter of recommendation for me. The application indicated that there was no official form. Send the letter directly to associate dean Norman F. Allen at Memphis State. Please mention the following in your letter: my academic preparation, my professional achievements, and my ability to do graduate study. My undergraduate grade point average was 3.52. I have only taken a couple of night courses in spanish since leaving school. I will be taking the appropriate entrance examinations soon. Wish me luck.

    Thank you for all the encouragement you've given me in the past.

Cordially,

INSTRUCTIONS: After completing Pretest IV.2, submit your paper to your instructor. Your instructor will evaluate your pretest and will let you know if you need to proceed further with the Capitalization section of Phase IV.

CAPITALIZATION

RULE: Capitalize all names of days of the week, months of the year, holidays, and periods of history.

EXAMPLES:

This year, *T*hanksgiving will fall on *T*hursday, *N*ovember 22.

Herbert Hoover was a political casualty of the *D*epression.

RULE: Capitalize the first word after a colon if the first word begins a complete sentence.

EXAMPLES:

The question is this: *A*re you proofreading carefully?

He purchased the following at the fruit market: *a* crate of peaches, apricots, and plums.

RULE: Capitalize the names of geographic regions and geographical names. Points on the compass are not capitalized when they indicate direction or when used in a descriptive sense.

EXAMPLES:

We will be moving from the *S*outh to the *W*est.

Go *s*outh on Oster Bay Drive, and then go *e*ast on Ocean Road.

RULE: Capitalize titles that immediately precede a name. Do not capitalize a title elsewhere in a sentence unless it is a title of distinction or it is used to refer to a specific person. Do not capitalize professional or business titles without the name of the person.

EXAMPLES:

On Wednesday, *P*resident Shaw will be the keynote speaker.

Sara Weinstein is the *p*resident of our club.

The *G*overnor will return tomorrow.

The *d*octor will return at nine o'clock.

RULE: Capitalize words used as an essential part of proper names.

EXAMPLES:

He attended Harvard *U*niversity.

Our family reunion will be at Kent *P*ark.

She works for the F and C *C*ompany.

RULE: Capitalize names of specific departments. Do not capitalize the names of general classifications of departments.

EXAMPLES:

The *P*ersonnel *D*epartment compiles that data for us.

She has had three years of experience working in a *p*ersonnel *d*epartment.

RULE: Capitalize all languages and the names of specific courses.

EXAMPLE:

I will be taking *T*ypewriting II and *S*panish, as well as classes in literature and math this fall.

RULE: In titles of books, plays, newspapers, periodicals, and articles, capitalize the *first* and the *last* word, and all other words except pronouns, articles, short conjunctions, short prepositions, and short verbs. (Prepositions of five or more letters are usually capitalized.)

EXAMPLE:

The *M*ysterious *A*ffair *at* *S*tyles was Hercule Poirot's first case.

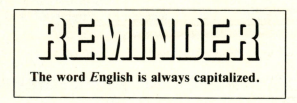

The word *E*nglish is always capitalized.

RULE: Capitalize abbreviations of capitalized words or acronyms formed from capitalized words.

EXAMPLES:

H. G. Wells lived in London.

I'll take the *GMAT* next month.

(GMAT is the acronym for [G]raduate [M]anagement [A]ptitude [T]est.)

RULE: Capitalize the first word of a complete direct quotation. Do not capitalize a quotation resumed within a sentence.

EXAMPLES:

She said, "*I*t is important to follow the directions carefully."

"Always do your best," Jerry said, "*a*nd it will pay off at review time."

EXERCISE IV.17: CAPITALIZATION

**APPLY
YOUR SKILLS**

INSTRUCTIONS: In the following business letter, circle the 23 letters that should be capitalized. If time permits, type the letter in rough-draft form to reinforce your mastery of the rules.

The letter goes to: Evelyn Mahoney, Office Manager/Base Manufacturing Company/4532 Sandalwood Court n.e./Grand Rapids, Michigan 49505

The letter is from: Alice G. Walters/Sales Manager

For the last ten years, Franklin Products company of grand rapids has been proud to serve your document production and reproduction needs. To show our appreciation, we invite you to an open house at our Lake Michigan drive office on Highway 11, just north of our main office. We'd be pleased if you would join us for refreshments on september 8 or 9 from 4 to 6 p.m.

Our entire staff will be on hand to show you our new sales department facilities. On both days, president Owen will be present to speak with you.

We all look forward to having you visit with us.

Sincerely,

PS: While at our open house, be sure to pick up copies of our latest brochures: "how to get results," "techniques for effective and efficient use of equipment," and "why we are number one."

INSTRUCTIONS: Check your answers with the Key to Exercise IV.17 in Appendix C to see if you capitalized the appropriate 23 letters.

REVIEW POINT

INSTRUCTIONS:

Transcribe Achievement Survey Tape IV.1 (Capitalization) in mailable form. You will be capitalizing a total of 47 letters. Then check your transcript with the Key to Achievement Survey Tape IV.1. Finally, complete a Mailability Analysis Chart and submit your transcript and the chart to your instructor. Note that on the accompanying cassette tapes, the Achievement Survey Tapes are designated as *AST*.

If you did not capitalize all the letters necessary, turn to the Practice Exercises in Appendix B for further drill on capitalization before taking the posttest.

INSTRUCTIONS:

Under supervision, transcribe Posttest IV.2 in mailable form. Submit your transcript to your instructor.

PRETEST IV.3: NUMBERS

INSTRUCTIONS: In the following memo, circle the 25 incorrectly expressed numbers. Write the correct form of each number in the space above it. Then type the memo in mailable form.

TO: Collegiate Deans and Departmental Executive Officers
FROM: Registrar's Office
SUBJECT: Enrollment Statistics

Nearly $\frac{1}{4}$ of the students who enrolled this semester were new to our campus. There were 2875 freshmen and 3122 transfer students—this is a potential of over $50,000,000 in revenue for our institution. 25 percent of the freshmen ranked in the top ten percent of their high school graduating classes.

The most popular undergraduate major continues to be business administration, with seven hundred eleven students enrolled. Engineering was 2d, with six hundred fifty-six students enrolled. The most popular graduate major was education, with an enrollment of 1029.

The average freshman enrolled for 2 4-hour classes and 1 three-hour course. As a rule, transfer students enrolled for 5 three-hour classes.

Enrolled students come from all fifty states and nine foreign countries. We hope to increase the foreign student enrollment to approximately 15 countries next year. Approximately seventy-five percent of the student body is made up of residents of our state.

If you wish a more detailed enrollment report, call our office at 555-4242 after the twenty-first between nine a.m. and four p.m. We'll be happy to send you a copy for only fifty cents. Payment can be billed to your college by using Purchasing Form No. Three, or you can send payment to 1 University Square Court.

INSTRUCTIONS: After completing Pretest IV.3, submit your paper to your instructor. Your instructor will evaluate your pretest and will let you know if you need to proceed further with the Number section of Phase IV.

NUMBERS AS FIGURES

RULE: Use figures for all exact numbers above ten.

EXAMPLE:

My collection has 52 mystery books.

RULE: Use figures for weights, dimensions, measures, percentages, and parts of books.

EXAMPLES:

Sophia shipped a box of records weighing 6 pounds 9 ounces.

A horizontal line of 5 inches has 50 pica spaces and 60 elite spaces.

The officials estimated that about 20 percent of the stock sustained smoke damage.

I found the exact quotation in Volume V, Section 4, paragraph 2, page 496.

RULE: Use figures for street numbers and in all house, apartment, and post office box numbers *except* one.

EXAMPLE:

We will move from One Wolfe Avenue Court to 18 Third Avenue.

RULE: Use figures for amounts of money.

EXAMPLES:

That candy bar cost 5 cents in 1964.

Send only $15.

REMINDER

If an amount of money is an exact dollar amount, do *not* add a decimal point and zeros.

RULE: Use figures in dates.

EXAMPLES:

Her birthday is the 22d.

Completion is scheduled for the 4th of February.

We will leave for Hawaii on August 11.

RULE: Use figures with abbreviations and symbols.

EXAMPLE:

Invoice No. 2416 has been processed and shipped.

RULE: Use figures with words for very large round numbers (millions and billions). Omitting the zeros makes reading easier.

EXAMPLE:

The price of the Philippine Islands was $20 million.

Use *th, st, d* only when the date precedes the month or when no month is given. Occasionally, *nd* is used rather than *d*.

EXERCISE IV.18: NUMBERS AS FIGURES

INSTRUCTIONS: In the following letter, circle the five numbers that should be expressed as figures. If time permits, type the letter in rough-draft form to reinforce your mastery of the rules.

APPLY YOUR SKILLS

The letter goes to: Mr. Donald J. Carlston/Arum Book Store/467 Fifth Avenue/Dallas, Texas 75203

The letter is from: Thomas Zajicek/Shipping Coordinator

Please accept our apology for shipping your order of February 12 for sixty-seven books (Invoice No. 2545E) to One Fifty-first Street instead of 467 Fifth Avenue in Dallas.

This shipment was only twenty-five percent of your total order and amounted to $729. Our present plans call for sending the remaining books out on March 5 or 6 but certainly no later than the eighth.

All of our twelve million customers are important to us. Please keep us informed as to how we can better serve you.

Sincerely,

INSTRUCTIONS: Check your answers with the Key to Exercise IV.18 in Appendix C to see if you correctly identified the five numbers that should be expressed as figures.

NUMBERS AS WORDS

RULE: Spell out a number at the beginning of a sentence.

EXAMPLE:

Forty people applied for the job.

RULE: Spell out numbers one through ten in a sentence.

EXAMPLE:

He purchased two tables and several books at the auction.

EXCEPTION:

If any number in a sentence must be expressed in figures, use figures for *all* numbers—including one through ten.

EXAMPLE: He purchased 2 tables and 12 books at the auction.

RULE: Spell out approximate numbers.

EXAMPLE:

Bring about twenty-five copies of the report to the meeting.

RULE: Spell out the time of day when a.m. or p.m. is not used.

EXAMPLES:

My flight leaves at eleven o'clock.

We'll meet at 10 a.m.

RULE: Spell out the shorter of two numbers when used together.

EXAMPLE:

The order called for 12 fifty-gallon drums and 25 ten-gallon cans.

(Note: Fifty is shorter than twelve; ten is shorter than twenty-five.**)**

RULE: Spell out isolated fractions.

EXAMPLE:

He completed two-thirds of the problems in the time allotted to him.

RULE: Spell out one-word or two-word numbers ending with the sounds *th, rd, nd,* or *st*, except when the numbers are used in a date.

EXAMPLE:

They will celebrate their thirty-fifth wedding anniversary on the 15th of December.

EXERCISE IV.19: NUMBERS AS WORDS

INSTRUCTIONS: Circle the nine numbers that should be expressed as words. If time permits, type the memo in rough-draft form to reinforce your mastery of the rules.

*APPLY
YOUR SKILLS*

TO: Jenny Hansmann
FROM: Van Abraham
SUBJECT: Update on Job Applications

Approximately 10 persons, or $\frac{2}{3}$ of the applicants who applied for the position of Administrative Assistant, have now been interviewed. Of the 14 persons who were interested in the position, 5 have taken the 4 3-hour courses in computer science or data processing. 3 of the 5 had an exceptionally fine record.

Miss Susan Lollaton, 1 of the 3 mentioned above, will be returning for a second interview on Wednesday, April 5, at 1:30 p.m.

After the 5th candidate has returned for the 2d interview, I'll bring you up to date on the selection process.

INSTRUCTIONS: Check your answers with the Key to Exercise IV.19 in Appendix C to see if you identified the nine numbers that should be expressed as words.

REVIEW POINT

INSTRUCTIONS:

Transcribe Achievement Survey Tape IV.2 (Numbers) in mailable form. You will be making 26 decisions about how to express numbers. Then check your transcript with the Key to Achievement Survey Tape IV.2. Finally, complete a Mailability Analysis Chart and submit your transcript and the chart to your instructor.

If you expressed any numbers incorrectly, turn to the Practice Exercises in Appendix B for further drill on numbers before taking the posttest.

INSTRUCTIONS:

Under supervision, transcribe Posttest IV.3 in mailable form. Submit your transcript to your instructor.

PUNCTUATION

Punctuation marks are signals designed to guide a reader, like traffic signs along a highway that direct a traveler through unfamiliar territory. The wrong mark of punctuation—like the wrong road sign—can mislead and confuse rather than clarify and enlighten.

Accuracy in punctuation—like accuracy in spelling—ranks near the top of the hierarchy of transcription skills. Because the rules are both definite and specific, a little study can go a long way and a lot of study will quickly turn you into something of an expert.

Be ready to verify punctuation when dictated and to supply it when not dictated. Guesswork should play no part in determining which mark of punctuation to use and when to use it. When in doubt, *always* refer to a good secretarial handbook or reference manual.

PRETEST IV.4: COMMA

INSTRUCTIONS: Read the following letter and insert the 27 missing commas. Then type the letter in mailable form.

The letter goes to: Miss Leticia Urbina/1400 Tiger Tail Road/San Antonio, Texas 78232

The letter is from: Gerry Strait/Word Processing Supervisor

I was happy to hear that you're studying word processing in your machine transcription class and that you've decided to investigate our company. I will respond to all the questions you asked and I would like to invite you to visit our department any workday before you turn in your final report.

We are a 20-person department and serve 10 other departments. The departments served include personnel auditing transportation legal real estate advertising marketing and merchandising.

Our originators provide input material into the word processing system by means of dictation or handwritten copy. Most originators use our central dictation system which is available on a 24-hour basis. Portable cassette units which can be checked out from our center are available for evening and weekend use.

There are three administrators in our center—a supervisor a controller and a coordinator. The controller's responsibility is to give each document a final accuracy check before sending it back to the originator. Each machine transcriptionist however is responsible for proofreading and checking the accuracy of all of the typed material. The center coordinator is responsible for all scheduling.

Our turnaround time is generally four hours. Sometimes there is a complicated time-consuming job that requires a 24-hour turnaround but it is rare that we do not achieve our 4-hour goal.

Several kinds of equipment are used in the center. By having a variety of machines we are not locked into the technology of any one system. If you come for a visit you will be able to see demonstrations of the different kinds of equipment we use.

Leticia if you have any further questions please let me know.
Sincerely,
PS: You might be interested in knowing that a word processing seminar will be held in Alamo Heights Texas sometime next month. A word processing machine exhibit is scheduled for March 17 1983 in Austin Texas and all interested persons are welcome.

INSTRUCTIONS: After completing Pretest IV.4, submit your paper to your instructor. Your instructor will evaluate your pretest and will let you know if you need to proceed further with the Comma section of Phase IV.

COMMA

Series Comma

RULE: To separate items in a series, use a comma after each item and before the conjunction.

EXAMPLE OF ITEMS IN A SERIES:
They are responsible for gathering, collating, classifying, and posting the data.

EXAMPLE OF PHRASES IN A SERIES:
Installation of a word processing center can result in reduced errors, reduced costs, higher quality production, added job satisfaction, and faster turnaround time.

EXERCISE IV.20: SERIES COMMA

INSTRUCTIONS: Insert the four commas missing in the following memo. If time permits, type the memo in rough-draft form to reinforce your mastery of the series comma rule.

APPLY YOUR SKILLS

TO: Department Heads
FROM: Purchasing
SUBJECT: Service Agreements

Any department may request service agreements to maintain company-owned typewriters and calculators. The department wanting a service agreement should submit a written request. The request should list the items of equipment with their correct names model numbers and serial numbers.

The Purchasing Department will contact the dealers negotiate the charges to be made and sign the agreements.

INSTRUCTIONS: Check your answers with the Key to Exercise IV.20 in Appendix C to see if you correctly inserted the four missing commas.

Introductory Comma

RULE: Insert a comma at the end of an introductory word, phrase, or dependent clause.

EXAMPLE OF COMMA AFTER INTRODUCTORY WORD:
Consequently, all entries will be made tomorrow.

EXAMPLE OF COMMA AFTER INTRODUCTORY PHRASE:
On the other hand, our telephone costs have increased over 100 percent.

EXAMPLE OF COMMA AFTER INTRODUCTORY DEPENDENT CLAUSE:
If you have any further questions about our product, please write again.

EXERCISE IV.21: INTRODUCTORY COMMA

APPLY YOUR SKILLS

INSTRUCTIONS: Insert the five commas missing in the following letter. If time permits, type the letter in rough-draft form to reinforce your mastery of the introductory comma rule.

The letter goes to: Mrs. Betty February/Route 3/Morgantown, Indiana 46160

The letter is from: Roger J. Catalog/President

Welcome to the Indiana State Personnel Managers Association (ISPMA)! It was with pleasure that I learned of your decision to join us. I hope you will become actively involved in our program. Through your participation in ISPMA you will gain the satisfaction of seeing an idea mature. Also you will broaden your professional skills and associations.

As a member of ISPMA you will be receiving our newsletter periodically. If you have any topics to suggest for inclusion in the newsletter please write me.

Once again welcome! I look forward to meeting and working with you in the coming year. Sincerely,

INSTRUCTIONS: Check your answers with the Key to Exercise IV.21 in Appendix C to see if you correctly inserted the five missing commas.

Explanatory Comma

RULE: Set off by commas a word, phrase, or clause that explains or identifies a preceding person or thing (sometimes referred to as *apposition*). The word, phrase, or clause is added to make the meaning clearer to the reader, but it is not absolutely essential to the sentence.

EXAMPLE OF AN EXPLANATORY WORD:
Today, Wednesday, we will issue the new directory.

EXAMPLE OF AN EXPLANATORY PHRASE:
"Today's Secretary," a one-day workshop for secretaries and clerical staff, will be led by Maria Martinez.

EXAMPLE OF AN EXPLANATORY CLAUSE:
Dr. Franklin, the physician who was on call last night, treated my injury at the hospital.

EXERCISE IV.22: EXPLANATORY COMMA

INSTRUCTIONS: Insert the four commas missing in the following memo. If time permits, type the memo in rough-draft form to reinforce your mastery of the explanatory comma rule.

APPLY YOUR SKILLS

TO: Vehicle Users
FROM: Motor Pool
SUBJECT: Company Vehicle Use—Speed Limit and Fuel Purchase

The Motor Pool has received a number of reports about speeding by drivers of company-owned vehicles. All users of company vehicles are reminded that the highway speed limit 55 miles per hour is federal law. Our attorney Frank Dallas has recommended that a conviction for speeding be followed by a suspension of driving privileges.

We would like to remind drivers that self-service gasoline pumps are to be used when gas is purchased on a company credit card. Saving a few cents a gallon should result in a reduction of our fuel costs by thousands of dollars over the year.

INSTRUCTIONS: Check your answers with the Key to Exercise IV.22 in Appendix C to see if you correctly inserted the four missing commas.

REVIEW POINT

INSTRUCTIONS:

Transcribe Achievement Survey Tape IV.3 (Series, Introductory, and Explanatory Commas) in mailable form. You will be inserting a total of 13 missing commas. Then check your transcript with the Key to Achievement Survey Tape IV.3. Finally, complete a Mailability Analysis Chart and submit your transcript and the chart to your instructor.

If you misplaced any commas, turn to the Practice Exercises in Appendix B for further drill on the series, introductory, and explanatory commas before proceeding to the next part.

Parenthetical Comma

RULE: Separate parenthetical material by commas.

EXAMPLE OF A PARENTHETICAL WORD:

Enough people, fortunately, have registered for the conference to cover our costs.

EXAMPLE OF A PARENTHETICAL PHRASE:

He is a man who, in my opinion, would make a fine employee of this firm.

EXAMPLE OF A PARENTHETICAL CLAUSE:

The meeting will be held next Thursday, if you approve of that date, right after lunch.

EXAMPLE OF A PARENTHETICAL EXPRESSION AT THE END OF A SENTENCE:

Our entire staff will be at the meeting, of course.

EXERCISE IV.23: PARENTHETICAL COMMA

APPLY YOUR SKILLS

INSTRUCTIONS: Insert the two commas missing in the following letter. If time permits, type the letter in rough-draft form to reinforce your mastery of the parenthetical comma rule.

The letter goes to: Mrs. Joleen Standeven / 1004 Gladlane Drive / Montgomery, Alabama 36111

The letter is from: Betty L. Birmingham / Circulation Director

It's hard to believe that a whole year has passed since you ordered your Christmas gift subscription. Although it may seem early in the season to be thinking again of Christmas and of gift-giving, we urge you to send us your gift instructions right away so that your special person can keep on receiving ACME for another happy year.

We must of course remind you that in order to insure prompt continuation of your gift subscription your order must reach us no later than December 10. Complete instructions and an order form are enclosed.

Sincerely,

INSTRUCTIONS: Check your answers with the Key to Exercise IV.23 in Appendix C to see if you correctly inserted the two missing commas.

Direct Address Comma

RULE: Use commas to set off a noun in a direct address.

EXAMPLE OF DIRECT ADDRESS IN THE MIDDLE OF A SENTENCE:

Thank you, Mrs. Farr, for completing and returning our questionnaire so promptly.

EXAMPLE OF DIRECT ADDRESS AT THE BEGINNING OF A SENTENCE:

Mrs. Farr, thank you for completing and returning our questionnaire so promptly.

EXAMPLE OF DIRECT ADDRESS AT THE END OF A SENTENCE:

Thank you for completing and returning our questionnaire so promptly, Mrs. Farr.

EXERCISE IV.24: DIRECT ADDRESS COMMA

INSTRUCTIONS: Insert the three commas missing in the following letter. If time permits, type the letter in rough-draft form to reinforce your mastery of the direct address comma rule.

APPLY
YOUR SKILLS

The letter goes to: Miss Sarah Goldberg/100 Indiana Avenue/Monaca, Pennsylvania 15061

The letter is from: Harry L. Steinwell/Salesperson

Thank you so much Miss Goldberg for your patronage. You have our assurance that we shall make every effort to maintain the friendly type of relationship so necessary for your continued confidence and good will.

All of us are eager to serve you at all times and in every way possible.

Thanks again Miss Goldberg.

Sincerely,

INSTRUCTIONS: Check your answers with the Key to Exercise IV.24 in Appendix C to see if you correctly inserted the three missing commas.

Modifier Comma

RULE: When two or more adjectives modify a noun, separate the adjectives with commas.

> **(Hint:** To determine if the comma is necessary between two consecutive adjectives, mentally put the word ''and'' between them. If the adjectives still make sense, the comma should be inserted; otherwise, omit the comma.)

EXAMPLE OF TWO ADJECTIVES MODIFYING A NOUN WHERE A COMMA IS NECESSARY:

Word processing centers can provide a sophisticated, systematic approach to handling information.

EXAMPLE OF TWO ADJECTIVES MODIFYING A NOUN WHERE A COMMA IS NOT NECESSARY:

She wore a new blue suit to her first job interview.

EXERCISE IV.25: MODIFIER COMMA

INSTRUCTIONS: Insert the two commas missing in the following letter. If time permits, type the letter in rough-draft form to reinforce your mastery of the modifier comma rule.

The letter goes to: Dr. Jose Negrete/College of Education/University of Wisconsin/Madison, Wisconsin 53706

The letter is from: Becky Baker/Administrative Associate

It is a pleasure to write a letter of recommendation for Roberto Segura. I feel that I can give a fair honest evaluation of his work and of his potential for a graduate fellowship in bilingual education.

Roberto is a very conscientious worker and has demonstrated excellent organizational capabilities. He is always willing to put forth extra time and effort to get things done. His initiative in all aspects of his work is highly commendable. He is a most pleasant cooperative worker.

It has been delightful working with him professionally and knowing him socially. Sincerely,

INSTRUCTIONS: Check your answers with the Key to Exercise IV.25 in Appendix C to see if you correctly inserted the two missing commas.

REVIEW POINT

INSTRUCTIONS:

Transcribe Achievement Survey Tape IV.4 (Parenthetical, Direct Address, and Modifier Commas) in mailable form. You will be inserting a total of 13 missing commas. Then check your transcript with the Key to Achievement Survey Tape IV.4. Finally, complete a Mailability Analysis Chart and submit your transcript and the chart to your instructor.

If you misplaced any commas, turn to the Practice Exercises in Appendix B for further drill on parenthetical, direct address, and modifier commas before proceeding to the next part.

Nonrestrictive Comma

RULE: Separate nonrestrictive matter (material not necessary to the meaning of the sentence) from the rest of the sentence by commas.

EXAMPLE:
Automatic typing equipment, which has powerful correction capabilities, cannot compensate for poor English skills.

EXERCISE IV.26: NONRESTRICTIVE COMMA

INSTRUCTIONS: Insert the two commas missing in the following letter. If time permits, type the letter in rough-draft form to reinforce your mastery of the nonrestrictive comma rule.

APPLY YOUR SKILLS

The letter goes to: The Reverend E. E. Raymond / Chaplain / The Episcopal Chaplaincy / Trinity Episcopal Church / 1500 Gordon Avenue / Charlottesville, Virginia 22903

The letter is from: Stella Samuels / Social Worker

I want to express my appreciation for your help in moving Frances Newman to her new apartment last week. The use of the truck which was a pleasant surprise proved to be a real time-saver.

We have always been appreciative of our relationship with the Episcopal Chaplaincy and look forward to its continuation.
Sincerely,

INSTRUCTIONS: Check your answers with the Key to Exercise IV.26 in Appendix C to see if you correctly inserted the two missing commas.

Independent Clauses Comma

RULE: Use a comma to separate two independent clauses joined by a conjunction.

EXAMPLE:
We acknowledge that after-working-hour purchases are sometimes necessary, but all such purchases should be confined to emergency situations only.

EXERCISE IV.27: INDEPENDENT CLAUSES COMMA

APPLY
YOUR SKILLS

INSTRUCTIONS: Insert the three commas missing in the following letter. If time permits, type the letter in rough-draft form to reinforce your mastery of the independent clauses comma rule.

The letter goes to: Hugh Gibson/One Sparkleberry Lane/Columbia, South Carolina 29206

The letter is from: Della Phillips/Personnel Director

I am very pleased to confirm our telephone conversation of this morning regarding your appointment to the position of Personnel Job Analyst. We feel that you can make a great contribution to our staff and we look forward to working with you.

Staff benefits are outlined in the enclosed booklets and a full description of all other benefits will be provided shortly after you begin employment with us. Please sign the enclosed employment contract and return it to us within ten days.

We look forward to welcoming you to our staff in the near future.

Sincerely,

INSTRUCTIONS: Check your answers with the Key to Exercise IV.27 in Appendix C to see if you correctly inserted the three missing commas.

Dates and States Commas

RULE: When typing a date in a sentence, use commas to set off the year from the rest of the sentence.

EXAMPLE:

The next finance meeting will be held on May 14, 1982, in the director's conference room.

RULE: When typing the name of a city and state in a sentence, use commas to set off the state from the rest of the sentence.

EXAMPLE:

We are planning meetings for our branch offices in Nashville, Tennessee, and Moline, Illinois.

EXERCISE IV.28: DATES AND STATES COMMAS

INSTRUCTIONS: Insert the five commas missing in the following memo. If time permits, type the memo in rough-draft form to reinforce your mastery of the dates and states comma rules.

APPLY YOUR SKILLS

TO: All Employees
FROM: Personnel Department
SUBJECT: Retirement Seminar

A free course for staff members who are making plans for retirement will be offered on February 28 19— in the auditorium of our Omaha Nebraska office. Husbands and wives are encouraged to attend.

The next retirement seminars have been scheduled for July 25 and December 28. These will be held at our office in Moline Illinois.

You are encouraged to attend one of these sessions if you plan to retire soon.

INSTRUCTIONS: Check your answers with the Key to Exercise IV.28 in Appendix C to see if you correctly inserted the five missing commas.

REVIEW POINT

INSTRUCTIONS:

Transcribe Achievement Survey Tape IV.5 (Nonrestrictive, Independent Clauses, and Dates and States Commas) in mailable form. You will be inserting a total of eight missing commas. Then check your transcript with the Key to Achievement Survey Tape IV.5. Finally, complete a Mailability Analysis Chart and submit your transcript and the chart to your instructor.

If you misplaced any commas, turn to the Practice Exercises in Appendix B for further drill on nonrestrictive, independent clauses, and dates and states commas before taking the posttest. You may also want to review the other Practice Exercises for the comma in Appendix B.

INSTRUCTIONS:

Under supervision, transcribe Posttest IV.4 in mailable form. Submit your transcript to your instructor.

PRETEST IV.5: APOSTROPHE

INSTRUCTIONS: Read the following memo and insert the 20 missing apostrophes. Then type the memo in mailable form.

TO: Mary Stanley, John Young, and John Wilson
FROM: Dick Peterson and Susan Rodgers
SUBJECT: Miscellaneous Items from the Chairpersons Desks

Please respond to Nancy, Betty, and Leslies request for comments concerning issues relevant to our clientele. Since Leslies report is due by the months end, turn in your comments within the next two days.

Plans are being made for the Staff Development Committees program for next year. Since we have received many negative comments about this years programs, let's provide some input for next years.

Budget time is here again. Please gather all information in keeping with the Presidents directive. Note that salary requests should be submitted to Bob Johnsons office. They will be reviewed by Mrs. Ludwigs staff and then by Ms. Martins.

Departmental budgets should include two columns of figures:
1. This years expenditures and
2. The past three years total expenditures.

You may obtain this information from either Mr. Gardners or Mr. Garrisons staff.

A few miscellaneous points:
1. It's summertime, which means time for socializing again. Everybodys ideas are needed; so jot yours down and turn them in to us.
2. This summers vacation schedules are due in the office by next Monday. All employees requests will be honored if at all possible, but it's important that you give at least three weeks notice.
3. The Williamsons vacation to Ireland is turning out to be a great success; they send greetings to everyone.

INSTRUCTIONS: After completing Pretest IV.5, turn your paper in to your instructor. Your instructor will evaluate your pretest and will let you know if you need to proceed further with the Apostrophe section of Phase IV.

APOSTROPHE

Singular Noun Possessives

RULE: To show possession (ownership) by a singular noun, add an apostrophe and *s*.

EXAMPLE:

My boss's desk faces the window.

EXERCISE IV.29: SINGULAR NOUN POSSESSIVES

CHECK YOURSELF

INSTRUCTIONS: In each of the following sentences, write the possessive word correctly in the blank provided. If necessary, add both an apostrophe and an *s*. If an apostrophe is not needed to show possession, write *Correct*.

1. My lawyers secretary is helpful.   _____
2. A clerks books will be audited.   _____
3. The only witness testimony will be heard today.   _____
4. Our father car is a "lemon."   _____
5. The physicians assistant wears white.   _____

INSTRUCTIONS: Check your answers with the Key to Exercise IV.29 in Appendix C.

Compound Noun Possessives

RULE: To show possession (ownership) by a compound noun, add an apostrophe and *s* to the end of the compound noun. (**Note:** A compound noun can be written as a solid, spaced, or hyphenated word.)

EXAMPLE:
The secretary-treasurer's books will be audited on February 15.

EXERCISE IV.30: COMPOUND NOUN POSSESSIVES

CHECK YOURSELF

INSTRUCTIONS: In each of the following sentences, write the possessive word correctly in the blank provided. If necessary, add an *s* to the word before adding the apostrophe. If an apostrophe is not needed to show possession, write *Correct*.

1. My brother-in-laws birthday is today.   _____
2. The district attorneys opinion was not popular.   _____
3. Our secretary-treasurer audit went well.   _____
4. The Secretary of States travels are exhausting.   _____
5. I received my stockholders report.   _____

INSTRUCTIONS: Check your answers with the Key to Exercise IV.30 in Appendix C.

Proper Name Possessives

RULE: To show possession (ownership) by a proper name in the singular, add an apostrophe and *s*.

EXAMPLE:

We are anxious to get Mary's report.

RULE: To show possession of a plural proper name, add an apostrophe to the plural of the name. (**Note:** To form the plural, add *s* to all names, except those ending in *s, x, z, ch,* or *sh.* For names ending in *s, x, z, ch,* or *sh,* add *es* to form the plural.)

EXAMPLES:

The Rodriguezes' apartment overlooks the Mississippi River.

The Huntzingers' family bakery is popular with all the children in the neighborhood.

RULE: To show possession where there is joint ownership by two or more persons, add an apostrophe and *s* to only the last proper noun in the series.

EXAMPLE:

Preparing the quarterly budget is Lowell, Leo, and Jane's responsibility.

RULE: To show separate ownership by two or more persons, add an apostrophe and *s* after each name.

EXAMPLE:

You will need to sort these papers for Marcella's and Gayle's files.

EXERCISE IV.31: PROPER NAME POSSESSIVES

CHECK YOURSELF

INSTRUCTIONS: In each of the following sentences, write the possessive word or words correctly in the blank provided. If an apostrophe is not needed to show possession, write *Correct*.

1. Sams and Ellas appointments were canceled.   _____

2. Patti and Bills letter was fun to read.   _____

3. Jenny Smiths essay won a blue ribbon.   _____

4. The Sanchezes son is four.   _____

5. Walterinas flight was delayed by the fog.   _____

INSTRUCTIONS: Check your answers with the Key to Exercise IV.31 in Appendix C.

Inanimate Object Possessives

RULE: Try to avoid using the possessive form with inanimate objects.

EXAMPLE:
They inspected the keyboard of the typewriter.
(NOT: They inspected the typewriter's keyboard.)

EXERCISE IV.32: INANIMATE OBJECT POSSESSIVES

INSTRUCTIONS: In each of the following sentences, reword the underscored phrase to avoid using the possessive form. Write the corrected phrases in the blanks.

CHECK
YOURSELF

1. The <u>newsletter's design</u> was outstanding.   _____

2. Our <u>building's elevators</u> are always dark.   _____

3. The <u>cabinet's key</u> is lost.   _____

4. The <u>folder's cover</u> was ripped.   _____

5. My <u>will's wording</u> is confusing.   _____

INSTRUCTIONS: Check your answers with the Key to Exercise IV.32 in Appendix C.

REVIEW POINT

INSTRUCTIONS:
Transcribe Achievement Survey Tape IV.6 (Singular Noun, Compound Noun, Proper Name, and Inanimate Object Possessives) in mailable form. You will be inserting a total of seven apostrophes. In addition, one sentence will have to be reworded. Then check your transcript with the Key to Achievement Survey Tape IV.6. Finally, complete a Mailability Analysis Chart and submit your transcript and the chart to your instructor.

If you misplaced any apostrophes or if you did not correctly reword the sentence, turn to the Practice Exercises in Appendix B for further drill on singular noun, compound noun, proper name, and inanimate object possessives before proceeding to the next part.

Plural Noun Possessives

RULE: To show possession (ownership) by a plural noun that is plural as it stands—called an *irregular* plural—add an apostrophe and *s*. (Examples: *children, men, women*.)

EXAMPLE:

They are interested in buying children's books.

RULE: To show possession (ownership) of a plural noun that is made plural by adding *s*—called a *regular* plural—add an apostrophe after the *s*.

EXAMPLE:

The stockholders' meeting will be held next Tuesday.

EXERCISE IV.33: PLURAL NOUN POSSESSIVES

**CHECK
YOURSELF**

INSTRUCTIONS: In each of the following sentences, write the possessive word correctly in the blank provided. If necessary, add *s* to the word before adding the apostrophe. If the apostrophe is not needed to show possession, write *Correct*.

1. All policyholders notices were issued.   _____

2. The womens coat department is having a sale.   _____

3. Our entire stock of boys bikes is on display.   _____

4. Several senators comments given at the hearing were published.   _____

5. Motorists licenses will now have a photograph affixed.   _____

INSTRUCTIONS: Check your answers with the Key to Exercise IV.33 in Appendix C.

Noun Understood Possessives

RULE: To show possession (ownership) if a noun in a sentence is understood but not actually given, use an apostrophe in its modifier.

EXAMPLE:

We went from the secretary's office to the treasurer's. (MEANING: We went from the secretary's office to the treasurer's *office*.)

EXERCISE IV.34: NOUN UNDERSTOOD POSSESSIVES

INSTRUCTIONS: In each of the following sentences, write the possessive word correctly in the blank space provided. If necessary, add *s* to the word before adding the apostrophe. If the apostrophe is not needed to show possession, write *Correct*.

CHECK YOURSELF

1. Compare this months with last months costs.   _____

2. Todays business was more than yesterdays.   _____

3. Victors estimates don't agree with Todds.   _____

4. Daras schedule is like Kristens.   _____

5. The childrens games are the same as the adults.   _____

INSTRUCTIONS: Check your answers with the Key to Exercise IV.34 in Appendix C.

Personal Pronoun and Indefinite Pronoun Possessives

RULE: To show possession (ownership) by a personal pronoun, no apostrophe is needed. (Examples: *hers, his, mine, its, whose, yours, ours, theirs.*)

EXAMPLE:
The sales figures you reviewed are hers.

RULE: To show possession (ownership) by an indefinite pronoun, add an apostrophe and *s*. (Examples: *anyone, everybody, one.*)

EXAMPLE:
Anybody's questions will be answered at the press conference.

EXERCISE IV.35: PERSONAL PRONOUN AND INDEFINITE PRONOUN POSSESSIVES

INSTRUCTIONS: In each of the following sentences, write the possessive word correctly in the blank space provided. If an apostrophe is not needed to show possession, write *Correct*.

CHECK YOURSELF

1. Yes, it is everybodys business.   _____

2. Those materials are yours.   _____

3. Ours are here; yours haven't arrived.   _____

4. Everyones desk is cleaned nightly.   _____

5. Hers is a good example; theirs needs improvement.   _____

INSTRUCTIONS: Check your answers with the Key to Exercise IV.35 in Appendix C.

Time and Measurement Possessives

RULE: To show possession (ownership) in cases of time or measurement, add either apostrophe plus *s* or *s* plus apostrophe.

EXAMPLES:

She bought 12 inches' worth of ribbon.

She was granted three years' leave of absence.

EXERCISE IV.36: TIME AND MEASUREMENT POSSESSIVES

CHECK YOURSELF

INSTRUCTIONS: In each of the following sentences, write the possessive word correctly in the blank space provided. If an apostrophe is not needed to show possession, write *Correct*.

1. He bought four gallons worth of gas.   _____

2. You will get two months supply free.   _____

3. There will be one weeks delay in shipment.   _____

4. Our days activities were well designed.   _____

5. She redeemed a dollars worth of coupons.   _____

INSTRUCTIONS: Check your answers with the Key to Exercise IV.36 in Appendix C.

REVIEW POINT

INSTRUCTIONS:

Transcribe Achievement Survey Tape IV.7 (Plural Noun, Noun Understood, Personal Pronoun and Indefinite Pronoun Possessives, and Time and Measurement Possessives) in mailable form. You will be inserting a total of six missing apostrophes. Then check your transcript with the Key to Achievement Survey Tape IV.7. Finally, complete a Mailability Analysis Chart and submit your transcript and the chart to your instructor.

If you misplaced any apostrophes, turn to the Practice Exercises in Appendix B for further drill on plural noun, noun understood, personal pronoun and indefinite pronoun possessives, and time and measurement possessives before taking the posttest. You may also want to review the other Practice Exercises for the apostrophe in Appendix B.

INSTRUCTIONS:

Under supervision, transcribe Posttest IV.5 in mailable form. Submit your transcript to your instructor.

PRETEST IV.6: COLON

INSTRUCTIONS: Read the following memo and insert the three missing colons. Then type the memo in mailable form.

TO:	H. Greg Wind, Editorial Assistant
FROM:	Roni Miller, Director
SUBJECT:	Changes in Fall Bulletin

The following items should be added to your copy before our fall bulletin goes to the printer

1. Enrollment is on a first-come, first-served basis first, students with advance reservations; second, students who attend the first class; third, students who register late.

2. Your employer may assist you in paying all or a portion of the cost of your tuition. In this vicinity, such assistance is available from the Department of Social Services, Fulton Industries, Great Plains Consultants, and Far West Associates.

3. The Parking Department has issued the following statement "Parking lots on the north side of Finkbine Hall and the west side of the Business Library are available for free student parking on Saturday and Sunday and after 5 p.m. every other evening. City parking meters need not be 'fed' any day after 5:30 p.m." I don't know where you want to insert the above quotation; however, I want it quoted precisely since there was so much confusion last year.

INSTRUCTIONS: After completing Pretest IV.6, submit your paper to your instructor. Your instructor will evaluate your pretest and will let you know if you need to proceed further with the Colon section of Phase IV.

COLON

RULE: Use the colon after an expression that introduces material following it, such as an explanation of a general statement, a list, or an enumeration.

EXAMPLE:
There are seven elements in the transcription process: displaying a professional attitude, listening, utilizing English skills, knowing equipment, typewriting, and formatting.

RULE: Do *not* use the colon if a series follows a verb or a preposition. (Examples of a preposition: *of, to, for, with, in, from.*)

EXAMPLES:
verb:
The features of this typewriter *include* versatility, compactness, and cost efficiency.

preposition:
The features of this typewriter consist *of* versatility, compactness, and cost efficiency.

RULE: Use the colon to introduce a long, direct quotation.

EXAMPLE:

Section 16 of the new law states: "It shall be a prohibited practice for an employer or designated company representative willfully to interfere with, restrain, or coerce employees in the exercise of rights granted by this act."

RULE: Use the colon before an explanation or an illustration of the preceding sentence.

EXAMPLE:

Your new portable dictation equipment has the right qualities: a weight of only 8 ounces and exceptional sound reproduction.

REMINDER

1. A typed colon is followed by two spaces.
2. If the material following a colon is a complete sentence, you must begin with a capital letter.

EXERCISE IV.37: COLON

CHECK YOURSELF

INSTRUCTIONS: In the following sentences, correct the punctuation by adding or deleting colons where necessary. If no change is needed, write *Correct* in the blank space.

1. The committee consisted of Ray Brady, Bill Aggson, Ednabell Yoder, and Sue Riba. _____

2. They will visit the following countries on their tour Germany, Switzerland, and Italy. _____

3. Three courses are required for students in the advanced secretarial program Office Management, Written Communications, and Records Management. _____

4. Mary is the author of "As I See It" and "Sometime Next June." _____

5. In view of the low attendance so far, we have decided to adopt the following new policy on meetings. Instead of starting at eight o'clock, we will begin at seven; and we will adjourn promptly at nine. _____

6. Section 5.2 of the Operations Manual reads: "All offices will be closed on legal holidays. (See also Section 56.)" _____

INSTRUCTIONS: Check your answers with the Key to Exercise IV.37 in Appendix C.

REVIEW POINT

INSTRUCTIONS:
Transcribe Achievement Survey Tape IV.8 (Colon) in mailable form. You will be inserting a total of three missing colons. Then check your transcript with the Key to Achievement Survey Tape IV.8. Finally, complete a Mailability Analysis Chart and submit your transcript and the chart to your instructor.

If you misplaced any colons, turn to the Practice Exercises in Appendix B for further drill on the colon before taking the posttest.

INSTRUCTIONS:
Under supervision, transcribe Posttest IV.6 in mailable form. Submit your transcript to your instructor.

PRETEST IV.7: SEMICOLON

INSTRUCTIONS: In the following bulletin, replace four commas with semicolons and add three semicolons where necessary. Then type the bulletin in mailable form.

HEADING: *BULLETIN NO. 37: SUMMER EMPLOYMENT*

1. Students who are interested in summer employment should contact Ernesto Cervantes, placement specialist, Mary Higuchi, career resources coordinator, or Phyllis VanRoekel, administrative assistant.

2. The suggested deadline date for submitting applications is March 10 the absolute deadline is April 15.

3. You should include a cover letter with your application it should be addressed to Ernesto Cervantes.

4. Responses to applications may be expected within six weeks unless you submit after the deadline date, for example, if you delay until April 15, you will not be notified until very late May.

5. Applicants with considerable experience will be given preference, however, you are encouraged to submit your application even though you may have had very little employment experience.

6. The meetings will be held on February 10, February 20, and March 1 no meetings will be held after March 1.

INSTRUCTIONS: After completing Pretest IV.7, submit your paper to your instructor. Your instructor will evaluate your pretest and will let you know if you need to proceed further with the Semicolon section of Phase IV.

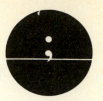

SEMICOLON

RULE: Use a semicolon to separate independent and closely related clauses when no conjunction connects the clauses.

EXAMPLE:

I wanted to leave the concert; they wanted to stay.

RULE: Use a comma to separate two independent clauses joined by a conjunction. However, when one or both of the independent clauses contains at least one comma, place a semicolon between the clauses instead.

EXAMPLE:

Letters of complaint were mailed on May 1, June 1, and July 1; *but* no reply came until July 29.

RULE: If an illustration is introduced by an expression such as *namely, that is, for example,* place a semicolon before the expression and a comma after the expression.

EXAMPLE:

There are only two things you need to do; namely, sign the card and send your check for $7.50.

RULE: If independent clauses are joined by an adverb used to join clauses, place a semicolon before the adverb and a comma after it. (Examples of adverbs used to join clauses: *however, therefore, accordingly, otherwise, consequently, nevertheless*.)

EXAMPLE:

Grandma received her third speeding ticket in a year's period of time; consequently, she had her license suspended for 18 months.

RULE: Use a semicolon to separate groups of items that contain commas within each group.

EXAMPLE:

Three officers could not attend the last meeting: Jean Jones, president; Elmer Shockey, secretary; and Charley Cronin, historian.

EXERCISE IV.38: SEMICOLON

INSTRUCTIONS: In the following sentences, correct the punctuation by adding or deleting semicolons where necessary. If no change is needed, write *Correct* in the blank.

CHECK YOURSELF

1. Betty is flying to New York; Barbara is flying to Dallas. _____

2. Most word processing centers have text-editing equipment, dictation equipment, and copiers; but I have heard of few that have stencil duplicators. _____

3. All work in our word processing center is logged in when it arrives, that is, the supervisor records the type of document and the name of the person to whom it is assigned. _____

4. The Typing Specialist in our word processing center keeps a record of the number of lines produced; therefore, it is possible to determine the progress the employee is making. _____

5. I plan to visit the Hughes Insurance Agency, Denver, the First National Bank, Omaha, and the Clemson Real Estate Office, Atlanta. _____

6. Yvonne Pederson is interested in the position of Correspondence Secretary in our office Lisa Lowenberg is not. _____

7. Your training period in our word processing center will extend over a three-month period namely, June, July, and August. _____

8. The Administrative Secretary dictated the memo, the Correspondence Secretary typed it. _____

INSTRUCTIONS: Check your answers with the Key to Exercise IV.38 in Appendix C.

REVIEW POINT

INSTRUCTIONS:

Transcribe Achievement Survey Tape IV.9 (Semicolon) in mailable form. You will be inserting a total of 12 missing semicolons. Then check your transcript with the Key to Achievement Survey Tape IV.9. Finally, complete a Mailability Analysis Chart and submit your transcript and the chart to your instructor.

If you misplaced any semicolons, turn to the Practice Exercises in Appendix B for further drill on the semicolon before taking the posttest.

INSTRUCTIONS:

Under supervision, transcribe Posttest IV.7 in mailable form. Submit your transcript to your instructor.

PRETEST IV.8: HYPHEN

INSTRUCTIONS: In the following two memos, insert the 18 missing hyphens. Then type the memos in mailable form.

Memo 1

TO: Members of the Support Staff
FROM: Roger Blakely, Manager
SUBJECT: Changes in Sick Leave and Vacation Policy

All support members should be aware of the following changes in policies concerning sick leave and vacation:

1. Effective mid July, eligible staff members may elect to change their monthly sick leave accrual (one and one half days) for one half day of vacation.

2. All staff members should check with the Personnel Office quarterly to see if their records are up to date. For example, for the quarter beginning mid July, staff should check their records between October 1 and 15. If you wish, you may check your record at midquarter time.

3. Part time employees may accrue that fractional portion of the full time entitlement where less than a complete month of service is involved.

4. One hundred forty four hours of vacation per year may be accrued by persons with 5 to 11 years of service.

Questions about any of the above statements may be noted on the enclosed form and returned to Personnel Service in the enclosed self addressed envelope.

Memo 2

TO: All Staff
FROM: Roger Blakely, Manager
SUBJECT: Reminders on Travel

Staff members should be thoroughly familiar with the following regulations which apply to in state and out of state travel:

1. When an employee is not away from home overnight, meal reimbursement represents taxable income.

2. We would like to reemphasize that requests from persons who wish to travel out of state should be submitted two weeks before departure.

3. You may find it necessary to stay at higher priced motels and hotels, but we suggest that you select those in a medium price range whenever possible.

4. It may seem tough minded; but with our increasing costs, it is absolutely necessary that employees exercise good judgment in selecting meals when on the road.

5. Whenever possible, use cars that are company owned.

6. An amount up to three fourths of your total anticipated travel expense will be advanced to you if you fill out and submit an Advance Travel Form.

A tip for our inexperienced travelers: Avoid friendly looking attractive people in well known hotels. Recently we've had several reports of pickpockets of this description.

INSTRUCTIONS: After completing Pretest IV.8, submit your paper to your instructor. Your instructor will evaluate your pretest and will let you know if you need to proceed further with the Hyphen section of Phase IV.

HYPHEN

Hyphen with Numbers

RULE: Use a hyphen between two numbers in place of the word *to* where the two numbers represent a continuous sequence.

EXAMPLES:

I'll be out of the office during the week of May 15-21.

Read the comments I wrote on pages 18-28.

(**Note:** Do not use a hyphen if the sequence is introduced by the word *from* or *between*. Example: I'll be at the meeting from 1 to 3:30 p.m.)

RULE: Use a hyphen with numbers between 21 and 99 that are spelled out.

EXAMPLE:

One hundred twenty-five students registered for the introductory economics course.

RULE: When a fraction is spelled out, use a hyphen to separate the numerator and the denominator.

EXAMPLE:

His last day of work is March 9; therefore, he will be paid one-fourth of his monthly wage for March.

EXERCISE IV.39: HYPHEN WITH NUMBERS

INSTRUCTIONS: In the following sentences, correct the punctuation by adding a hyphen or by deleting a hyphen and adding a word where necessary. If no change is needed, write *Correct* in the blank space.

CHECK YOURSELF

1. His office is somewhere between rooms 400-412. _____

2. Thirty five employees will be promoted in July. _____

3. I was surprised to hear that one third of our staff do not carry health insurance. _____

4. We'll be in Nashville from September 13-19. _____

5. The conference is scheduled to run between 9 a.m. and 5 p.m. _____

INSTRUCTIONS: Check your answers with the Key to Exercise IV.39 in Appendix C.

Hyphen with Prefixes and Suffixes

RULE: Use a hyphen after *self* when *self* serves as a prefix.

EXAMPLE:

> The return envelope was self-addressed.

> (**Note:** Do not use a hyphen after *self* if *self* serves as the base word and a suffix is added. Example: *They are selfish.*)

RULE: Use a hyphen after a prefix added to a word that begins with a capital letter.

EXAMPLES:

> Your semester report is due in mid-January.

> Your semester report is due in midwinter.

RULE: Use a hyphen when the prefix or suffix added to the root word results in a sequence of two *a*'s or two *i*'s. (Examples of prefixes and suffixes: *extra, inter, non, over, anti, semi, ment, less, like.*)

EXAMPLES:

> The intensive care facility classified the patient as semi-invalid.

> Our youngest child is the nonconformist in the family.

EXERCISE IV.40: HYPHEN WITH PREFIXES AND SUFFIXES

CHECK YOURSELF

INSTRUCTIONS: In the following sentences, correct the punctuation by adding or deleting hyphens where necessary. If no change is needed, write *Correct*.

1. Marjorie will take her mid-summer vacation in July.   _____

2. Any employer is interested in hiring people who are self starters.   _____

3. He seemed only semi-independent when they released him from the intensive care center.   _____

4. I will have two weeks off beginning in midAugust.   _____

5. I need to check the anti-freeze before winter comes.   _____

INSTRUCTIONS: Check your answers with the Key to Exercise IV.40 in Appendix C.

Hyphen with Compound Adjectives Preceding and Following Nouns

RULE: Place a hyphen between the words of a compound adjective when it precedes a noun.

EXAMPLE:

The up-to-date registration forms were filed.

RULE: Do not place a hyphen between the words of a compound adjective when it follows a noun.

EXAMPLE:

The registration forms are up to date.

RULE: Do not add a hyphen when the first word in a modifier is an adverb ending in *ly*. However, add a hyphen when the first word in a modifier is an *adjective* ending in *ly*.

EXAMPLES:

The white sale features greatly reduced prices on bed linens.

The child was carrying a friendly-looking old dog.

Hint: When you are not certain whether a modifier ending in *ly* is an adjective or an adverb, try using the modifier *alone* with the noun. If it can be used alone, it is an adjective.

EXAMPLES:

The white sale features *greatly reduced prices* on bed linens.
features greatly prices. (No hyphen needed)

The child was carrying a *friendly-looking old dog*.
carrying a friendly old dog. (Hyphen needed)

RULE: Add a hyphen to a compound adjective composed of an adjective plus either a noun ending in *ed* or a participle.

EXAMPLES:

The hats worn in the play are old-fashioned.

It was the best-looking car.

EXERCISE IV.41: HYPHEN WITH COMPOUND ADJECTIVES PRECEDING AND FOLLOWING NOUNS

CHECK YOURSELF

INSTRUCTIONS: In the following sentences, correct the punctuation by adding or deleting hyphens where necessary. If no change is needed, write *Correct* in the blank space.

1. Word processing centers that are well-organized are usually ones that produce lots of work.   _____

2. It is a well known fact that businesses that implement word processing often cut their costs by 25 percent after the first year.   _____

3. The day by day routine in an office can be challenging and interesting.   _____

4. Keeping a procedures manual up to date is the duty of our supervisor.   _____

5. There was a friendly sounding knock at the door.   _____

6. People, procedures, and equipment—these are closely related elements in any word processing system.   _____

7. The sculpture was very life-like.   _____

8. John and George are enjoying their air cooled office.   _____

INSTRUCTIONS: Check your answers with the Key to Exercise IV.41 in Appendix C.

REVIEW POINT

INSTRUCTIONS:

Transcribe Achievement Survey Tape IV.10 (Hyphen) in mailable form. You will be inserting a total of 11 missing hyphens. Then check your transcript with the Key to Achievement Survey Tape IV.10. Finally, complete a Mailability Analysis Chart and submit your transcript and the chart to your instructor.

If you misplaced any hyphens, turn to the Practice Exercises in Appendix B for further drill on the hyphen before taking the posttest.

INSTRUCTIONS:

Under supervision, transcribe Posttest IV.8 in mailable form. Submit your transcript to your instructor.

PRETEST IV.9: DASH

INSTRUCTIONS: In the following memo, insert the six dashes missing. Then type the memo in mailable form.

TO:	V. C. Eltoft
FROM:	K. S. Hwang
SUBJECT:	Summary Report on Advertising

    For the month of February, our sales rose 15 percent 3 percent more than anticipated. This increase was due largely in the opinion of the Sales Department Manager to increased radio advertising. Commercials were added on the following two local radio stations: WJN and WYR. Present plans in fact, both present and future plans call for still more use of radio commercials.

    I suggest we continue to evaluate all advertising media. Newspapers, magazines, TV, radio these are the wheels which make our business run.

INSTRUCTIONS: After completing Pretest IV.9, submit your paper to your instructor. Your instructor will evaluate your pretest and will let you know if you need to proceed further with the Dash section of Phase IV.

DASH

RULE: Separate parenthetical material from the rest of the sentence with dashes (instead of commas) to give emphasis.

EXAMPLE:

Students of a second language should have frequent practice—daily practice— if they wish to become proficient in the second language.

RULE: Use the dash before words that summarize the preceding part of the sentence.

EXAMPLE:

Ideal build, perfect balance, lightning reflexes, speed—he has everything to be the world's best long-distance runner.

EXERCISE IV.42: DASH

INSTRUCTIONS: Insert the four dashes missing in the following memo. If time permits, type the memo in rough-draft form to reinforce your mastery of the dash rules.

TO: Sales Department Staff
FROM: Pat Dixon, Administrative Assistant
SUBJECT: Our Move to Fourth Floor

Boxes, boxes, and more boxes—I'm sure you're tired of seeing them and shoving them around. I do have good news for you! The latest word is that we will move on Thursday next Thursday, that is—for sure.

You've all worked hard to prepare for this move I knew you would and you'll be happy to be settled in our new quarters. After my tour of them yesterday—it was a short one—I'm convinced that it's all been worth it. Colorful dividers, soft brown carpeting, and the newest in beautiful modular furniture these are some of the things you have to look forward to.

INSTRUCTIONS: Check your answers with the Key to Exercise IV.42 in Appendix C to see if you correctly inserted the four missing dashes.

REVIEW POINT

INSTRUCTIONS:

Transcribe Achievement Survey Tape IV.11 (Dash) in mailable form. You will be inserting a total of seven missing dashes. Then check your transcript with the Key to Achievement Survey Tape IV.11. Finally, complete a Mailability Analysis Chart and submit your transcript and the chart to your instructor.

If you misplaced any dashes, turn to the Practice Exercises in Appendix B for further drill on the dash before taking the posttest.

INSTRUCTIONS:

Under supervision, transcribe Posttest IV.9 in mailable form. Submit your transcript to your instructor.

PRETEST IV.10: QUOTATION MARKS

INSTRUCTIONS: In the following memo, insert the five pairs of quotation marks missing and, where necessary, delete or correct the placement of existing quotation marks. Then type the memo in mailable form.

TO: Ruth L. Moultrie, Associate Editor
FROM: Justin Collier, Assistant Editor
SUBJECT: Comments on *Marketing Practices in the Northeastern States*

According to your instructions, I have reviewed the Tyson book, *Marketing Practices in the Northeastern States*. On the whole, the book is well written; however, I have the following comments and criticisms:

1. Chapter 2, Grocery Store Market Practices, is poorly organized.
2. Chapter 3 is a real "loser!" Something must be done with it.
3. Chapter 5 needs better transition between sections. As I remember, we tried to "pound this in" when we told our authors last fall, For goodness sake, work for readability!
4. Chapter 6: Some sections with possible problems are Economic Forecasts for Vermont, Projected Sales for 1990, and Sales Trends in Southwest Vermont; however, with some extra editing on our part, we may be able to overcome these problems.
5. You will find the following tables in the section marked "Statistics for Maine:" "Population by Area", "Population by County", and "Population by City". These were the ones you wanted Tyson to add.

I'll be available next week to discuss this further.

INSTRUCTIONS: After completing Pretest IV.10, submit your paper to your instructor. Your instructor will evaluate your pretest and will let you know if you need to proceed further with the Quotation Marks section of Phase IV.

QUOTATION MARKS

RULE: Place quotation marks at the beginning and at the end of a direct quotation.

EXAMPLES:

"Of course," the reporter said, "he has unbelievable maturity for his age."

The reporter continued saying, "That's something you can't teach."

RULE: Place quotation marks around the titles of short stories, short poems, songs, articles from periodicals, and subdivisions of books.

(**Note:** Quotation marks are occasionally used with the titles of books, periodicals, and newspapers; use underscoring or italics instead.)

EXAMPLE:

"These Summer Nights" was first published in *El Nahuatzen*.

RULE: Quotation marks are sometimes placed around words used in a special sense.

EXAMPLE:

> Never be late for or forget an interview, for such mistakes are the "kiss of death."

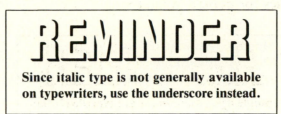

REMINDER

Since italic type is not generally available on typewriters, use the underscore instead.

The following rules show how to use quotation marks with other punctuation marks.

RULE: Always put the period or the comma inside closing quotation marks.

EXAMPLES:

> The saleswoman said, "I believe the sales of cross-country ski equipment will increase fivefold this year."

> "It's an excellent winter sport for bicyclists and backpackers who want to stay in shape," he said.

RULE: Always place the semicolon or colon outside closing quotation marks.

EXAMPLES:

> Eric spoke on "Building Speed in Typing"; Erin, on "Building Accuracy in Typing."

> You will find the following books in the section of the library marked "References": census of population, sales tax reports, and county directories.

RULE: Place a question mark or an exclamation point inside closing quotation marks only if the quoted material is a question or an exclamation.

EXAMPLES:

> We always ask, "Is it different?"

> They were screaming, "We found it!"

RULE: Place a question mark or an exclamation point outside closing quotation marks if the entire sentence is a question or an exclamation.

EXAMPLES:

> Did he say, "It is different"?

> It is a real "treasure"!

RULE: Use single quotation marks for quoted material within a quotation.

EXAMPLES:

> Mary replied, "What did he mean when he said, 'No news is good news'?"

> "I don't remember saying, 'I just finished reading Chapter 6.'"

> Bill commented, "Marquita read the article 'Watch Your Language' while on the airplane."

EXERCISE IV.43: QUOTATION MARKS

INSTRUCTIONS: Insert the seven sets of single and double quotation marks missing in the following letter. If time permits, type the letter in rough-draft form to reinforce your mastery of the rules for quotation marks.

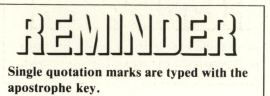

REMINDER

Single quotation marks are typed with the apostrophe key.

The letter goes to: Miss Julie Scott/4578 Kings Cove/Cincinnati, Ohio 45230

The letter is from: Tedi J. Ames/Manager

Dear Julie:

Congratulations on your new job! I first found out about it when I read People and Places, one of the regular columns in the *Press-Citizen*. You'll enjoy working for Louise Stroud. She's a real ''go-getter,'' and I'm sure she is an excellent word processing manager.

We had some good laughs during the Word Processing National Convention—especially when she said, I hear you're moving to my town. Not a chance, I said, but have you ever thought about moving to New York? You have to know Louise better to get the idea of that conversation.

Louise asked me if I'd read your article, How We Started Word Processing. She thinks it's a real zinger, and I agree.

One more thing. She told me that she's writing an article entitled What Is New in Word Processing; it's scheduled to be out next month. Are you helping with it?

Best of luck, Julie. See you one of these days.

Sincerely,

INSTRUCTIONS: Check your answers with the Key to Exercise IV.43 in Appendix C to see if you correctly inserted the missing seven sets of single or double quotation marks.

REVIEW POINT

INSTRUCTIONS:

Transcribe Achievement Survey Tape IV.12 (Quotation Marks) in mailable form. You will be inserting a total of six sets of double or single quotation marks. Then check your transcript with the Key to Achievement Survey Tape IV.12. Finally, complete a Mailability Analysis Chart and submit your transcript and the chart to your instructor.

If you misplaced any quotation marks, turn to the Practice Exercises in Appendix B for further drill on quotation marks before taking the posttest.

INSTRUCTIONS:

Under supervision, transcribe Posttest IV.10 in mailable form. Submit your transcript to your instructor.

STUDENT'S TALLY SHEET/PHASE V

Name _____

Target Completion Date _____

STUDENT'S ACTIVITY	DATE COMPLETED	STUDENT'S QUESTIONS AND COMMENTS
STUDY **Introduction to Phase V**		
STUDY **Welcome to Your New Job!**		
STUDY **Training for the Job**		

BEGINNING OF **Office Procedures and Training Manual**

FAMILIARIZE yourself with **Job Descriptions**		
STUDY **Organizational Chart of Graham Office Services** (Figure A)		
REVIEW **Personnel Policies**		
STUDY **Employee Performance Appraisal Form** (Figure B)		
COMPLETE **Staff Development Assignment**		
STUDY **Work Flow**		
STUDY **Completed Job Instruction Sheet** (Figure C)		
KNOW purpose for recording **Production Rate**		

STUDENT'S ACTIVITY	DATE COMPLETED	STUDENT'S QUESTIONS AND COMMENTS
KNOW meaning of **Turnaround Time**		
STUDY **Completed Daily Record Form** (Figure D)		
STUDY **Example of Line Count Procedure** (Figure E)		
REVIEW policy on **Confidential Work**		
STUDY **Procedures for Producing Correspondence**		
REVIEW **List of Our Customers**		
STUDY **Transcription Training**		

END OF Office Procedures and Training Manual

PROCEED with transcription training, using Trainee's Progress Report Forms		
READ about **The Office of Tomorrow**		

PERSONAL GOALS FOR PHASE V

1. _____

2. _____

INSTRUCTOR'S COMMENTS: _____

_____

_____

PHASE V

PHASE V

YOU'RE EMPLOYED!

INTRODUCTION

IN PHASES I THROUGH IV of this text-workbook, you learned about the importance of the transcription specialist in the communication process. You also saw how your growth in professionalism and decision-making skills can lead to increased cost efficiency, improved job effectiveness, and steady promotion. In addition, you reviewed your English and proofreading skills and brushed up on typewriting and formatting.

Let's assume you are now ready to step into a position in the business world where you will be able to use your skills and decision-making abilities. In Phase V, you are asked to exercise your imagination and picture yourself as a transcription specialist working in a real office setting. You'll proceed through a series of activities designed to simulate actual on-the-job operations that use the skills you have acquired.

The goals of these Phase V activities are to reinforce your competence, boost your confidence, and provide the practical experience necessary for your success as an employee.

After completing Phase V, you will

- Be familiar with typical office settings and procedures.

- Be capable of setting realistic production goals for mailability within a time framework.

- Be fully aware of your value as a professional transcription specialist in any business organization.

So, WELCOME TO THE WORLD OF BUSINESS!

WELCOME TO YOUR NEW JOB!

After completing your secretarial and machine transcription courses, you applied for a position as Transcription Specialist I with Graham Office Services in Oak River, Iowa, a city of 75,000 population. The advertisement you answered read as follows:

> WANTED: TRANSCRIPTIONIST. Must be well qualified and responsible. Typing 60 wpm; accuracy of utmost importance. Machine transcription experience required; shorthand not required but helpful. Good English skills essential. Need real professional, oriented to teamwork. Write Box 10, *Oak River Dispatch*. Salary open.

You did an impeccable job of preparing your application letter and résumé, and it paid off. A week after mailing them, you were called in for an interview with Gerry Graham, Manager and owner of Graham Office Services. Two days later Mrs. Graham notified you that you had the job. (She also mentioned that you were selected from among 13 applicants!)

The Office Setting

Graham Office Services was founded four years ago. It offers word processing services to local businesses, including those in a number of small outlying towns. Mrs. Graham, an experienced administrative secretary, decided to locate the firm in the heart of the city—at Center Plaza One, a seven-story building.

Graham's offices, located on the second floor of the building, are attractively decorated in "earth" tones. The walls are soft beige; the carpeting, rich brown; and the drapes, beige with splashes of brown and yellow. Several large plants in marbled orange and yellow urns enhance the open landscape setting.

All desks have a walnut finish and are modular in style. Dividers provide privacy for the employees. Other furniture and equipment blend in with the open landscape, both in space and color. A floor plan of the office is shown in Figure V.1.

You will find Graham Office Services a pleasant place in which to work. There is an atmosphere of congeniality: The surroundings are cheerful and the staff is friendly and cooperative; yet the office is operated in a professional, businesslike manner.

Opportunities for promotion and merit raises are good, provided employees demonstrate growth on the job and exemplify professionalism at all times. All employees receive thorough training in production procedures.

The services required by most of Graham's customers involve machine transcription skills. Occasionally, however, Graham will do straight copy work. Jobs are measured by line count, and a customer is charged by the number of lines in the completed document. Gerry Graham is proud of the job the staff is doing in producing error-free documents in record time.

A number of businesses in Center Plaza One and in its vicinity have their telephones wired to provide access to Graham's centralized dictation system, which uses cassette tapes. The customers who use desk-top or portable dictation units hand-carry or mail their completed dictation tapes to Graham.

The Employees

Your co-workers at Graham Office Services are:

> Gerry Graham, Manager
> Lisa Denton, Assistant Manager/Receptionist
> Willie Washington, Transcription Specialist II
> Ana Somoza, Transcription Specialist I
> Chris Mortley, Transcription Operator
> Kelly Olson, Transcription Operator
> Paul Julander, Clerk/Messenger
> Jackie Abikowski, Office Education Student Trainee

The Equipment

As a Transcription Specialist I, you will use the following equipment on your job:

- A typewriter. This may be a standard electric machine, a correcting typewriter, or a text-editing typewriter with or without a visual display screen.[1]
- A transcribing unit which uses cassette tapes.
- An electronic calculator.

---

[1]Equipment plays an important part in your work as a transcription specialist. However, the skills you have mastered in Phases I–IV are much more important than the kind of equipment you will use.

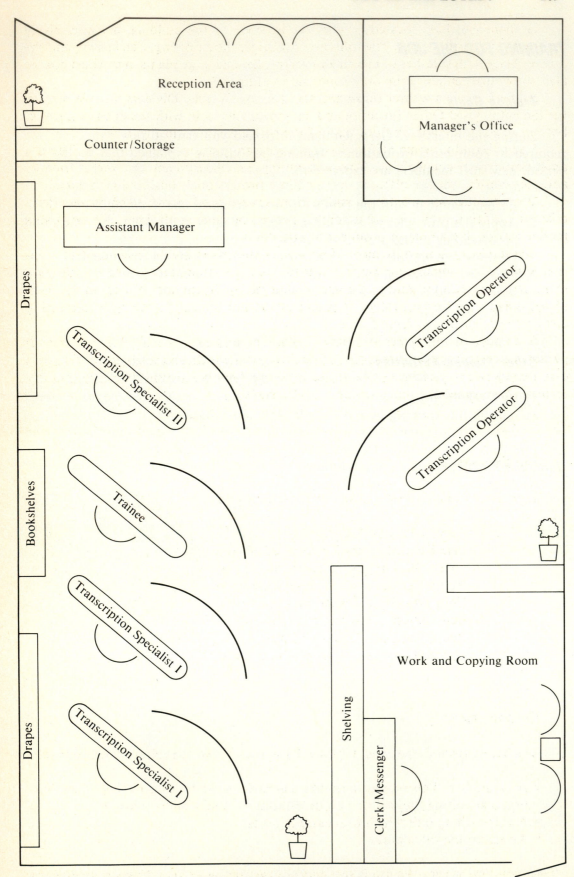

Figure V.1 FLOOR PLAN OF GRAHAM OFFICE SERVICES

TRAINING FOR THE JOB

Trainee Goals

During the interview, Gerry Graham informed you that all new employees are required to complete a probationary training period. She explained that during this period, new staff members are expected to:

1. Become familiar with the firm's *Office Procedures and Training Manual*.
2. Apply the principles of typewriting, English skills, formatting, listening, and proofreading in the process of turning out mailable documents.
3. Demonstrate competence in the operation of transcribing equipment.
4. Develop professional job attitudes, evidenced by a high level of skill in transcription and a desire to perform every assigned task efficiently.

Other Trainee Activities

Gerry Graham also explained that you would be expected to do some professional reading during this training period. In addition, she requested that you visit another office and try to interview at least one secretary there about transcription techniques and problems. Use the Staff Development Assignment provided in the *Office Procedures and Training Manual*, which follows, as the guide for completing this assignment.

GRAHAM OFFICE SERVICES ■ Center Plaza One/Oak River, Iowa 52410/(319) 555-1252

OFFICE PROCEDURES AND TRAINING MANUAL

Welcome to the staff of Graham Office Services! We hope you will enjoy working here. Your duties will be much easier if you first familiarize yourself with the contents of this manual. Keep the manual available for ready reference at all times.

CONTENTS

LIST OF FIGURES

JOB DESCRIPTIONS

MANAGER:

Exercises complete responsibility for all managerial aspects of the office, hires staff, selects equipment, develops office procedures, studies costs, recruits and communicates with customers, makes final decisions on staff evaluations and merit raises.

ASSISTANT MANAGER:

Logs in (records) incoming work and logs out completed work; determines work flow; trains new employees; does customer billing; supervises employees; keeps production records of employees; in emergency situations, does typing; receives callers; handles telephone calls; acts as substitute manager in Manager's absence.

TRANSCRIPTION SPECIALIST II:

Transcribes dictation, including confidential material; is familiar with specialized terminology; formats and revises complicated documents and statistical material; is fully responsible for document accuracy; works with minimum supervision; supervises student trainee.

TRANSCRIPTION SPECIALIST I:

Transcribes dictation, including occasional confidential material; is familiar with specialized terminology; formats and revises complicated documents and statistical material; is fully responsible for document accuracy.

TRANSCRIPTION OPERATOR:

Does routine transcription and types text from various types of source information.

CLERK/MESSENGER:

Operates copier; delivers completed work when necessary; performs miscellaneous clerical tasks; does occasional simple typing jobs.

OFFICE EDUCATION STUDENT TRAINEE:

Does routine typing and transcribing, and performs general clerical duties.

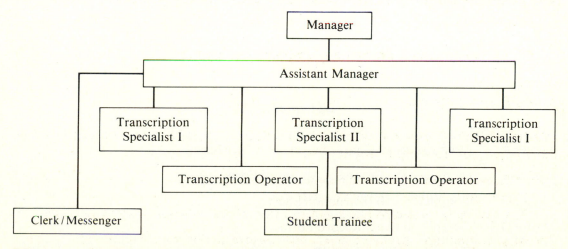

Figure A   ORGANIZATIONAL CHART OF GRAHAM OFFICE SERVICES

2

PERSONNEL POLICIES

Office Hours.   The office is open from 8 a.m. to 5 p.m. Employees may elect to work a flexible schedule. Employees are entitled to a 15-minute break each morning and each afternoon and to one hour for lunch. Lunch hours are staggered.

Absences.   Employees are expected to be punctual at all times. Call as soon as you know that you are too ill to report for work. In cases of absences other than for illness (doctor's appointments, funeral leave, etc.), notify your supervisor ahead of time. If possible, you will be given the opportunity to make up the lost time.

Vacation.   Employees are entitled to two weeks of vacation after one year of employment and to three weeks after five years of employment. In addition, employees are eligible for ten paid holidays a year: two personal holidays, New Year's Day, Memorial Day, Independence Day, Labor Day, Thanksgiving, the Friday following Thanksgiving, Christmas, and an additional day at Christmas time.

Appearance and Attitude.   Although Graham Office Services has no specific dress code, employees are expected to come to work suitably attired. Because we are a service business, good customer relations are vitally important; therefore, all employees are expected to treat our clients in a courteous manner at all times.

The Team Concept.   Our service center is a joint effort. Always remember that you are a member of a team and that a spirit of cooperation is a necessary ingredient of every team effort.

Evaluation.   Trainee job performance is evaluated periodically at the discretion of the supervisor. After the training period, employees are evaluated for merit raises on a yearly basis. (See Employee Performance Appraisal Form, Figure B.)

STAFF DEVELOPMENT ASSIGNMENT

A. *Professional Reading*

INSTRUCTIONS: From the list of periodicals recommended by your supervisor, select three articles for reading, as follows:

1. one article related to equipment.
2. one article related to human relations.
3. one article related to management of an office or word processing center.

Report your findings—orally or in writing—as directed by your supervisor.

3

B. *Site Visit*

INSTRUCTIONS: Visit either a word processing center or an office where secretaries do machine transcription as part of their job responsibilities. On another sheet of paper, copy and respond to the following items. Then submit your responses to your supervisor.

1. Describe the dictating and transcribing equipment used.
2. Describe the typewriters used.
3. Describe the type of production records maintained.
4. What job titles are used?
5. What education and experience are required for an entry-level transcriptionist's position?
6. Describe the technical skills and personal qualities needed by an applicant.
7. What is the nature of the training program for new employees?
8. What equipment changes are being planned?

WORK FLOW

All work to be completed by Graham Office Services is accompanied by a Job Instruction Sheet (JIS), which is reviewed by the Assistant Manager. (See Figure C for a sample of a completed Job Instruction Sheet for a former customer.) The Assistant Manager then logs in the job and assigns it to the transcriptionist. The transcriptionist completes the work, proofreads it, and makes corrections before returning it to the Assistant Manager for approval and logging out.

Occasionally, a transcriptionist may work directly with the originator on an assignment—especially if the originator works in close proximity to Center Plaza One. Employees are also available to go to an originator's office to take shorthand dictation.

PRODUCTION RATE

Each transcriptionist is required to submit a Daily Record Form, showing the number of lines of copy produced. In evaluating an employee's performance, the Assistant Manager will note the general production trend of the transcriptionist, rather than the daily or weekly line count.

Transcriptionists who are concerned about their production rates are encouraged to confer with the Assistant Manager. The Assistant Manager, in turn, may ask the employee to keep a record of the kinds of errors made on work returned—for example,

GRAHAM OFFICE SERVICES ■ Center Plaza One/Oak River, Iowa 52410/(319) 555-1252

EMPLOYEE PERFORMANCE APPRAISAL FORM

Name of Transcriptionist _____ Date _____

PERSONAL QUALITIES	Needs Improvement	Acceptable	Good	Exceptional
Professional Attitude (Cooperation/Teamwork) Comments:	1 2 3	4 5 6	7 8 9	10 11 12
Ability to Follow Directions Comments:	1 2 3	4 5 6	7 8 9	10 11 12
Initiative/Use of Time Comments:	1 2 3	4 5 6	7 8 9	10 11 12
Quality of Work (Accuracy/Neatness) Comments:	1 2 3	4 5 6	7 8 9	10 11 12
Use of Work Area/Equipment Comments:	1 2 3	4 5 6	7 8 9	10 11 12
Punctuality and Attendance Comments:	1 2 3	4 5 6	7 8 9	10 11 12

PERSONAL SKILLS				
Typing/Keyboarding Comments:	1 2 3	4 5 6	7 8 9	10 11 12
Ability to Apply English Skills Comments:	1 2 3	4 5 6	7 8 9	10 11 12
Proofreading Comments:	1 2 3	4 5 6	7 8 9	10 11 12
Spelling Comments:	1 2 3	4 5 6	7 8 9	10 11 12
Ability to Correct Typed Material Comments:	1 2 3	4 5 6	7 8 9	10 11 12
Ability to Communicate Verbally Comments:	1 2 3	4 5 6	7 8 9	10 11 12

Supervisor _____

Figure B EMPLOYEE PERFORMANCE APPRAISAL FORM

5

GRAHAM OFFICE SERVICES ■ Center Plaza One/Oak River, Iowa 52410/(319) 555-1252

JOB INSTRUCTION SHEET

Firm Name _Sample_ _____ Telephone Number _____

INSTRUCTIONS: Fill in all information requested. Be specific in indicating special instructions (examples: _rush, confidential, rough draft_). Also, include any instructions that were omitted in the dictation process.

TYPE OF DOCUMENT	FORM IN WHICH SUBMITTED	SPECIAL INSTRUCTIONS	EVALUATION (for office use only)
1 Letter	tape	full block	M C R
2 Letter	tape	full block	M C R
3 Report with a Table	tape	4 carbons, please!	M C R
4 Invoice	tape	Use special form with NCR paper.	M C R
5 Outline	handwritten rough draft	2 carbon copies	M C R
6 Table	handwritten rough draft	Type lengthwise on page.	M C R
7 Financial Statement	typed rough copy		M C R
8			M C R
9			M C R
10			M C R
11			M C R

TIME RECORD: (to be completed by transcriptionist)
Name: _(your name)_
Date Started: _7/5/—_
Date Completed: _7/5/—_
Total No. of Minutes: _105_

TAPE NO. _O_ SIDE NO. _O_

MAILABILITY RECORD: (to be completed by supervisor)
No. of items approved as MAILABLE (M): _____
No. of items returned for CORRECTION (C): ___
No. of items returned for RETYPING (R): _____

Job approved by: _____ Date: _____
(initials)

Figure C COMPLETED JOB INSTRUCTION SHEET

spelling, punctuation, or typographical errors. If it seems advisable, the transcriptionist may then be placed on probation.

See Figure D for a sample of a completed Daily Record Form. (Use a line count guide to assist you in determining the number of lines you produce. See Figure E, which illustrates how lines are counted.)

TURNAROUND TIME

Turnaround time is computed as the number of minutes or hours it takes to process a job from the time it arrives at the office until it is delivered to the customer. Turnaround time will generally be four hours for the average-length job at Graham Office Services. However, work that arrives at the office after 3 p.m. will not be delivered until the following business day.

CONFIDENTIAL WORK

Only two staff members are designated to type or transcribe confidential work—the Assistant Manager and the Transcription Specialist II (occasionally a Transcription Specialist I). Those persons are cautioned NOT TO DIVULGE ANY INFORMATION about the documents they produce. Unauthorized divulging of information in violation of this policy may lead to the dismissal of the employee guilty of the infraction.

PROCEDURES FOR PRODUCING CORRESPONDENCE

Follow the guidelines below unless you receive special instructions from the customer or your supervisor.

1. Margins   Use a 70-space line for elite; use a 60-space line for pica.

2. File copy   Make one file copy of every document, unless otherwise instructed.

3. Corrections on copies   All errors on copies are to be corrected.

4. Letter style   Use full-block with mixed punctuation.

5. Position of date on letter	Type the date a double space below the last line of letterhead, or at least two inches from top of the page.
6. Spacing after date	The number of blank lines between the date and inside address should be adjusted according to the length of the letter.
7. Mailing notations	Type in all caps and center vertically below the date and above the inside address.
8. Name of states in inside address and on envelopes	Use two-letter abbreviations.
9. Style of attention line	Type *ATTENTION:*
10. Style of subject line	Type *SUBJECT:*
11. Typing the word *versus* in legal documents	Abbreviate *v.*
12. Salutation	Type either the name of the individual, or *Ladies and Gentlemen*, or use simplified style. Use *Ms.* only where a woman's marital status is not known.
13. Complimentary closing	Use *Sincerely.*
14. Executive's title	Type below the name.
15. Company name after closing	Do not use; type only the dictator's name and title.
16. Reference initials	Use only lower case letters for the typist's initials.
17. Enclosure notation	Type *Enclosure:* or *Enclosures:* and list the enclosure or enclosures.
18. Carbon or photocopy notation	Type *c:* and list names of the recipients.
19. Postscript notation	Type *PS:*
20. Blind carbon copy notation	Type *bc:* in the upper left corner of the copies only.
21. Signatures	All of an executive's documents must be signed by the executive.
22. Envelopes	Type address in all caps, using modern style.

8

GRAHAM OFFICE SERVICES ■ 101 Center Plaza One/Oak River, Iowa 52410/(319) 555-1252

DAILY RECORD FORM

Tape No. _O_ Side No. _O_ Firm Name (_Sample – corresponds with sample JIS._) Name of Transcriptionist (_your name_)

Date	Beginning Time	Description of Item L=letter M=memo R=report/manuscript F=form I=invoice S=financial statement O=other (specify)	LINE COUNTS* Letters† Memos Reports (Multiply lines by 2)	Forms Other Materials (Multiply lines by 3)	Tables Invoices Financial Statements (Multiply lines by 4)	Carbon Copies (Multiply copies by 5)	Envelopes Labels (Multiply items by 5)	Total Lines	Ending Time	Total Production Time per Item, in Minutes
7/5	9 a.m.	L (see figure)	23×2=46	—	—	2×5=10	1×5=5	61	9:15	15 min.
	9:15	L	20×2=40	—	—	8×5=10 (include file copy)	2×5=10	60	9:30	15 min.
	9:30	R with T	60×2=120	—	5×4=20	4×5=20	—	160	10:05	35 min.
	10:25	I	—	—	6×4=24	2×5=10	1×5=5	39	10:35	10 min.
	10:35	O-outline	—	12×3=36	—	2×5=10	—	46	10:45	10 min.
	10:45	T	—	—	17×4=68	1×5=5	—	73	11:05	20 min.
	11:05	S	—	—	59×4=236	1×5=5	—	241	12noon	55 min.

TOTALS FOR TAPE: LINES **680** MINUTES **160**

*1/4 line or more counts as 1 line.
†Opening lines count for a total of three lines and closing lines count for a total of three lines.

Figure D COMPLETED DAILY RECORD FORM

9

TIEJENS TRAVEL SERVICE

105 Center Plaza Two
Oak River, Iowa 52410
(319) 555-3777

Date

Acme Airlines
612 Avenue of the Americas
New York, NY 10020

Ladies and Gentlemen:

SUBJECT: Luxembourg Thru-Fare

We were most pleased to discover that you are now offering a new
group Thru-Fare for $478 out of Chicago to Luxembourg. As part
of a university community, we expect a great demand for this low-
priced, easily booked fare. In anticipation of this demand, we
would like to reserve blocks of space on your flights from Chicago
to Luxembourg to coincide with the spring break and the closing of
the spring semester at Oak River University.

Specifically, we would like the following:

1. A block of 25 group-10 seats for the March 22 flight out of
    Chicago.

2. A block of 25 group-10 seats for your flight out of Chicago
    on May 21. If the flight does not operate on May 21, we
    would like reservations for May 22.

3. A block of 15 group-10 seats for a May 25 flight. If these
    are not available on the 25th, would you please make reser-
    vations for the 24th.

Our clients are anxious to get information about reservations;
therefore, we would appreciate hearing from you within the next
week.

Sincerely,

Maura R. Tiejens
Manager

xx

Figure E   EXAMPLE OF LINE COUNT PROCEDURE

10

OUR CUSTOMERS

The names of the firms for which you will be working, along with the names of their dictators, are listed below. You will want to refer to this listing often to make sure that names and titles are spelled correctly.

Check the *Special Instructions* column before you begin an assignment.

LIST OF CUSTOMERS

FIRM	NAME	JOB POSITION TITLE	SPECIAL INSTRUCTIONS
ENTERTAINMENT All-Star Spotlight P.O. Box 206B What Cheer, Iowa 50268	Alvin J. Levrington	Agency Manager	Make two file copies of all correspondence.
ACCOUNTING Barr and Beach Certified Public Accountants 605 Center Plaza One Oak River, Iowa 52410	Shirley Williams Beach, CPA Marvin E. Barr, CPA	Manager Senior Accountant	Use simplified letter style.
OFFICE SUPPLIES & EQUIPMENT Bates Office Supply, Inc. 124 East Washington Street Oak River, Iowa 52410	Louise M. Lubaroff Kenneth Kjarsgaard	Manager Assistant Manager	None
REAL ESTATE City Realtors and Property Management 500 Center Plaza One Oak River, Iowa 52410	Judith R. Boyd, CPM Theresa Espinoza Anthony M. Rocca	Director, Property Management Sales Agent Sales Agent	Use open punctuation. Sign and mail all correspondence.
EDUCATIONAL ASSOCIATION Educational Secretaries of America 400 Center Plaza One Oak River, Iowa 52410	Edward Howell Angela Williston	Executive Director Local Arrangements Chairperson	Use open punctuation.

FIRM	NAME	JOB POSITION TITLE	SPECIAL INSTRUCTIONS

MEDICINE
Family Practice Associates
102 Center Plaza One
Oak River, Iowa 52410
	Rebecca E.
	  Greenwald, M.D.
	J. Richard
	  Rosenberger, M.D.
	Silas C. Shelton,
	  M.D.
			None

BANKING Fourth National Bank Hills, Iowa 52235	Starkey N. Culp Martha Hoffman	President Vice President	Use simplified letter style.
OFFICE SERVICES Graham Office Services 101 Center Plaza One Oak River, Iowa 52410	Gerry Graham	Manager	None
NONPROFIT ORGANIZATION Green Life Foundation 709 Center Plaza One Oak River, Iowa 52410	Reginald R. Fitzgerald Daniel L. Kickingbird	Executive Director Associate Director and Treasurer	Use modified block letter style.
INSURANCE Hartman Insurance Agency 505 Center Plaza One Oak River, Iowa 52410	Norman Hartman Norma Hartman- Hartvigsen Harold M. Hartvigsen	Manager District Agent District Agent	Use modified block letter style.

MANUFACTURING
Heinrich Electric Company
Heinrich Causeway and
  I-380
Swisher, Iowa 52338
	Udo Ivan Heinrich,
	  Sr.
	Udo Ivan Heinrich,
	  Jr.
	Udo Ivan Heinrich,
	  III
		President
		
		Vice President
		
		Chairman of
		Security
			Style will vary with the dictator.

EMPLOYMENT M and N Employment Service 100 Center Plaza Two Oak River, Iowa 52410	Lynn W. Mansfield Pat R. Turnipseed	President Vice President	Use simplified letter style. Use *Patrick* in the typed signature.

PRINTING AND PUBLISHING
MacQueen Printing and
  Publishing Service
205 Center Plaza Two
Oak River, Iowa 52410
	Finley D. Marshal
	Maurita Scott
		Manager
		Production
		  Manager
			Style will vary with the dictator.

FIRM	NAME	JOB POSITION TITLE	SPECIAL INSTRUCTIONS
LAW			
Marner, Thirtyacre and Troyer Law Offices 606 B Avenue Kalona, Iowa 52247	Jonas V. Marner Dewey M. Thirtyacre Trudy E. Troyer	Senior Partner Senior Partner Junior Partner	None
INTERNATIONAL CORPORATION			
Multinational Food Exports, Inc. 15677 South Village Roadway Cedar Rapids, Iowa 52406	Arturo Lopez	President	Sign and mail all correspondence.
HOTEL			
The Plaza Inn Center Plaza Two Oak River, Iowa 52410	Franklyn Doodlesack Su Kim	General Manager Sales and Catering Manager	Use simplified letter style.
GOVERNMENT			
Rutherford, (The Honorable) M. Bradley 310 Center Plaza One Oak River, Iowa 52410	M. Bradley Rutherford Phoebe Harris	Senator Legislative Aide	Use simplified letter style.
TRAVEL			
Tiejens Travel Service 105 Center Plaza Two Oak River, Iowa 52410	Maura R. Tiejens Brent W. Schaapveld Tim O'Brien	Manager Assistant Manager Manager, Customer Relations	Use *Timothy* in the typed signature.

TRANSCRIPTION TRAINING

During your training period, you will be transcribing from cassette tapes and, in a few instances, doing some typing from handwritten or rough-draft copy. The handwritten and rough-draft materials, as well as certain papers accompanying the dictation, are referred to as *working papers*. The working papers, as well as the stationery you will need for transcription from these tapes, will be found in the *Packet of Trainee Materials*.

Job Instruction Sheets will accompany the dictation from each business firm. You will want to review each one thoroughly before starting to work.

Tape 1, Side 1	Nonprofit Organization
Side 2	Insurance
Tape 2, Side 1	Banking
Side 2	Accounting
Tape 3, Side 1	Educational Association
Side 2	Real Estate
Tape 4, Side 1	Manufacturing
Side 2	Printing and Publishing
Test Tape, Side 1	MIDWAY APPRAISAL, Part A
Side 2	MIDWAY APPRAISAL, Part B
Tape 5, Side 1	Medicine
Side 2	Law
Tape 6, Side 1	Hotel
Side 2	Office Supplies and Equipment
Tape 7, Side 1	Office Services
Side 2	Entertainment
Tape 8, Side 1	Travel
Side 2	Employment
Tape 9, Side 1	Government
Side 2	International
Test Tape, Side 1	FINAL EVALUATION, Part A
Side 2	FINAL EVALUATION, Part B

You are now ready to begin transcribing. Follow the detailed instructions provided on each of the Trainee's Progress Report Forms.

END OF OFFICE MANUAL

TRAINEE'S PROGRESS REPORT FORM / TAPE 1, SIDE 1
(NONPROFIT ORGANIZATION)

Name_____

Target Completion Date _____

DISTINCTIVE FEATURES: This is your orientation to transcription. You will be transcribing from "perfect" dictation. Dictators will indicate all punctuation and will spell difficult words; they will also give you assistance on special instructions. No logging is required on the Daily Record Form.

TRAINEE'S ACTIVITY	COMPLETED	TRAINEE'S QUESTIONS AND COMMENTS
REVIEW Job Instruction Sheet		
ASSEMBLE all materials and reference books		
INSERT Tape 1, Side 1 into transcribing machine		
MAKE machine adjustments		
LISTEN to instructions		
TRANSCRIBE all documents according to instructions		
PROOFREAD and MAKE corrections on typewriter		
CHECK Mailability Analysis Chart		
COMPLETE Job Instruction Sheet		
SUBMIT all Tape 1, Side 1 papers in a folder to supervisor		

GRAHAM OFFICE SERVICES ■ Center Plaza One/Oak River, Iowa 52410/(319) 555-1252

JOB INSTRUCTION SHEET

Firm Name *Green Life Foundation* Telephone Number (319) 555-1980

INSTRUCTIONS: Fill in all information requested. Be specific in indicating special instructions (examples: *rush, confidential, rough draft*). Also, include any instructions that were omitted in the dictation process.

TYPE OF DOCUMENT	FORM IN WHICH SUBMITTED	SPECIAL INSTRUCTIONS	EVALUATION (for office use only)
1 average letter to Dr. J. Richard Rosenberger	dictated on tape		M C R
2 short letter to Grace Stone	dictated on tape	Certificate will be enclosed by our office.	M C R
3 average length letter to Jane Matthews	dictated on tape	Agreement and General Provisions will be enclosed by our office.	M C R
4 average length letter to Lowell Miller	dictated on tape		M C R
5 average length letter to Douglas Jorgensen	dictated on tape		M C R
6 short memo to Center Plaza One Tenants	dictated on tape	IT'S TRIPLETS!	M C R
7			M C R
8			M C R
9			M C R
10			M C R
11			M C R

TIME RECORD: (to be completed by transcriptionist)

Name: _____

Date Started: _____

Date Completed: _____

Total No. of Minutes: _____

TAPE NO. *1* SIDE NO. *1*

MAILABILITY RECORD: (to be completed by supervisor)

No. of items approved as MAILABLE (M): _____

No. of items returned for CORRECTION (C): ___

No. of items returned for RETYPING (R): _____

Job approved by: _____ Date: _____
(initials)

TRAINEE'S PROGRESS REPORT FORM / TAPE 1, SIDE 2
(INSURANCE)

Name_____

Target Completion Date _____

DISTINCTIVE FEATURES: As you continue your orientation to transcription, you will still be transcribing from "perfect" dictation. No logging is required on the Daily Record Form.

TRAINEE'S ACTIVITY	COMPLETED	TRAINEE'S QUESTIONS AND COMMENTS
REVIEW Job Instruction Sheet		
ASSEMBLE all materials and reference books		
INSERT Tape 1, Side 2 into transcribing machine		
MAKE machine adjustments		
LISTEN to instructions		
TRANSCRIBE all documents according to instructions		
PROOFREAD and MAKE corrections on typewriter		
CHECK Mailability Analysis Chart		
COMPLETE Job Instruction Sheet		
SUBMIT all Tape 1, Side 2 papers in a folder to supervisor		

GRAHAM OFFICE SERVICES ■ Center Plaza One/Oak River, Iowa 52410/(319) 555-1252

JOB INSTRUCTION SHEET

Firm Name *Hartman Insurance Agency* Telephone Number (319) 555-3865

INSTRUCTIONS: Fill in all information requested. Be specific in indicating special instructions (examples: *rush, confidential, rough draft*). Also, include any instructions that were omitted in the dictation process.

TYPE OF DOCUMENT	FORM IN WHICH SUBMITTED	SPECIAL INSTRUCTIONS	EVALUATION (for office use only)
1 average length letter to Bruce Wright	dictated on tape	Estate Planning brochures will be enclosed by our office.	M C R
2 average length letter to Margaret O'Connor	dictated on tape	Brochures will be enclosed by our office. Prepare copy for Ronald Smith.	M C R
3 average length memo to Russell Schaeffer	dictated on tape		M C R
4 short letter to Timothy Gallagher	dictated on tape	Subject is Claim No. 299 114	M C R
5 short memo to Mary Alice Chinetti	dictated on tape	The enclosure is dictated next.	M C R
6 biographical sketch of Leonard N. Henry	dictated on tape	Center heading lines, double space between heading lines, double space body.	M C R
7 average length letter to Mike & Gayle Weinstein	dictated on tape		M C R
8 average length letter to Lydia Bowers	dictated on tape	Excess Umbrella Liability Policy and Invoice will be enclosed by our office.	M C R
9			M C R
10			M C R
11			M C R

TIME RECORD: (to be completed by transcriptionist)	MAILABILITY RECORD: (to be completed by supervisor)
Name: _____ Date Started: _____ Date Completed: _____ Total No. of Minutes: _____	No. of items approved as MAILABLE (M): _____ No. of items returned for CORRECTION (C): __ No. of items returned for RETYPING (R): _____
TAPE NO. *1* SIDE NO. *2*	Job approved by: _____ Date: _____ (initials)

TRAINEE'S PROGRESS REPORT FORM / TAPE 2, SIDE 1
(BANKING)

Name_____

Target Completion Date _____

DISTINCTIVE FEATURES: This dictation is similar to that given on the job. Dictators will occasionally indicate spelling and punctuation; in most cases, they will explain special instructions. However, you will need to rely on yourself for some decisions. No logging is required on the Daily Record Form.

TRAINEE'S ACTIVITY	COMPLETED	TRAINEE'S QUESTIONS AND COMMENTS
REVIEW Job Instruction Sheet		
ASSEMBLE all materials and reference books		
INSERT Tape 2, Side 1 into transcribing machine		
MAKE machine adjustments		
LISTEN to instructions		
TRANSCRIBE all documents according to instructions		
PROOFREAD and MAKE corrections on typewriter		
CHECK Mailability Analysis Chart		
COMPLETE Job Instruction Sheet, being sure to record ending date		
SUBMIT all Tape 2, Side 1 papers in a folder to supervisor		

GRAHAM OFFICE SERVICES ■ Center Plaza One/Oak River, Iowa 52410/(319) 555-1252

JOB INSTRUCTION SHEET

Firm Name *Fourth National Bank* Telephone Number *(319) 555-4694*

INSTRUCTIONS: Fill in all information requested. Be specific in indicating special instructions (examples: *rush, confidential, rough draft*). Also, include any instructions that were omitted in the dictation process.

TYPE OF DOCUMENT	FORM IN WHICH SUBMITTED	SPECIAL INSTRUCTIONS	EVALUATION (for office use only)
1 *very short letter to Cynthia Oliver*	*on tape*		M C R
2 *same letter to Evan Pierce*	*directions on tape*	*Variables: Account No. 8392 12, August 21, and $439.49*	M C R
3 *medium letter to Mark Fritz*	*on tape*	*Subject is Checking Account No. 6782 57.*	M C R
4 *medium letter to Wayne Murphy*	*on tape*	*Public Law 91-508 is mentioned in paragraph 2.*	M C R
5 *medium letter to Clement R. Meadows*	*on tape*		M C R
6 *medium letter to Lee Chee*	*on tape*	*Credit Card Statement will be enclosed by us.*	M C R
7 *letter to be printed*	*on tape and draft*	*See working paper for edited draft.*	M C R
8 *brochure copy*	*on tape*	*Type in rough-draft form.*	M C R
9 *short letter to Jerry Graham*	*on tape*	*Magazine article will be enclosed by us.*	M C R
10			M C R
11			M C R

TIME RECORD: (to be completed by transcriptionist)

Name: _____

Date Started: _____

Date Completed: _____

Total No. of Minutes: _____ _____

TAPE NO. *2* SIDE NO. *1*

MAILABILITY RECORD: (to be completed by supervisor)

No. of items approved as MAILABLE (M): _____

No. of items returned for CORRECTION (C): __

No. of items returned for RETYPING (R): _____

Job approved by: _____ Date: _____
(initials)

TRAINEE'S PROGRESS REPORT FORM / TAPE 2, SIDE 2
(ACCOUNTING)

Name_____

Target Completion Date _____

DISTINCTIVE FEATURES: Same features as Tape 2, Side 1.

TRAINEE'S ACTIVITY	COMPLETED	TRAINEE'S QUESTIONS AND COMMENTS
REVIEW Job Instruction Sheet		
RECORD beginning date on Job Instruction Sheet		
ASSEMBLE all materials and reference books		
INSERT Tape 2, Side 2 into transcribing machine		
MAKE machine adjustments		
LISTEN to instructions		
TRANSCRIBE all documents according to instructions		
PROOFREAD and MAKE corrections on typewriter		
CHECK Mailability Analysis Chart		
COMPLETE Job Instruction Sheet, being sure to record ending date		
SUBMIT all Tape 2, Side 2 papers in a folder to supervisor		

GRAHAM OFFICE SERVICES ■ Center Plaza One/Oak River, Iowa 52410/(319) 555-1252

JOB INSTRUCTION SHEET

Firm Name *Barr and Beach Certified Public Accountants* Telephone Number (319) 555-2098

INSTRUCTIONS: Fill in all information requested. Be specific in indicating special instructions (examples: *rush, confidential, rough draft*). Also, include any instructions that were omitted in the dictation process.

TYPE OF DOCUMENT	FORM IN WHICH SUBMITTED	SPECIAL INSTRUCTIONS	EVALUATION (for office use only)
1 short letter to Patricia Zimmerman	on tape		M C R
2 same letter to Eduardo Olvera	directions on tape	Variables: participation loan to Raymond Lee Rose for $40,789	M C R
3 short letter to American Express Co.	on tape	Listing will be enclosed by us.	M C R
4 short letter to Citicorp Service, Inc.	on tape	Listing will be enclosed by us.	M C R
5 medium letter to Theodore & Angela Steward	on tape		M C R
6 note to financial statement	on tape	Type in rough-draft form. Use 70-space line.	M C R
7 balance sheet	on tape and draft	See working paper for edited draft.	M C R
8 medium letter to Kevin Kent	on tape	Postage-paid reply card will be enclosed by us.	M C R
9			M C R
10			M C R
11			M C R

TIME RECORD: (to be completed by transcriptionist)

Name: _____

Date Started: _____

Date Completed: _____

Total No. of Minutes: _____

TAPE NO. 2 SIDE NO. 2

MAILABILITY RECORD: (to be completed by supervisor)

No. of items approved as MAILABLE (M): _____

No. of items returned for CORRECTION (C): _____

No. of items returned for RETYPING (R): _____

Job approved by: _____ Date: _____
(initials)

TRAINEE'S PROGRESS REPORT FORM / TAPE 3, SIDE 1
(EDUCATIONAL ASSOCIATION)

Name_____

Target Completion Date _____

DISTINCTIVE FEATURES: Same features as Tape 2, Side 1. You should type envelopes for this tape.

TRAINEE'S ACTIVITY	COMPLETED	TRAINEE'S QUESTIONS AND COMMENTS
REVIEW Job Instruction Sheet		
RECORD beginning date on Job Instruction Sheet		
ASSEMBLE all materials and reference books		
INSERT Tape 3, Side 1 into transcribing machine		
MAKE machine adjustments		
LISTEN to instructions		
TRANSCRIBE all documents and type envelopes according to instructions		
PROOFREAD and MAKE corrections on typewriter		
CHECK Mailability Analysis Chart		
COMPLETE Job Instruction Sheet, being sure to record ending date		
SUBMIT all Tape 3, Side 1 papers in a folder to supervisor		

GRAHAM OFFICE SERVICES ■ Center Plaza One/Oak River, Iowa 52410/(319) 555-1252

JOB INSTRUCTION SHEET

Firm Name *Educational Secretaries of America*   Telephone Number *(319) 555-7191*

INSTRUCTIONS: Fill in all information requested. Be specific in indicating special instructions (examples: *rush, confidential, rough draft*). Also, include any instructions that were omitted in the dictation process.

TYPE OF DOCUMENT	FORM IN WHICH SUBMITTED	SPECIAL INSTRUCTIONS	EVALUATION (for office use only)
1 Letter to Carol McLaren — average length	dictation on tape	Transcribe in final form. We will enclose the brochure.	M C R
2 Financial report for convention	handwritten copy	Type in final form. See working paper for handwritten copy.	M C R
3 Short memo to Office Staff	dictation on tape	Type in final form.	M C R
4 Executive Director's Report	dictation on tape	Transcribe in rough-draft form.	M C R
5 Letter to Diane K. Moore — average length	dictation on tape	Type in final form. We will enclose the invitation.	M C R
6 List of Advisory Committee	rough draft	Type in final form. See working paper for rough-draft copy.	M C R
7 Letter to Pearl A. Victor — average length	dictation on tape	Type in final form. We will enclose the membership form and envelope.	M C R
8 Short memo to Presidents of Chapters	dictation on tape	Type in final form.	M C R
9 Letter to Nobel and Booker, Inc.	dictation on tape	Type this letter and the next two letters in final form.	M C R
10 Same letter to Bowen Systems, Inc.	directions on tape	Address is 245 Fremont Building; 341 Market Street; San Francisco, CA 94105.	M C R
11 Same letter to American Offices, Inc.	directions on tape	Address is 2462 Arapahoe; Denver, CO 80202.	M C R

TIME RECORD: (to be completed by transcriptionist)

Name: _____

Date Started: _____

Date Completed: _____

Total No. of Minutes: _____

TAPE NO. **3** SIDE NO. **L**

MAILABILITY RECORD: (to be completed by supervisor)

No. of items approved as MAILABLE (M): _____

No. of items returned for CORRECTION (C): ___

No. of items returned for RETYPING (R): _____

Job approved by: _____ Date: _____
                 (initials)

TRAINEE'S PROGRESS REPORT FORM/TAPE 3, SIDE 2
(REAL ESTATE)

Name_____

Target Completion Date _____

DISTINCTIVE FEATURES: Same features as Tape 3, Side 1.

TRAINEE'S ACTIVITY	COMPLETED	TRAINEE'S QUESTIONS AND COMMENTS
REVIEW Job Instruction Sheet		
RECORD beginning date on Job Instruction Sheet		
ASSEMBLE all materials and reference books		
INSERT Tape 3, Side 2 into transcribing machine		
MAKE machine adjustments		
LISTEN to instructions		
TRANSCRIBE all documents and type envelopes according to instructions		
PROOFREAD and MAKE corrections on typewriter		
CHECK Mailability Analysis Chart		
COMPLETE Job Instruction Sheet, being sure to record ending date		
SUBMIT all Tape 3, Side 2 papers in a folder to supervisor		

GRAHAM OFFICE SERVICES ■ **Center Plaza One/Oak River, Iowa 52410/(319) 555-1252**

JOB INSTRUCTION SHEET

Firm Name *City Realtors and Property Management*   Telephone Number *(319) 555-3090*

INSTRUCTIONS: Fill in all information requested. Be specific in indicating special instructions (examples: *rush, confidential, rough draft*). Also, include any instructions that were omitted in the dictation process.

TYPE OF DOCUMENT	FORM IN WHICH SUBMITTED	SPECIAL INSTRUCTIONS	EVALUATION (for office use only)
1 *Letter to the Al Moores—two pages*	*dictation on tape*	*Transcribe in final form.*	M C R
2 *Memo to Oak River Press—very short*	*dictation on tape*	*Transcribe in final form. Enclosure is dictated next.*	M C R
3 *News item enclosure*	*dictation on tape*	*Double space this item.*	M C R
4 *Letter to Melinda R. Davis—short*	*dictation on tape*	*Type in final form. See working papers for the table to be enclosed.*	M C R
5 *One-page manuscript on Willow Bluff*	*dictation on tape*	*Transcribe in rough-draft form.*	M C R
6 *List of Board of Realtors—short item*	*handwritten copy*	*Instructions are on the tape. See working paper for handwritten copy.*	M C R
7 *Letter to Gene and Marcia Schaaf—average length*	*dictation on tape*	*Type in final form.*	M C R
8			M C R
9			M C R
10			M C R
11			M C R

TIME RECORD: (to be completed by transcriptionist)

Name: _____

Date Started: _____

Date Completed: _____

Total No. of Minutes: _____

TAPE NO. *3* SIDE NO. *2*

MAILABILITY RECORD: (to be completed by supervisor)

No. of items approved as MAILABLE (M): _____

No. of items returned for CORRECTION (C): ___

No. of items returned for RETYPING (R): _____

Job approved by: _____ Date: _____
                    (initials)

TRAINEE'S PROGRESS REPORT FORM/TAPE 4, SIDE 1
(MANUFACTURING)

Name_____

Target Completion Date _____

DISTINCTIVE FEATURES: Same features as Tape 2, Side 1. You should type envelopes for this tape.

TRAINEE'S ACTIVITY	COMPLETED	TRAINEE'S QUESTIONS AND COMMENTS
REVIEW Job Instruction Sheet		
RECORD beginning date on Job Instruction Sheet		
ASSEMBLE all materials and reference books		
INSERT Tape 4, Side 1 into transcribing machine		
MAKE machine adjustments		
LISTEN to instructions		
TRANSCRIBE all documents and type envelopes according to instructions		
PROOFREAD and MAKE corrections on typewriter		
CHECK Mailability Analysis Chart		
COMPLETE Job Instruction Sheet, being sure to record ending date		
SUBMIT all Tape 4, Side 1 papers in a folder to supervisor		

GRAHAM OFFICE SERVICES ▪ Center Plaza One/Oak River, Iowa 52410/(319) 555-1252

JOB INSTRUCTION SHEET

Firm Name *Heinrich Electric Company* Telephone Number *(319) 555-4387*

INSTRUCTIONS: Fill in all information requested. Be specific in indicating special instructions (examples: *rush, confidential, rough draft*). Also, include any instructions that were omitted in the dictation process.

TYPE OF DOCUMENT	FORM IN WHICH SUBMITTED	SPECIAL INSTRUCTIONS *ALL MAILABLE!*	EVALUATION (for office use only)
1 Letter to Ronald Lyle Stilliman	tape	Prepare a carbon copy for Alice Wheat-Moore.	M C R
2 Notice of Annual Meeting of Shareholders	tape	Type "NOTICE IS HEREBY GIVEN" in all caps!	M C R
3 Holiday Greeting	tape	Type message in all caps.	M C R
4 Letter with table to Adam Matthew Hartwell	tape and handwritten	See working paper for handwritten table.	M C R
5 Marketing, Service, & Engineering Personnel Memo	tape		M C R
6 Warranty	tape	Double space.	M C R
7 Agenda	handwritten	Please double space! See working paper for handwritten copy.	M C R
8 Memo to All Staff	tape	Underscore "DO NOT KEEP THE KEYS."	M C R
9 Line Graph	handwritten	Use formatting creativity. See working paper for handwritten copy.	M C R
10			M C R
11			M C R

TIME RECORD: (to be completed by transcriptionist)	MAILABILITY RECORD: (to be completed by supervisor)
Name: _____ Date Started: _____ Date Completed: _____ Total No. of Minutes: _____	No. of items approved as MAILABLE (M): _____ No. of items returned for CORRECTION (C): _____ No. of items returned for RETYPING (R): _____
TAPE NO. 4 SIDE NO. 1	Job approved by: _____ Date: _____ (initials)

TRAINEE'S PROGRESS REPORT FORM/TAPE 4, SIDE 2
(PRINTING AND PUBLISHING)

Name_____

Target Completion Date _____

DISTINCTIVE FEATURES: Same features as Tape 4, Side 1.

TRAINEE'S ACTIVITY	COMPLETED	TRAINEE'S QUESTIONS AND COMMENTS
REVIEW Job Instruction Sheet		
RECORD beginning date on Job Instruction Sheet		
ASSEMBLE all materials and reference books		
INSERT Tape 4, Side 2 into transcribing machine		
MAKE machine adjustments		
LISTEN to instructions		
TRANSCRIBE all documents and type envelopes according to instructions		
PROOFREAD and MAKE corrections on typewriter		
CHECK Mailability Analysis Chart		
COMPLETE Job Instruction Sheet, being sure to record ending date		
SUBMIT all Tape 4, Side 2 papers in a folder to supervisor		

GRAHAM OFFICE SERVICES ■ Center Plaza One/Oak River, Iowa 52410/(319) 555-1252

JOB INSTRUCTION SHEET

Firm Name *Mac Queen Printing and Publishing* Telephone Number *(319) 555-6468*

INSTRUCTIONS: Fill in all information requested. Be specific in indicating special instructions (examples: *rush, confidential, rough draft*). Also, include any instructions that were omitted in the dictation process.

TYPE OF DOCUMENT	FORM IN WHICH SUBMITTED	SPECIAL INSTRUCTIONS *ALL MAILABLE!*	EVALUATION (for office use only)
1 *Letter to Subscribers*	*tape*	*Type "AMBROSE" in all caps and underscore.*	M C R
2 *Short letter to Mrs. Zelda McDonald*	*tape*	*Prepare a carbon copy to Rosewood, Inc.*	M C R
3 *Letter to Harold Johnson*	*tape*	*Subject: Invoice No. 3458.*	M C R
4 *Memo to All Employees*	*tape*		M C R
5 *Letter to Readers*	*tape*	*Type on the left 2/3 of page only — leave right 1/3 empty for art work.*	M C R
6 *Memo to Finley Marshal*	*tape*		M C R
7 *Letter and list to Andy Hiram Beebe*	*tape and handwritten*	*See working paper for list. Any format you choose is o.k. for list.*	M C R
8 *Flyers*	*tape*	*Arrange four or five on a single sheet of paper for offset press printing.*	M C R
9 *Letter to Marva Kathleen Johnson*	*tape*		M C R
10 *Bar Graph*	*handwritten*	*See working paper for handwritten copy. Use formatting creativity.*	M C R
11			M C R

TIME RECORD: (to be completed by transcriptionist)

Name: _____

Date Started: _____

Date Completed: _____

Total No. of Minutes: _____

TAPE NO. *4* SIDE NO. *2*

MAILABILITY RECORD: (to be completed by supervisor)

No. of items approved as MAILABLE (M): _____

No. of items returned for CORRECTION (C): _____

No. of items returned for RETYPING (R): _____

Job approved by: _____ Date: _____
(initials)

TRAINEE'S PROGRESS REPORT FORM/TEST TAPE, SIDE 1 OR SIDE 2

Name _____

Target Completion Date _____

MIDWAY APPRAISAL

DISTINCTIVE FEATURES: YOU WILL TRANSCRIBE THIS TAPE UNDER SUPER-VISION. Your supervisor will let you know when ten minutes remain in the transcription period; use that time for proof-reading. SEE YOUR SUPERVISOR BEFORE YOU BEGIN TRANSCRIBING.

TRAINEE'S ACTIVITY	SIDE 1	SIDE 2	SUPERVISOR'S COMMENTS
REVIEW Job Instruction Sheet			
ASSEMBLE all materials and reference books			
INSERT Test Tape. DO NOT LISTEN TO ANY PART OF TAPE UNTIL YOU ARE INSTRUCTED TO DO SO			
TURN on transcribing machine			
TRANSCRIBE all documents in mailable form. No envelopes are to be typed			
PROOFREAD when time is called by supervisor			
RECORD total time on Job Instruction Sheet when you finish proofreading or when your supervisor indicates the end of the appraisal period			
SUBMIT all Midway Appraisal papers in a folder to supervisor			

YOUR SUPERVISOR WILL RECOMMEND ANY REVIEW WORK TO BE COMPLETED AFTER THIS MIDWAY APPRAISAL.

ADVANCE to Tape 5 _____   **RETAKE Midway Appraisal** _____

GRAHAM OFFICE SERVICES ■ Center Plaza One/Oak River, Iowa 52410/(319) 555-1252

JOB INSTRUCTION SHEET

Firm Name ___MIDWAY APPRAISAL, Part A___ Telephone Number _____

INSTRUCTIONS: Fill in all information requested. Be specific in indicating special instructions (examples: *rush, confidential, rough draft*). Also, include any instructions that were omitted in the dictation process.

TYPE OF DOCUMENT	FORM IN WHICH SUBMITTED	SPECIAL INSTRUCTIONS	EVALUATION (for office use only)
1 Short memo to Finance Committee Members from Reginald R. Fitzgerald	dictation on tape		M C R
2 Very short letter to Royal Fields from Norman Hartman	dictation on tape		M C R
3 Short letter to Lesley Shaw from Martha Hoffman	dictation on tape	Subject is "New Account."	M C R
4 Short letter to Louis E. Conner from Shirley Williams Beach	dictation on tape	Summary sheet to be enclosed later.	M C R
5 Short memo to Tania Berdo and Ted Turk from Angela Williston	dictation on tape		M C R
6 Average-length letter to Reid Bates from Anthony M. Rocca	dictation on tape	In closing, use title "Chairperson, Community Recognition Dinner" for Rocca.	M C R
7 Very short letter to Traci M. Nielson from Udo Ivan Heinrich, Sr.	dictation on tape	Check will be enclosed later.	M C R
8 Average-length letter to Professor Mary Frederick from Finley D. Marshal	dictation on tape		M C R
9			M C R
10			M C R
11			M C R

TIME RECORD: (to be completed by transcriptionist)

Name: _____

Date Started: _____

Date Completed: _____

Total No. of Minutes: _____

TAPE NO. __TEST__ SIDE NO. __1__ (Part A)

MAILABILITY RECORD: (to be completed by supervisor)

No. of items approved as MAILABLE (M): _____

No. of items returned for CORRECTION (C): ___

No. of items returned for RETYPING (R): _____

Job approved by: _____ Date: _____
(initials)

GRAHAM OFFICE SERVICES ■ **Center Plaza One/Oak River, Iowa 52410/(319) 555-1252**

JOB INSTRUCTION SHEET

Firm Name _MIDWAY APPRAISAL, Part B_____ Telephone Number_____

INSTRUCTIONS: Fill in all information requested. Be specific in indicating special instructions (examples: *rush, confidential, rough draft*). Also, include any instructions that were omitted in the dictation process.

TYPE OF DOCUMENT	FORM IN WHICH SUBMITTED	SPECIAL INSTRUCTIONS	EVALUATION (for office use only)
1 Short letter to Helen Monroe from Daniel L. Kickingbird	dictation on tape		M C R
2 Short letter to Randall Troyer from Norma Hartman-Hartvigsen	dictation on tape	Business card will be enclosed later.	M C R
3 Short letter to Paul F. Kelley from Martha Hoffman	dictation on tape	Subject is "FNB Christmas Club."	M C R
4 Very short letter to Bank-America Travelers Checks from Shirley Williams Beach	dictation on tape	Subject is "Audit of Account No. 345 678."	M C R
5 Short memo to Secretaries of All Chapters from Edward Howell	dictation on tape		M C R
6 Average-length memo to All Tenants from Judith R. Boyd	dictation on tape		M C R
7 Short letter to Edward Bixby from Udo Ivan Heinrich, Jr.	dictation on tape		M C R
8 Average-length letter to Jeremiah Dudley from Finley D. Marshal	dictation on tape		M C R
9			M C R
10			M C R
11			M C R

TIME RECORD: (to be completed by transcriptionist)

Name: _____

Date Started: _____

Date Completed:_____

Total No. of Minutes: _____

TAPE NO. _TEST_ **SIDE NO.** _2_ (Part B)

MAILABILITY RECORD: (to be completed by supervisor)

No. of items approved as MAILABLE (M): _____

No. of items returned for CORRECTION (C): __

No. of items returned for RETYPING (R): _____

Job approved by:_____Date:_____
                (initials)

TRAINEE'S PROGRESS REPORT FORM/TAPE 5, SIDE 1
(MEDICINE)

Name_____

Target Completion Date _____

DISTINCTIVE FEATURES: Same features as Tape 2, Side 1.

TRAINEE'S ACTIVITY	COMPLETED	TRAINEE'S QUESTIONS AND COMMENTS
REVIEW Job Instruction Sheet		
RECORD beginning date on Job Instruction Sheet		
PREPARE for transcription*		
TRANSCRIBE all documents and type envelopes according to instructions		
PROOFREAD†		
CHECK Mailability Analysis Chart		
COMPLETE Job Instruction Sheet, being sure to record ending date		
SUBMIT all Tape 5, Side 1 papers in a folder to supervisor		

*PREPARE *for transcription* means assemble all materials and reference books, insert the tape, make machine adjustments, and listen to instructions.

†PROOFREAD means proofread all documents (and envelopes, when required) *and* make any necessary corrections on the typewriter.

GRAHAM OFFICE SERVICES ■ Center Plaza One/Oak River, Iowa 52410/(319) 555-1252

JOB INSTRUCTION SHEET

Firm Name *Family Practice Associates* Telephone Number (319) 555-2022

INSTRUCTIONS: Fill in all information requested. Be specific in indicating special instructions (examples: *rush, confidential, rough draft*). Also, include any instructions that were omitted in the dictation process.

TYPE OF DOCUMENT	FORM IN WHICH SUBMITTED	SPECIAL INSTRUCTIONS	EVALUATION (for office use only)
1 very short letter to Elaine Hayes	dictation	See working paper for report to be completed for enclosure	M C R
2 short letter to Juanita Fowler	dictation	See working paper for report to be completed for enclosure.	M C R
3 letter to Sidney O. Link	dictation		M C R
4 letter to Anita Gallery	dictation		M C R
5 letter to be printed	dictation	Put "Attending Physician's Statement" in quotation marks each time dictated.	M C R
6 letter to Gary Brumley	dictation		M C R
7 short letter to Craig Novotny	dictation		M C R
8 very short letter to Visiting Nurses	dictation		M C R
9 letter to Glenn C. Bother	dictation	cholecystectomy	M C R
10 short letter to Bradley I. Wilson	dictation		M C R
11			M C R

TIME RECORD: (to be completed by transcriptionist)

Name: _____

Date Started: _____

Date Completed: _____

Total No. of Minutes: _____

TAPE NO. **5** SIDE NO. **1**

MAILABILITY RECORD: (to be completed by supervisor)

No. of items approved as **MAILABLE (M)**: _____

No. of items returned for **CORRECTION (C)**: __

No. of items returned for **RETYPING (R)**: _____

Job approved by: _____ Date: _____
(initials)

TRAINEE'S PROGRESS REPORT FORM/TAPE 5, SIDE 2
(LAW)

Name_____

Target Completion Date _____

DISTINCTIVE FEATURES: Same features as Tape 2, Side 1.

TRAINEE'S ACTIVITY	COMPLETED	TRAINEE'S QUESTIONS AND COMMENTS
REVIEW Job Instruction Sheet		
RECORD beginning date on Job Instruction Sheet		
PREPARE for transcription*		
TRANSCRIBE all documents and type envelopes according to instructions		
PROOFREAD†		
CHECK Mailability Analysis Chart		
COMPLETE Job Instruction Sheet, being sure to record ending date		
SUBMIT all Tape 5, Side 2 papers in a folder to supervisor		

*PREPARE for transcription means assemble all materials and reference books, insert the tape, make machine adjustments, and listen to instructions.
†PROOFREAD means proofread all documents (and envelopes, when required) and make any necessary corrections on the typewriter.

GRAHAM OFFICE SERVICES ■ Center Plaza One/Oak River, Iowa 52410/(319) 555-1252

JOB INSTRUCTION SHEET

Firm Name *Marner, Thirtyacre, and Troyer Law Offices*   Telephone Number (319) 555-2715

INSTRUCTIONS: Fill in all information requested. Be specific in indicating special instructions (examples: *rush, confidential, rough draft*). Also, include any instructions that were omitted in the dictation process.

TYPE OF DOCUMENT	FORM IN WHICH SUBMITTED	SPECIAL INSTRUCTIONS	EVALUATION (for office use only)
1 letter to Ellis and Emma Shalla	dictation	Our office will enclose the will.	M C R
2 letter to Richard Miller	dictation		M C R
3 short letter to Daniel Jimenez	dictation	Copies of Articles of Incorporation and $50 check will be enclosed by us.	M C R
4 Very short memo to Mark J. and Candy T. Jacques	dictation	Enclosure is dictated next.	M C R
5 Enclosure (Paragraph 7, Condition of Premises)	dictation	Capitalize the words "Lessee" and "Lessor" every time they are in text.	M C R
6 letter to The Honorable Alfred R. Collins	dictation	Prepare carbon copies for Ingrid Anderson and Keith Jablonski.	M C R
7 short letter to Small Claims Division	dictation	Copies of the Original Notice will be enclosed by our office.	M C R
8			M C R
9			M C R
10			M C R
11			M C R

TIME RECORD: (to be completed by transcriptionist)

Name: _____

Date Started: _____

Date Completed: _____

Total No. of Minutes: _____

TAPE NO. 5 SIDE NO. 2

MAILABILITY RECORD: (to be completed by supervisor)

No. of items approved as MAILABLE (M): _____

No. of items returned for CORRECTION (C): __

No. of items returned for RETYPING (R): _____

Job approved by: _____ Date: _____
(initials)

TRAINEE'S PROGRESS REPORT FORM/TAPE 6, SIDE 1
(HOTEL)

Name_____

Target Completion Date _____

DISTINCTIVE FEATURES: This transcription task will require careful listening and thoughtful decision making on your part. Dictators ordinarily insert little or no punctuation and give few spelling helps. Some dictators make grammatical errors, and it will be your responsibility to make decisions as to the corrections needed. Occasionally, you will encounter "problem" dictators who, for example, do not speak plainly or are thoughtless about their dictation habits (e.g., information may be omitted or a radio may be turned on during the dictation). You are required to complete the Daily Record Form.

TRAINEE'S ACTIVITY	COMPLETED	TRAINEE'S QUESTIONS AND COMMENTS
REVIEW Job Instruction Sheet		
RECORD beginning date on Job Instruction Sheet		
PREPARE for transcription		
RECORD beginning time on Daily Record Form when you start transcribing each document		
TRANSCRIBE each document according to instructions		
PROOFREAD		
COMPLETE remaining columns on Daily Record Form		
CHECK Mailability Analysis Chart		
COMPLETE Job Instruction Sheet		
COMPUTE total lines you transcribed and your total production minutes for the tape		
SUBMIT all Tape 6, Side 1 papers in a folder to supervisor		

GRAHAM OFFICE SERVICES ■ Center Plaza One/Oak River, Iowa 52410/(319) 555-1252

JOB INSTRUCTION SHEET

Firm Name _The Plaza Inn_ _____ Telephone Number _(319) 555-1800_

INSTRUCTIONS: Fill in all information requested. Be specific in indicating special instructions (examples: *rush, confidential, rough draft*). Also, include any instructions that were omitted in the dictation process.

TYPE OF DOCUMENT	FORM IN WHICH SUBMITTED	SPECIAL INSTRUCTIONS	EVALUATION (for office use only)
1 Letter from Kim to Udo Ivan Heinrich, Jr. (two pages)	on tape	Enclosure is list of dinner menus— see working paper.	M C R
2 List of forthcoming events (one page)	rough draft	See working paper.	M C R
3 Welcome letter to prospective customers from Kim	on tape	Enclosure coupon to be filled in on typewriter— see working paper.	M C R
4 letter from Doodlesack to Mrs. Ellsworth Eye	on tape		M C R
5 letter from Doodlesack to Joseph Peters	on tape		M C R
6 letter from Doodlesack to Frances R. Farmington	on tape	We will enclose check.	M C R
7			M C R
8			M C R
9			M C R
10			M C R
11			M C R

TIME RECORD: (to be completed by transcriptionist)

Name: _____

Date Started: _____

Date Completed: _____

Total No. of Minutes: _____

TAPE NO. **6** SIDE NO. **1**

MAILABILITY RECORD: (to be completed by supervisor)

No. of items approved as MAILABLE (M): _____

No. of items returned for CORRECTION (C): __

No. of items returned for RETYPING (R): _____

Job approved by: _____ Date: _____
(initials)

TRAINEE'S PROGRESS REPORT FORM/TAPE 6, SIDE 2
(OFFICE SUPPLIES AND EQUIPMENT)

Name_____

Target Completion Date _____

DISTINCTIVE FEATURES: Same as Tape 6, Side 1.

TRAINEE'S ACTIVITY	COMPLETED	TRAINEE'S QUESTIONS AND COMMENTS
REVIEW Job Instruction Sheet		
RECORD beginning date on Job Instruction Sheet		
PREPARE for transcription		
RECORD beginning time on Daily Record Form when you start transcribing each document		
TRANSCRIBE each document according to instructions		
PROOFREAD		
COMPLETE remaining columns on Daily Record Form		
CHECK Mailability Analysis Chart		
COMPLETE Job Instruction Sheet		
COMPUTE total lines you transcribed and your total production minutes for the tape		
SUBMIT all Tape 6, Side 2 papers in a folder to supervisor		

GRAHAM OFFICE SERVICES ■ Center Plaza One/Oak River, Iowa 52410/(319) 555-1252

JOB INSTRUCTION SHEET

Firm Name _Bates Office Supply, Inc._ Telephone Number _(319)555-0123_

INSTRUCTIONS: Fill in all information requested. Be specific in indicating special instructions (examples: _rush, confidential, rough draft_). Also, include any instructions that were omitted in the dictation process.

TYPE OF DOCUMENT	FORM IN WHICH SUBMITTED	SPECIAL INSTRUCTIONS	EVALUATION (for office use only)
1 letter from Kjarsgaard to Mrs. Mary Foster	on tape		M C R
2 letter from Kjarsgaard to Mr. Frank La Belle	on tape		M C R
3 letter from Kjarsgaard to Ms. Jolene Wagner	on tape		M C R
4 letter from Kjarsgaard to Mr. Kevin M. Landers	on tape		M C R
5 table (very short)	on tape	Heading should read "INFORMATION ON NEW COPIERS."	M C R
6 order form for newsletter	on tape	For order form, see working paper. Information for form is on tape.	M C R
7 letter about meeker film from Lubaroff	on tape	Three letters with variables — addressee, name of convention, city, and date.	M C R
8			M C R
9			M C R
10			M C R
11			M C R

TIME RECORD: (to be completed by transcriptionist)

Name: _____

Date Started: _____

Date Completed: _____

Total No. of Minutes: _____

TAPE NO. **6** SIDE NO. **2**

MAILABILITY RECORD: (to be completed by supervisor)

No. of items approved as MAILABLE (M): _____

No. of items returned for CORRECTION (C): ___

No. of items returned for RETYPING (R): _____

Job approved by: _____ Date: _____
(initials)

TRAINEE'S PROGRESS REPORT FORM/TAPE 7, SIDE 1
(OFFICE SERVICES)

Name_____

Target Completion Date _____

DISTINCTIVE FEATURES: Same as Tape 6, Side 1.

TRAINEE'S ACTIVITY	COMPLETED	TRAINEE'S QUESTIONS AND COMMENTS
REVIEW Job Instruction Sheet		
RECORD beginning date on Job Instruction Sheet		
PREPARE for transcription		
RECORD beginning time on Daily Record Form when you start transcribing each document		
TRANSCRIBE each document according to instructions		
PROOFREAD		
COMPLETE remaining columns on Daily Record Form, computing the total lines and total production time for each document		
CHECK Mailability Analysis Chart		
COMPLETE Job Instruction Sheet		
COMPUTE total lines you transcribed and your total production minutes for the tape		
SUBMIT all Tape 7, Side 1 papers in a folder to supervisor		

GRAHAM OFFICE SERVICES ■ Center Plaza One/Oak River, Iowa 52410/(319) 555-1252

JOB INSTRUCTION SHEET

Firm Name *Graham Office Services*   Telephone Number *(319) 555-1252*

INSTRUCTIONS: Fill in all information requested. Be specific in indicating special instructions (examples: *rush, confidential, rough draft*). Also, include any instructions that were omitted in the dictation process.

TYPE OF DOCUMENT	FORM IN WHICH SUBMITTED	SPECIAL INSTRUCTIONS	EVALUATION (for office use only)
1 *Mailing labels*	*instructions on tape*	*Use our mailing labels. See working papers.*	M C R
2 *Cards for file*	*instructions on tape*	*Use 3×5 cards. See sample in working papers.*	M C R
3 *Telephone listing*	*instructions on tape*	*Any format is o.k.— just so it's readable and usable.*	M C R
4 *Letter to Kane (average)*	*tape*		M C R
5 *Internal letter (average)*	*tape*	*Carbon to Samantha Epp —CONFIDENTIAL—*	M C R
6 *Letter (short)*	*tape*	*Use simplified style for this letter only.*	M C R
7 *4 invoices*	*tape*	*Use our invoices with company logo. See working papers.*	M C R
8 *Memo (short)*	*tape*		M C R
9 *2 letters (short)*	*tape*	*New collection letter with variables dictated.*	M C R
10			M C R
11			M C R

TIME RECORD: (to be completed by transcriptionist)

Name: _____

Date Started: _____

Date Completed: _____

Total No. of Minutes: _____

TAPE NO. *7* SIDE NO. *1*

MAILABILITY RECORD: (to be completed by supervisor)

No. of items approved as MAILABLE (M): _____

No. of items returned for CORRECTION (C): __

No. of items returned for RETYPING (R): _____

Job approved by: _____ Date: _____
    (initials)

TRAINEE'S PROGRESS REPORT FORM / TAPE 7, SIDE 2
(ENTERTAINMENT)

Name_____

Target Completion Date _____

DISTINCTIVE FEATURES: Same as Tape 6, Side 1.

TRAINEE'S ACTIVITY	COMPLETED	TRAINEE'S QUESTIONS AND COMMENTS
REVIEW Job Instruction Sheet		
RECORD beginning date on Job Instruction Sheet		
PREPARE for transcription		
RECORD beginning time on Daily Record Form when you start transcribing each document		
TRANSCRIBE each document according to instructions		
PROOFREAD		
COMPLETE remaining columns on Daily Record Form, computing the total lines and total production time for each document		
CHECK Mailability Analysis Chart		
COMPLETE Job Instruction Sheet		
COMPUTE total lines you transcribed and your total production minutes for the tape		
SUBMIT all Tape 7, Side 2 papers in a folder to supervisor		

GRAHAM OFFICE SERVICES ■ Center Plaza One/Oak River, Iowa 52410/(319) 555-1252

JOB INSTRUCTION SHEET

Firm Name *All-Star Spotlight*   Telephone Number (515) 555-9019

INSTRUCTIONS: Fill in all information requested. Be specific in indicating special instructions (examples: *rush, confidential, rough draft*). Also, include any instructions that were omitted in the dictation process.

TYPE OF DOCUMENT	FORM IN WHICH SUBMITTED	SPECIAL INSTRUCTIONS	EVALUATION (for office use only)
1 List of events	tape	Use two columns: "Event" and "Date"	M C R
2 Outline for workshop	draft	One page, please! See working papers.	M C R
3 Dance tickets	draft	See sample in working papers.	M C R
4 Form letter (very long)	tape	Type ready for offset reproduction.	M C R
5 Form letter (long)	tape	Type ready for offset reproduction. Type NEW and FAMILIAR in all caps.	M C R
6 Letter (short)	tape		M C R
7 Contract letter to Dixon	typed sample; variables dictated	See contract form in working papers. (CONFIDENTIAL INFORMATION) We'll insert legal contract and return envelope.	M C R
8			M C R
9			M C R
10			M C R
11			M C R

TIME RECORD: (to be completed by transcriptionist)

Name: _____

Date Started: _____

Date Completed: _____

Total No. of Minutes: _____

TAPE NO. 7 SIDE NO. 2

MAILABILITY RECORD: (to be completed by supervisor)

No. of items approved as MAILABLE (M): _____

No. of items returned for CORRECTION (C): __

No. of items returned for RETYPING (R): _____

Job approved by: _____ Date: _____
(initials)

TRAINEE'S PROGRESS REPORT FORM/TAPE 8, SIDE 1
(TRAVEL)

Name_____

Target Completion Date _____

DISTINCTIVE FEATURES: Same as Tape 6, Side 1.

TRAINEE'S ACTIVITY	COMPLETED	TRAINEE'S QUESTIONS AND COMMENTS
REVIEW Job Instruction Sheet		
RECORD beginning date on Job Instruction Sheet		
PREPARE for transcription		
RECORD beginning time on Daily Record Form when you start transcribing each document		
TRANSCRIBE each document according to instructions		
PROOFREAD		
COMPLETE remaining columns on Daily Record Form, computing the total lines and total production time for each document		
CHECK Mailability Analysis Chart		
COMPLETE Job Instruction Sheet		
COMPUTE total lines you transcribed and your total production minutes for the tape		
SUBMIT all Tape 8, Side 1 papers in a folder to supervisor		

GRAHAM OFFICE SERVICES ■ Center Plaza One/Oak River, Iowa 52410/(319) 555-1252

JOB INSTRUCTION SHEET

Firm Name *Tiejens Travel Service*   Telephone Number *(319)555-3777*

INSTRUCTIONS: Fill in all information requested. Be specific in indicating special instructions (examples: *rush, confidential, rough draft*). Also, include any instructions that were omitted in the dictation process.

TYPE OF DOCUMENT	FORM IN WHICH SUBMITTED	SPECIAL INSTRUCTIONS	EVALUATION (for office use only)
1 *Letter — very long — to Peterson*	*tape*		M C R
2 *Copy for brochure (manuscript form.)*	*tape*	*Heading: "TWO EXCITING EVENTS FOR YOUR SUMMER"*	M C R
3 *Information for tour reservation forms*	*tape*	*Forms will be found on working paper.*	M C R
4 *Letter — short — to B. Blackstone*	*tape*		M C R
5 *Memo — short — to Padavan, Elliot, Lemmon & Sorensen*	*tape*		M C R
6 *Letter — average — to Ginberg*	*tape*		M C R
7 *Letter — average — to Madison Airlines*	*tape*	*Enclosures: Two Passenger Lists (see working papers).*	M C R
8 *Letter — average — to Lovelace, O'Hara & Swensen*	*tape*	*Variables: article title, magazine, and number of pages.*	M C R
9			M C R
10			M C R
11			M C R

TIME RECORD: (to be completed by transcriptionist)

Name: _____

Date Started: _____

Date Completed: _____

Total No. of Minutes: _____

TAPE NO. **8** SIDE NO. **1**

MAILABILITY RECORD: (to be completed by supervisor)

No. of items approved as MAILABLE (M): _____

No. of items returned for CORRECTION (C): __

No. of items returned for RETYPING (R): _____

Job approved by: _____ Date: _____
                  (initials)

TRAINEE'S PROGRESS REPORT FORM/TAPE 8, SIDE 2
(EMPLOYMENT)

Name_____

Target Completion Date _____

DISTINCTIVE FEATURES: Same as Tape 6, Side 1.

TRAINEE'S ACTIVITY	COMPLETED	TRAINEE'S QUESTIONS AND COMMENTS
REVIEW Job Instruction Sheet		
RECORD beginning date on Job Instruction Sheet		
PREPARE for transcription		
RECORD beginning time on Daily Record Form when you start transcribing each document		
TRANSCRIBE each document according to instructions		
PROOFREAD		
COMPLETE remaining columns on Daily Record Form, computing the total lines and total production time for each document		
CHECK Mailability Analysis Chart		
COMPLETE Job Instruction Sheet		
COMPUTE total lines you transcribed and your total production minutes for the tape		
SUBMIT all Tape 8, Side 2 papers in a folder to supervisor		

GRAHAM OFFICE SERVICES ■ Center Plaza One/Oak River, Iowa 52410/(319) 555-1252

JOB INSTRUCTION SHEET

Firm Name *M and N Employment Service* ___ Telephone Number *(319) 555-8132*

INSTRUCTIONS: Fill in all information requested. Be specific in indicating special instructions (examples: *rush, confidential, rough draft*). Also, include any instructions that were omitted in the dictation process.

	TYPE OF DOCUMENT	FORM IN WHICH SUBMITTED	SPECIAL INSTRUCTIONS	EVALUATION (for office use only)
1	Letter — short — to Karous	tape		M C R
2	Letter — average — to Rivers	tape		M C R
3	Letter — average — to Coleman	tape		M C R
4	Letter — average — to Reynolds	tape		M C R
5	Letter — average — to Klemme	tape	We will enclose the forms and brochures.	M C R
6	Outline — short	tape	For talk to National Secretaries Association.	M C R
7	Table — one page	handwritten	See working paper.	M C R
8	Table — one page	rough draft	See working paper.	M C R
9	Letter — average — to customers	tape		M C R
10				M C R
11				M C R

TIME RECORD: (to be completed by transcriptionist)

Name: _____

Date Started: _____

Date Completed: _____

Total No. of Minutes: _____

TAPE NO. *8* SIDE NO. *2*

MAILABILITY RECORD: (to be completed by supervisor)

No. of items approved as **MAILABLE (M):** _____

No. of items returned for **CORRECTION (C):** __

No. of items returned for **RETYPING (R):** _____

Job approved by: _____ Date: _____
                  (initials)

TRAINEE'S PROGRESS REPORT FORM/TAPE 9, SIDE 1
(GOVERNMENT)

Name_____

Target Completion Date _____

DISTINCTIVE FEATURES: Same as Tape 6, Side 1. However, you are <u>not</u> required to complete a Daily Record Form.

TRAINEE'S ACTIVITY	COMPLETED	TRAINEE'S QUESTIONS AND COMMENTS
REVIEW Job Instruction Sheet		
RECORD beginning date on Job Instruction Sheet		
PREPARE for transcription		
TRANSCRIBE all documents		
PROOFREAD		
CHECK Mailability Analysis Chart		
COMPLETE Job Instruction Sheet		
SUBMIT all Tape 9, Side 1 papers in a folder to supervisor		

GRAHAM OFFICE SERVICES ■ Center Plaza One/Oak River, Iowa 52410/(319) 555-1252

JOB INSTRUCTION SHEET

Firm Name _Senator M. Bradley Rutherford_ Telephone Number _(319) 555-0313_

INSTRUCTIONS: Fill in all information requested. Be specific in indicating special instructions (examples: *rush, confidential, rough draft*). Also, include any instructions that were omitted in the dictation process.

	TYPE OF DOCUMENT	FORM IN WHICH SUBMITTED	SPECIAL INSTRUCTIONS	EVALUATION (for office use only)
1	Letter	Dictated		M C R
2	Letter	Dictated	Carbon to the President of U.S.	M C R
3	Letter	Dictated		M C R
4	Letter	Dictated		M C R
5	Resolution	Dictated	See sample format on working paper.	M C R
6	Speech	Dictated	This is page 4. It is URGENT!!	M C R
7	Cover Page and Committee Listing	Dictated and Rough Draft	See working paper for listing draft.	M C R
8	Form Letter	Dictated	For the Senator's signature.	M C R
9	Letter	Dictated		M C R
10			THANKS!	M C R
11				M C R

TIME RECORD: (to be completed by transcriptionist)

Name: _____
Date Started: _____
Date Completed: _____
Total No. of Minutes: _____

TAPE NO. _9_ SIDE NO. _L_

MAILABILITY RECORD: (to be completed by supervisor)

No. of items approved as MAILABLE (M): _____
No. of items returned for CORRECTION (C): __
No. of items returned for RETYPING (R): _____

Job approved by: _____ Date: _____
                (initials)

TRAINEE'S PROGRESS REPORT FORM / TAPE 9, SIDE 2
(INTERNATIONAL)

Name_____

Target Completion Date _____

DISTINCTIVE FEATURES: Same as Tape 9, Side 1.

TRAINEE'S ACTIVITY	COMPLETED	TRAINEE'S QUESTIONS AND COMMENTS
REVIEW Job Instruction Sheet		
RECORD beginning date on Job Instruction Sheet		
PREPARE for transcription		
TRANSCRIBE all documents		
PROOFREAD		
CHECK Mailability Analysis Chart		
COMPLETE Job Instruction Sheet		
SUBMIT all Tape 9, Side 2 papers in a folder to supervisor		

GRAHAM OFFICE SERVICES ■ Center Plaza One/Oak River, Iowa 52410/(319) 555-1252

JOB INSTRUCTION SHEET

Firm Name _Multinational Food Exports_ Telephone Number _(319) 555-0500_

INSTRUCTIONS: Fill in all information requested. Be specific in indicating special instructions (examples: _rush, confidential, rough draft_). Also, include any instructions that were omitted in the dictation process.

	TYPE OF DOCUMENT	FORM IN WHICH SUBMITTED	SPECIAL INSTRUCTIONS	EVALUATION (for office use only)
1	Letter	Dictated	Two carbons: Mozella Taylor and Takoko Moriyama	M C R
2	Letter	Dictated	A carbon to Kris Langley-Wolfe	M C R
3	Title page	Rough Draft	See draft on working paper.	M C R
4	Section of Manual	Dictated		M C R
5	Employee Notice	Dictated	For bulletin board.	M C R
6	News Release	Dictated	URGENT!!	M C R
7	Letter	Dictated		M C R
8	Section of Personnel Manual	Rough Copy	See copy on working papers. Instructions on tape.	M C R
9				M C R
10				M C R
11				M C R

TIME RECORD: (to be completed by transcriptionist)	MAILABILITY RECORD: (to be completed by supervisor)
Name: _____ Date Started: _____ Date Completed: _____ Total No. of Minutes: _____	No. of items approved as **MAILABLE** (M): _____ No. of items returned for **CORRECTION** (C): __ No. of items returned for **RETYPING** (R): _____ Job approved by: _____ Date: _____ (initials)

TAPE NO. _9_ SIDE NO. _2_

TRAINEE'S PROGRESS REPORT FORM / TEST TAPE, SIDE 1 OR SIDE 2

Name _____

Target Completion Date _____

FINAL EVALUATION

DISTINCTIVE FEATURES: YOU WILL TRANSCRIBE THIS TAPE UNDER SUPER-VISION. Your supervisor will let you know when ten minutes remain in the transcription period; use that time for proof-reading. SEE YOUR SUPERVISOR BEFORE YOU BEGIN TRANSCRIBING.

TRAINEE'S ACTIVITY	SIDE 1	SIDE 2	SUPERVISOR'S COMMENTS
REVIEW Job Instruction Sheet			
INSERT Test Tape. DO NOT LISTEN TO ANY PART OF TAPE UNTIL YOU ARE INSTRUCTED TO DO SO			
TURN on transcribing machine			
TRANSCRIBE all documents in mailable form. No envelopes are to be typed			
PROOFREAD when time is called by supervisor			
RECORD total time on Job Instruction Sheet when you finish proofreading or when your supervisor indicates the end of the final evaluation period			
SUBMIT All Final Evaluation papers in a folder to supervisor			

RETAKE Final Evaluation _____

GRAHAM OFFICE SERVICES ■ **Center Plaza One/Oak River, Iowa 52410/(319) 555-1252**

JOB INSTRUCTION SHEET

Firm Name _FINAL EVALUATION, Part A_____ Telephone Number_____

INSTRUCTIONS: Fill in all information requested. Be specific in indicating special instructions (examples: *rush, confidential, rough draft*). Also, include any instructions that were omitted in the dictation process.

TYPE OF DOCUMENT	FORM IN WHICH SUBMITTED	SPECIAL INSTRUCTIONS	EVALUATION (for office use only)
1 Very short letter to Elizabeth Archer from Silas C. Shelton	dictation on tape		M C R
2 Very short memo to the Clerk of Court from Trudy E. Troyer	dictation on tape		M C R
3 Short letter to Mrs. Benjamin P. Bell from Franklyn Doodlesack	dictation on tape		M C R
4 Short letter to Deacon Jones from Louise M. Lubaroff	dictation on tape		M C R
5 Very short memo to All Employees from Gerry Graham	dictation on tape		M C R
6 Short letter to Anita Worsfold from Alvin J. Levrington	dictation on tape	Type "All-Star Spotlight" in all caps.	M C R
7 Short letter to Mrs. Calvin Mether from Timothy O'Brien	dictation on tape		M C R
8 Very short letter to Mrs. Virginia Nash from Lynn W. Mansfield	dictation on tape		M C R
9 Short announcement to be sent to the printers from M. Bradley Rutherford	dictation on tape	Double space the body; use "Kindest personal regards" as complimentary close.	M C R
10 Average-length memo to All Employees from Arturo Lopez	dictation on tape		M C R
11			M C R

TIME RECORD: (to be completed by transcriptionist)

Name: _____

Date Started: _____

Date Completed:_____

Total No. of Minutes: _____

TAPE NO. _TEST_ SIDE NO. _1_ (Part A)

MAILABILITY RECORD: (to be completed by supervisor)

No. of items approved as MAILABLE (M): _____

No. of items returned for CORRECTION (C): __

No. of items returned for RETYPING (R): _____

Job approved by:_____ Date:_____
(initials)

GRAHAM OFFICE SERVICES ■ **Center Plaza One/Oak River, Iowa 52410/(319) 555-1252**

JOB INSTRUCTION SHEET

Firm Name FINAL EVALUATION, Part B _____ Telephone Number _____

INSTRUCTIONS: Fill in all information requested. Be specific in indicating special instructions (examples: *rush, confidential, rough draft*). Also, include any instructions that were omitted in the dictation process.

TYPE OF DOCUMENT	FORM IN WHICH SUBMITTED	SPECIAL INSTRUCTIONS	EVALUATION (for office use only)
1 Very short letter to Melinda Hunt from Silas C. Shelton	dictation on tape		M C R
2 Very short memo to Clerk of Court from Trudy E. Troyer	dictation on tape		M C R
3 Short letter to Claiborne Kincaid from Su Kim	dictation on tape		M C R
4 Short memo to Preferred Customer from Louise M. Lubaroff	dictation on tape		M C R
5 Short memo to Office Staff from Gerry Graham	dictation on tape		M C R
6 Short letter to Jay Marshall from Alvin J. Levrington	dictation on tape	Put "The City Limits Band" in quotation marks.	M C R
7 Short memo to Office Staff from Brent W. Schaapveld	dictation on tape		M C R
8 Short letter to Dr. Noel H. Maxwell from Lynn W. Mansfield	dictation on tape		M C R
9 Short announcement to be sent to the printers by Senator Rutherford	dictation on tape	Double space body; use "Best wishes for continued success" as complimentary close.	M C R
10 Short memo to Mozella May Taylor and Takoko Moriyama from Arturo Lopez	dictation on tape		M C R
11			M C R

TIME RECORD: (to be completed by transcriptionist)

Name: _____

Date Started: _____

Date Completed: _____

Total No. of Minutes: _____

TAPE NO. TEST SIDE NO. 2 (Part B)

MAILABILITY RECORD: (to be completed by supervisor)

No. of items approved as MAILABLE (M): _____

No. of items returned for CORRECTION (C): __

No. of items returned for RETYPING (R): _____

Job approved by: _____ Date: _____
                (initials)

THE END OF THE BEGINNING!

Congratulations! You are now at the end of an extensive transcription training program that will serve as a beginning of your career as a professional transcription specialist in the business world. Together with your supervisor (instructor), review your specific performance by going over each item on your Employee Performance Appraisal Form in the *Office Procedures and Training Manual*. Make notes about any areas where improvement is needed; then follow the suggestions of your supervisor to make you an even more productive professional employee.

REMINDER

Do your best at all times and take pride in your accomplishments!

THE OFFICE OF TOMORROW

As a professional transcription specialist in tomorrow's office you can expect to be presented with exceptional employment opportunities because you are entering the world of work at a time when there is a tremendous demand for qualified office personnel. The figures in the following quotation dramatize this need:

The Department of Labor reports that more jobs are opening up in the secretarial field than in any of the other 299 work classifications on which it keeps tabs. Although there are already a record 3.6 million secretaries on public and private payrolls, new positions are being created at a rate of 440,000 a year. But while secretarial schools are filled, almost 20% of the new jobs are going begging.[2]

A look at the office of tomorrow reveals that it will be an exciting place in which to work. With access to new technology capable of producing documents at record speeds and applying new management techniques which make jobs more challenging, the transcriptionist will have opportunities to fulfill career goals never before defined or imagined.

This new office will also be characterized by heavier work loads on the part of transcriptionists and those performing related tasks. Meeting the challenge of these heavier work loads will pay off in terms of additional opportunities to climb career ladders which often lead to management-level positions. However, in our goal-oriented environment, you will have an obligation to know and identify with the needs of your firm and to keep up to date on new developments. In other words, you need to develop a broad-based professional attitude.

[2]*Time*, September 3, 1979, p. 55. Reprinted by permission from TIME, The Weekly Newsmagazine; Copyright Time Inc. 1979.

Here are three concrete ways in which you can develop and continue to improve this professional work attitude:

1. Read professional journals. Reading about the latest innovations will help you keep current about changes in your field. (See Appendix A for a suggested list of periodicals.)
2. Join professional organizations. Interacting with colleagues can be both educational and stimulating. (A list of selected professional organizations will be found in Appendix A.)
3. Enroll in educational programs. There are numerous opportunities to participate in regular classes, seminars, and workshops, which will enhance both your professional and social growth.

Activities such as those described above will help you move ahead in your career and will effectively demonstrate your professionalism to all who work with you.

APPENDIXES

APPENDIX A
SOURCES OF INFORMATION

WORD SOURCES

Dictionaries

1. *The American Heritage Dictionary of the English Language*. Boston: Houghton Mifflin, 1973. (Desk-sized dictionary)
2. *The Random House Dictionary of the English Language*. New York: Random House, 1971. (Unabridged dictionary)
3. *Webster's New Collegiate Dictionary*. Rev. ed. Springfield, Mass.: Merriam, 1977. (Desk-sized dictionary)

Thesaurus

Roget, Peter M. *Roget's International Thesaurus*. 4th ed. New York: Crowell, 1977. (Pocket-sized and desk-sized editions)

Word Books (Pocket-sized editions)

1. Byers, Edward E. *10,000 Medical Words, Spelled and Divided for Quick Reference*. New York: McGraw-Hill, 1972.
2. Kurtz, Margaret A., Dorothy Adams, and Jeanette Vezeau. *10,000 Legal Words, Spelled and Divided for Quick Reference*. New York: McGraw-Hill, 1971.
3. Leslie, Louis A. *20,000 Words, Spelled and Divided for Quick Reference*. 7th ed. New York: McGraw-Hill, 1977.
4. *The Word Book*. Boston: Houghton Mifflin, 1976.

REFERENCE SOURCES

Secretarial Handbooks and Reference Manuals

1. Clark, James L., and Lyn R. Clark. *How 2: A Handbook for Office Workers*. 2nd ed. Belmont, Calif.: Wadsworth, 1979.
2. Merriam-Webster Editorial Staff. *Webster's Secretarial Handbook*. Springfield, Mass.: Merriam, 1976.

3. Nanassy, Louis C., William Selden, and Jo Ann Lee. *Reference Manual for Office Workers.* Encino, Calif.: Glencoe, 1977.
4. Sabin, William A. *Reference Manual for Stenographers and Typists.* 5th ed. New York: McGraw-Hill, 1977.
5. Whalen, Doris H. *The Secretary's Handbook.* 3rd ed. New York: Harcourt Brace Jovanovich, 1978.

Style Manuals

1. Fernald, James C. *Funk & Wagnalls Standard Handbook of Synonyms, Antonyms and Prepositions.* Rev. ed. New York: Funk & Wagnalls, 1975.
2. Hodges, John C., and Mary E. Whitten. *Harbrace College Handbook.* 8th ed. New York: Harcourt Brace Jovanovich, 1977.
3. Turabian, Kate L. *A Manual for Writers of Term Papers, Theses, and Dissertations.* 4th ed. Chicago: Univ. of Chicago Press, 1973.
4. United States Government Printing Office. *Style Manual.* Washington, D. C.: Government Printing Office, 1973.

OTHER SOURCES

Postal Directory

National Zip Code and Post Office Directory. Washington, D.C.: United States Postal Service. (Published annually)

City Directories

(Individual directories are published by R. L. Polk & Co., St. Louis, Mo.)

Airline Guide

Official Airline Guide. Oak Brook, Ill.: Official Airline Guides. (Published twice monthly)

Hotels and Motels

Hotel and Motel Red Book. New York: American Hotel Assn. Directory Corp. (Published annually)

Almanac

The World Almanac and Book of Facts. New York: Newspaper Enterprise Assn. (Published annually)

Encyclopedias

1. Harris, William H., and Judith S. Levey, eds. *The New Columbia Encyclopedia.* 4th ed. New York: Columbia Univ. Press, 1975.
2. Preece, Warren E., ed. *Encyclopaedia Britannica.* Chicago: Encyclopaedia Britannica, 1974.

Maps

Rand McNally Commercial Atlas and Marketing Guide. Chicago: Rand McNally. (Published annually)

Etiquette

1. Post, Elizabeth. *The New Emily Post's Etiquette.* 12th ed. New York: Funk & Wagnalls, 1975.
2. Reardon, Maureen E. *The New Etiquette.* New York: Popular Library, 1978.

PUBLICATIONS OF PROFESSIONAL INTEREST

1. *Administrative Management.* Geyer-McAllister Publications, 51 Madison Ave., New York, N.Y. 10010. (Published monthly)
2. *Modern Office Procedures.* Industrial Publishing Co., 614 Superior Ave., W., Cleveland, Ohio 44113. (Published monthly)
3. *Office Product News.* United Technical Publications, 645 Stewart Ave., Garden City, N.Y. 11530. (Published monthly)
4. *The Office.* Office Publications, 1200 Summer St., Stamford, Conn. 06904. (Published monthly)
5. *The Secretary.* The National Secretaries Assn., 2400 Pershing Road, Kansas City, Mo. 64108. (Published monthly)
6. *Word Processing.* Office Products Div., IBM Corp., Parson's Pond Drive, Franklin Lakes, N.J. 07417. (Published monthly)
7. *Word Processing & Information Systems.* Geyer-McAllister Publications, 51 Madison Ave., New York, N.Y. 10010. (Published monthly)
8. *Words.* International Word Processing Assn., Maryland Road, Willow Grove, Pa. 19090. (Published bimonthly)

ORGANIZATIONS OF PROFESSIONAL INTEREST

1. Administrative Management Society. Willow Grove, Pa. 19090.
2. International Word Processing Association. Maryland Road, Willow Grove, Pa. 19090.
3. National Association of Educational Secretaries. 1801 No. Moore St., Arlington, Va. 22209.
4. National Association of Legal Secretaries. 3005 East Skelly Drive, Suite 120, Tulsa, Okla. 74105.
5. National Federation of the Blind, Division of Secretaries and Transcribers. P.O. Box 4422, Baltimore, Md. 21223.
6. National Registry of Medical Secretaries. P. O. Box 360, Newton Highlands, Mass. 02161.
7. The National Secretaries Association. 2440 Pershing Road, Kansas City, Mo. 64108.
8. The Word Processing Society. P.O. Box 92553, Milwaukee, Wis. 53202.

APPENDIX B
PRACTICE EXERCISES

PRACTICE EXERCISE 1: HOMONYMS AND WORDS SIMILAR IN SOUND

INSTRUCTIONS: Circle the correct word, or (if time allows) type the sentences on a separate piece of paper, selecting the correct word.

1. No to/too/two word processing centers are identical.

2. Please accept/except my apologies.

3. Your job responsibilities will include helping students choose/chose an on-the-job training experience.

4. Submit your ad/add by Wednesday.

5. College students may contribute to the support of a household in addition/edition to their college expenses.

6. We need to hire an additional six surgery attendance/attendants for the 7 a.m. shift.

7. The city council/counsel/consul meets every Thursday evening.

8. It is defined as an elicit/illicit act.

9. There/Their/They're are long-range goals on file.

10. We are always in a state of continual/continuous shortage of supplies.

11. Your assistance/assistants was helpful during the registration process.

12. This practice may lead/led to improvements in our staff development program.

13. Submit all change-of-status forms to the personal/personnel office.

14. We recommend that the physical/fiscal education class be a required course.

15. We will adapt/adept/adopt a new record-keeping system on July 1.

16. The counseling experience affects/effects most of the participants positively.

17. We will precede/proceed with the staff selection procedure.

18. The legislature will vote on our capital/capitol appropriations next month.

19. I will be hear/here until 5 p.m.

20. We were uncertain, but we felt that the statement was a lay/lie.

21. What is the lessee/lesser/lessor of the two amounts?

22. Please sit beside/besides me at the afternoon conference session.

23. In my opinion, we pay a decent/descent/dissent hourly wage.

24. All our correspondence/correspondents must apply for passports.

25. What would your advice/advise be on the matter?

26. Move it farther/further to the back of the auditorium.

27. Its/It's too early to make a decision.

28. Your/You're termination reports need to be submitted by the 15th of this month.

29. You are asked to indicate the principal/principle cause of the accident on the form.

30. The children were instructed not to loose/lose/loss the keys.

31. They were all introduced very formally/formerly at the banquet.

32. The transcriptionist should forward/foreword the correspondence to me.

33. I would appreciate it if you would do/due this for me.

34. We plan on spending our weak's/week's vacation in Montana.

35. Do you really want to quiet/quit/quite your job?

36. He disapproved/disproved of the decision of the committee.

37. I asked all guilty parties to step forth/fourth.

38. I will see you later/latter.

39. The motion was passed/past unanimously.

40. He moved the chair, but the desk was stationary/stationery.

41. I was bothered by his allusion/illusion to my tardiness in sending the report.

42. The biannual/biennial reports are due in May and December.

43. I was conscience/conscious of the fact that the manager of the office left late.

44. Dr. Grey sees a great number of patience/patients each day.

45. The cite/sight/site for the new building was selected.

46. We need a better device/devise for collating the materials.

47. The final entrance/entrants for the drawing have been selected.

48. Our staff was very much involved in the peace/piece movement.

49. That color complements/compliments your personality.

50. The verdict of the grand jury was that the party would not be persecuted/prosecuted.

51. Weather/Whether John will resign is still an unanswered question.

52. The secretary signed the meeting minutes "Respectfully/Respectively yours."

53. Whose/Who's chairperson of the committee?

54. She would rather meet in the morning than/then in the afternoon.

INSTRUCTIONS: Check your answers with the Key to Practice Exercise 1 in Appendix C.

PRACTICE EXERCISE 2: ONE OR TWO WORDS

INSTRUCTIONS: Circle the correct word, or (if time allows) type the sentences on a separate piece of paper, selecting the correct word.

1. Mary all ways/always takes the bus to work.

2. His coming in late seems to be an every day/everyday occurrence.

3. No body/Nobody of knowledge on that subject is available.

4. A lot/Allot of the staff are taking vacations in August.

5. When you are in town some time/sometime/sometimes, visit our word processing center.

6. Some one/Someone of us will pick you up at seven o'clock.

7. We were all ready/already to leave for the conference when the car arrived.

8. Our office may be/maybe purchasing a text-editing typewriter.

9. It is all right/alright if you leave a few minutes early today.

10. You can complete the assignment in any way/anyway you choose.

11. We were all together/altogether when we were traveling in Switzerland.

12. Any one/Anyone of you can be chairperson of the committee.

INSTRUCTIONS: Check your answers with the Key to Practice Exercise 2 in Appendix C.

PRACTICE EXERCISE 3: WORD DIVISION

INSTRUCTIONS: Circle the correct word division. In some cases, there will be more than one correct word division given.

1. can't	can'-t	ca-n't
2. patio	pat-io	pa-tio
3. Elizabeth	Eliz-abeth	Eliza-beth
4. similar	sim-ilar	simi-lar
5. creative	cre-ative	crea-tive
6. December, 1982	December,- 1982	Decem-ber, 1982
7. resignation	resig-nation	resigna-tion
8. passed	pass-ed	pas-sed
9. o'clock	o'-clock	o'clo-ck
10. Peterson	Peter-son	Pe-terson
11. separate	sep-arate	sepa-rate
12. prescription	pre-scription	prescrip-tion

13. accommodate	accom-modate	ac-commodate
14. S. L. Schneider	S. L. - Schneider	S. L. Sch-neider
15. retroactive	re-troactive	retro-active
16. 245,652	245,-652	245,6-52
17. briefly	brief-ly	br-iefly
18. solved	solv-ed	sol-ved
19. along	a-long	alon-g
20. ass't.	ass'-t.	as-s't.

INSTRUCTIONS: Check your answers with the Key to Practice Exercise 3 in Appendix C.

PRACTICE EXERCISE 4: CAPITALIZATION

INSTRUCTIONS: Circle each letter that needs to be capitalized. If time allows, type the sentences on a separate piece of paper, capitalizing the appropriate words.

1. The hearing is scheduled for thursday, march 29, and friday, march 30, at the Federal building in provo, utah.

2. "language," she sighed, "is hard to define."

3. Kansu is china's northwest corridor to western regions.

4. It was described in the *journal of the american medical association*.

5. Lee Jones, executive vice president, will serve as chairperson.

6. We'll send you a copy of the article, "plan for the future," free of charge.

7. In any venture, the lack of a plan can be serious: it can mean failure.

8. Wellman company headquarters will be moving to the northwest.

9. The payroll department has the lowest staff turnover.

10. Please check the applicants' credentials to identify those who have taken eight quarters of spanish.

11. When will professor Buchwald submit her travel vouchers?

12. We will interview some journalists from the north.

13. I attended Columbia university for graduate studies.

14. Kerry Bates, director of nutrition services of Scott Memorial Hospital, recommends a low-fat diet for everyone.

15. "Stop at your nearest dealer," urged the commercial, "and get a closer look at our product."

INSTRUCTIONS: Check your answers with the Key to Practice Exercise 4 in Appendix C.

PRACTICE EXERCISE 5: EXPRESSING NUMBERS

INSTRUCTIONS: Write the numbers in the correct form where necessary, or (if time permits) type the sentences on a separate piece of paper, correctly expressing the numbers.

1. He published his first piano composition at age twelve. _____

2. She will conduct the 27-member chamber orchestra. _____

3. The children's performance will be given Saturday at eleven o'clock. _____

4. The custodian used three gallons of liquid wax on the lobby floor. _____

5. A full-size sheet of paper measures eight and one-half by eleven inches. _____

6. Our factory is located at 15 1st Avenue; our outlet store, at 1 West 59th Street. _____

7. We hope to have it competitively priced at about $8.00. _____

8. It will be released on the fifteenth of March. _____

9. Bring four sandwiches, eight apples, and twelve drinks. _____

10. The project was only three-fourths completed by the deadline date. _____

11. Did you locate Purchase Order No. 4512 in the files? _____

12. Over 20,000,000 persons participated in the recent poll. _____

13. 275 musicians attended the concert. _____

14. The company plans to purchase five typewriters, 14 desks, 3 4-drawer files, and 20 calculators. _____

15. Mr. Sandcastle plans to order 6 2-drawer files and 12 4-drawer files. _____

16. She estimated that 2/3 of the office staff would vote for flexible hours. _____

17. Bob's 2nd color choice was brown. _____

18. He expects to have about 15 small packages in the briefcase he'll take on Flight 102 at nine o'clock. _____

19. Do you plan to resign by the fifth of June? _____

20. 25 percent of our staff members are out of work today with the flu. _____

INSTRUCTIONS: Check your answers with the Key to Practice Exercise 5 in Appendix C.

PRACTICE EXERCISE 6: SERIES COMMA

INSTRUCTIONS: Insert the missing commas, or (if time permits) type the sentences on a separate piece of paper, inserting the missing commas where necessary.

1. We will discuss human relations in the office different problem-solving and decision-making techniques and building team skills.

2. The following persons have been awarded 20-year service pins: Harold Frank Charlotte Healey Joseph Sebastian and Heidi Gruber.

3. All faculty staff students and area residents will be able to donate blood on January 29 and 30 during the annual blood drive.

4. The basketball teams for the charity game will be made up of city officials candidates for public office and several disc jockeys and television personalities.

5. Current unclaimed lost-and-found items include a watch a camera and a woman's winter coat.

6. An examination of policies relating to land water and energy in Montana's future will be the focus of the one-day meeting on July 24.

7. The service is intended to provide a liaison person for patients and their families in time of confusion doubt or worry.

8. The registration fee covers a conference packet attendance at all sessions and a Friday evening banquet.

9. Nominations shall include a brief description of the candidate's qualifications past and present service to the organization consent to serve and the candidate's reason for seeking election.

10. He comes to our department with an impressive background in scholarship teaching academic administration and government.

INSTRUCTIONS: Check your answers with the Key to Practice Exercise 6 in Appendix C.

PRACTICE EXERCISE 7: INTRODUCTORY COMMA

INSTRUCTIONS: Insert the missing commas, or (if time permits) type the sentences on a separate piece of paper, inserting the missing commas where necessary.

1. Over the next few years solar energy will make a significant contribution to our energy supply.

2. However let me point out the fallacies in these statistics.

3. By including more data in the record-keeping book reconciling the monthly financial statements has become much easier.

4. When I have a lot of work to do I have some trouble prioritizing the assignments.

5. If you wish to place names in nomination for national offices you should submit them on the enclosed form by May 29.

6. For more information concerning eligibility requirements call the Donor Bank at 555-6710.

7. If you wish to enroll for the payroll deduction plan for Savings Bonds please contact Nancy Barnes.

8. If it is necessary to make a personal call from a company phone it must be operator-assisted and charged to a home phone number.

9. While at the Department of Labor she was on leave from Tulane University.

10. As of the last of the year there has been no judicial interpretation of the new law.

INSTRUCTIONS: Check your answers with the Key to Practice Exercise 7 in Appendix C.

PRACTICE EXERCISE 8: EXPLANATORY COMMA

INSTRUCTIONS: Insert the missing commas, or (if time permits) type the sentences on a separate piece of paper, inserting the missing commas where necessary.

1. The Alumni Service Awards will be presented during Alumni Weekend February 27 and 28.

2. The book will be available at a reduced price $5 per copy if you buy ten or more.

3. Marion Scott coordinator for staff development and training will speak at our council meeting.

4. Our summer hours 7:30 a.m. to 4 p.m. will be effective June 15 through August 15.

5. The United Way began its campaign on September 15 with a goal of $85,000 15 percent more than was given last year.

6. Craft an outdoor festival is intended to encourage interest in the arts.

7. A travel guide for the handicapped Access to the World is now available in the Bookmobile.

8. Costs for increased staff fringe benefits approximately 15 percent above last year's were factors in the budget increases.

9. The four charter members Roy Kern, Marilee Sloan, Peter Kraus, and Davis Flynn will be honored at the banquet.

10. Mr. Jones president will address the convention.

INSTRUCTIONS: Check your answers with the Key to Practice Exercise 8 in Appendix C.

PRACTICE EXERCISE 9: PARENTHETICAL COMMA

INSTRUCTIONS: Insert the missing commas, or (if time permits) type the sentences on a separate piece of paper, inserting the missing commas where necessary.

1. Congress frankly has occasionally done a less than admirable job.

2. Higher education historically has functioned as a chief means of social mobility.

3. Actually we know that the tests only have value as diagnostic instruments.

4. You should if possible begin inquiring about housing prior to your arrival.

5. Obviously such factors were used in the evaluation of the secretarial candidate.

6. Anyone interested in these issues especially professionals in programs for handicapped persons should attend the conference.

7. This program funded by the Department of Education has been approved for three years.

8. Therefore I find it extremely difficult to understand your resistance.

9. Your projected costs if negotiations are successful can be adjusted downward.

10. There was no increase in departmental allocations for this fiscal year as you are well aware.

INSTRUCTIONS: Check your answers with the Key to Practice Exercise 9 in Appendix C.

PRACTICE EXERCISE 10: DIRECT ADDRESS COMMA

INSTRUCTIONS: Insert the missing commas, or (if time permits) type the sentences on a separate piece of paper, inserting the missing commas where necessary.

1. There is no charge Mr. Stein for this office call.

2. Read this report Steve and take some notes on it for me.

3. Carol did you know that it is most important to brush your teeth at night?

4. Stop it Francis!

5. Sir come on in.

6. Katie will you please finish typing that report before you go out for lunch.

7. You're getting too old to still dress alike Leonard and Lenard.

8. You know Mr. Franklin at Capital Motors.

9. Helen please come into my office when you have a minute.

10. Guess who is here Brenda.

INSTRUCTIONS: Check your answers with the Key to Practice Exercise 10 in Appendix C.

PRACTICE EXERCISE 11: MODIFIER COMMA

INSTRUCTIONS: Insert the missing commas, or (if time permits) type the sentences on a separate piece of paper, inserting the missing commas where necessary.

1. Estella Meeks is a dependable efficient secretary.

2. Many customers return again and again because of our courteous complete service.

3. His rude surly office behavior makes everyone uneasy.

4. The older deeper roots of a reseeded lawn need more watering than the roots of a newly planted lawn.

5. A sign of heat stroke in a dog is dry hot skin.

6. Ozone is a tasteless pungent gas used in purifying water.

7. An adequately sized architecturally barrier-free facility is needed for senior citizens.

8. I'm acquainted with several knowledgeable responsible people who would be willing to serve on the committee.

9. It is a low-interest federally insured loan.

10. The hand-framed cabled vest is reasonably priced.

INSTRUCTIONS: Check your answers with the Key to Practice Exercise 11 in Appendix C.

PRACTICE EXERCISE 12: NONRESTRICTIVE COMMA

INSTRUCTIONS: Insert the missing commas, or (if time permits) type the sentences on a separate piece of paper, inserting the missing commas where necessary.

1. This jewelry which comes from Spain is inexpensive and sells well.

2. Mrs. Price whose job takes her out of town frequently is now in Minneapolis.

3. Your lawn fertilizer should contain nitrogen which gives grass its deep green color and thickness.

4. Joe Abramson who is a well-known and well-liked employee will retire next month.

5. The statement from the Food and Drug Administration which wrote and will enforce the rules said that it was designed to protect consumers.

6. Ballots with self-addressed envelopes will be mailed from the national office.

7. Nasal decongestants which provide immediate relief to people with clogged noses can cause tissues to swell once the initial effect wears off.

8. We feel that Santa with his rosy red cheeks and laugh will make a perfect public relations person.

9. This form which is available from your counselor must be completed and returned to the guidance office by the date specified on the form.

10. More students than ever are participating in foreign study which offers unique laboratory conditions.

INSTRUCTIONS: Check your answers with the Key to Practice Exercise 12 in Appendix C.

PRACTICE EXERCISE 13: INDEPENDENT CLAUSES COMMA

INSTRUCTIONS: Insert the missing commas, or (if time permits) type the sentences on a separate piece of paper, inserting the missing commas where necessary.

1. Tax cuts are a good method of stimulating the U.S. economy and some people feel that we need them at the present time.

2. I congratulate the honor students for their outstanding achievements and express my best wishes to them for their future success.

3. These changes are very evident and they are changing the character of our industry.

4. The slate of candidates will be mailed to the membership in July and a written reminder of voting procedures will be sent to all voting members in August.

5. I have deadlines to meet and I would appreciate your cooperation in meeting your deadlines so that I will be able to meet mine.

6. The merchandise delivered is not the quality we use nor is it the quantity requested.

7. It was our first trip to the Grand Canyon but it won't be our last to Arizona.

8. You are permitted to sell your contract for services but this may prove to be very difficult to do.

9. Take a look at the schedule and we think you will find a topic that whets your curiosity.

10. A senior center does exist but it is located in a deteriorated structure.

INSTRUCTIONS: Check your answers with the Key to Practice Exercise 13 in Appendix C.

PRACTICE EXERCISE 14: DATES AND STATES COMMAS

INSTRUCTIONS: Insert the missing commas, or (if time permits) type the sentences on a separate piece of paper, inserting the missing commas where necessary.

1. President Thompson announced that the Recognition Reception held on July 5 1981 had the highest attendance.

2. My resignation will be effective July 31, and I will be moving to Eugene Oregon.

3. All full- or part-time permanent employees who have been employed for one year prior to June 15 1980 are eligible to apply.

4. This will verify that Patricia Rowell was employed by our office beginning August 1, 1979 through December 12 of this year.

5. All employees having accumulated compensatory time due for the period from July 1 1981 through June 10 1982 should report their total unpaid compensatory hours on their June 13 time cards.

6. Dallas Texas is a popular convention location.

7. She moved from Morrison Iowa to Morrison Illinois.

8. I attended the Midwestern Energy Conference at the Pick-Congress Hotel in Chicago on November 19–21 1980.

9. There was an earthquake in the Santa Barbara California area on August 13 1978.

10. The General Assembly enacted legislation on July 1, 1980 relating to smoking in public buildings.

INSTRUCTIONS: Check your answers with the Key to Practice Exercise 14 in Appendix C.

PRACTICE EXERCISE 15: SINGULAR NOUN POSSESSIVES

INSTRUCTIONS: Insert the missing apostrophes, or (if time permits) type the sentences on a separate piece of paper, inserting the missing apostrophes where necessary.

1. I am my brothers keeper.

2. The doctors office is open on Saturday mornings.

3. The clients name was misspelled.

4. My mothers parents are naturalized U.S. citizens.

5. The childs toys were left out in the rain.

6. The lawyers advice was sound.

7. The eyewitnesss report was filed with the police.

8. The students paper was turned in on time.

9. That ladys luggage was put on the plane to Tampa.

10. My secretarys work piled up during her illness.

INSTRUCTIONS: Check your answers with the Key to Practice Exercise 15 in Appendix C.

PRACTICE EXERCISE 16: COMPOUND NOUN POSSESSIVES

INSTRUCTIONS: Insert the missing apostrophes, or (if time permits) type the sentences on a separate piece of paper, inserting the missing apostrophes where necessary.

1. My mother-in-laws flower garden never has a weed in it.

2. The editor-in-chiefs article was controversial.

3. The attorney generals opinion will be published next week.

4. The district attorneys office is in the courthouse.

5. The Vice Presidents report is attached to the meeting minutes.

6. His brother-in-laws will named his wife as executor.

7. A businesswomans portfolio was left on the bus.

8. That salesmans salary is considered too high by the other sales personnel.

9. My sister-in-laws name is the same as mine, and it is sometimes confusing.

10. That stockholders comments were misunderstood by the other stockholders.

INSTRUCTIONS: Check your answers with the Key to Practice Exercise 16 in Appendix C.

PRACTICE EXERCISE 17: PROPER NAME POSSESSIVES

INSTRUCTIONS: Insert the missing apostrophes, or (if time permits) type the sentences on a separate piece of paper, inserting the missing apostrophes where necessary.

1. Nevelsons work will be displayed at the Museum of Art.

2. Andy and Sids complaint will be considered.

3. Do you know Stephen Smiths phone number?

4. Ruths and Letitias cars are identical.

5. Miss Alexanders and Mr. Boyds employment papers are ready for review.

6. The Walter Hoffbergs home is on the left side of Elm Drive.

7. Do you screen Mr. Josephs and Mr. Baskervilles calls?

8. Lisa and Larry Trenches restaurant opens tomorrow.

9. Susie and Rons apartment is nicely decorated.

10. Phillips and Rays report was concise.

INSTRUCTIONS: Check your answers with the Key to Practice Exercise 17 in Appendix C.

PRACTICE EXERCISE 18: INANIMATE OBJECT POSSESSIVES

INSTRUCTIONS: Rewrite the phrases without using the possessive form, or (if time permits) type the sentences on a separate piece of paper without using the possessive form.

1. The lease's terms were unclear.   _____

2. The car's left side was extensively damaged in the accident.   _____

3. The street's closure caused traffic congestion on First Avenue.   _____

4. The cover of the notebook is blue. _____

5. The résumé's format is outstanding. _____

6. The letter's complimentary closing is out of date. _____

7. The paper's weight is not correct for this machine. _____

8. The building's door is locked at 5 p.m. daily. _____

9. The dictionary's pages are falling out. _____

10. The calendar's pages measure 3 1/2 by 6 inches. _____

INSTRUCTIONS: Check your answers with the Key to Practice Exercise 18 in Appendix C.

PRACTICE EXERCISE 19: PLURAL NOUN POSSESSIVES

INSTRUCTIONS: Insert the missing apostrophes, or (if time permits) type the sentences on a separate piece of paper, inserting the missing apostrophes where necessary.

1. The women's department was just remodeled.

2. It was considered a gentlemens agreement.

3. The three postal carriers routes are posted monthly.

4. Contributors gifts are acknowledged the same day they are received.

5. Doctors prescriptions are nontransferable.

6. The secretaries recommendations will be considered.

7. We are the largest manufacturer of ladies shoes.

8. Police officers uniforms are usually blue.

9. Several customers accounts are past due.

10. All infants apparel is half price.

INSTRUCTIONS: Check your answers with the Key to Practice Exercise 19 in Appendix C.

PRACTICE EXERCISE 20: NOUN UNDERSTOOD POSSESSIVES

INSTRUCTIONS: Insert the missing apostrophes, or (if time permits) type the sentences on a separate piece of paper, inserting the missing apostrophes where necessary.

1. Sharons was the best report handed in.

2. Todays weather is just like yesterdays.

3. This year's science projects are better than last year's.

4. I'm Mary Lous friend but not Katies.

5. Lloyds grades are better than Eddies.

6. Marjories paper was typed; Lulas was handwritten.

7. The womens tennis team challenged the mens.

8. Whitebrooks sales are better than Clanceys.

9. This months expenditures are less than last months.

10. Marians typewriter is cleaned weekly and covered nightly; Terrys is not.

INSTRUCTIONS: Check your answers with the Key to Practice Exercise 20 in Appendix C.

PRACTICE EXERCISE 21: PERSONAL PRONOUN AND INDEFINITE PRONOUN POSSESSIVES

INSTRUCTIONS: Insert the missing apostrophes, or (if time permits) type the sentences on a separate piece of paper, inserting the missing apostrophes where necessary.

1. Whose report is that?

2. That attached billing is yours.

3. Sports are frequently activities engaged in during ones leisure time.

4. The accident was nobodys fault.

5. Neither of the salesmen has his records up to date.

6. It's nobody's business.

7. Has either of the secretaries had her afternoon break?

8. Anyones receipts will be in the file cabinet.

9. Ours arrived yesterday; hers arrived today.

10. Everyones happiness is important.

INSTRUCTIONS: Check your answers with the Key to Practice Exercise 21 in Appendix C.

PRACTICE EXERCISE 22: TIME AND MEASUREMENT POSSESSIVES

INSTRUCTIONS: Insert the missing apostrophes, or (if time permits) type the sentences on a separate piece of paper, inserting the missing apostrophes where necessary.

1. He will be docked a days pay.

2. Give me a dollars worth.

3. Today's customers are more sophisticated.

4. This years festival will be held from January 29 through February 4.

5. This gives you an idea of a typical days work.

6. I expect an hours work for an hours pay.

7. I need four yards worth.

8. You must give us two weeks notice to assure delivery.

9. Yesterdays sunset was beautiful.

10. It will appear in next months issue of our newsletter.

INSTRUCTIONS: Check your answers with the Key to Practice Exercise 22 in Appendix C.

PRACTICE EXERCISE 23: COLON

INSTRUCTIONS: Insert the missing or delete the unnecessary colons, or (if time permits) type the sentence on a separate piece of paper, making the necessary changes.

1. Three important skills we look for in a worker are: speed, accuracy, and neatness.

2. The following items are also carried in our lumberyard building hardware, hand tools, electrical supplies, plumbing supplies, and cabinet hardware.

3. My ready references are these: *Harbrace College Handbook; A Manual for Writers of Term Papers, Theses, and Dissertations;* and *Roget's International Thesaurus.*

4. These holiday hours will be maintained by the library December 23, 10 a.m. to 5 p.m.; December 24, 10 a.m. to noon; and it will remain closed through December 26.

5. The rules about dropping courses are explained in the catalog in three places:
   a. Section 2, Item A;
   b. Section 5, Item B; and
   c. Section 11, Item C.

6. They drove to the northeast part of town via this route Kirkwood Street to Gilbert Street, Gilbert to Church Street, and Church to Johnson Street.

7. Most often a letter consists of: the date line, an inside address, a salutation, the body, a complimentary closing, the writer's name and title, and reference initials.

8. My supervisor always gives me prompt feedback on my work: Everything is returned with comments the same day I give it to her.

9. Unfortunately, rather than ability and experience, the following combination frequently determines promotions vacancies, the type of business, and timing.

10. Change Article II, Section 1, (3) to read: "The Treasurer shall represent the Board in, and be responsible for, the receipt and expenditure of funds in accordance with the directive established by the Executive Board."

INSTRUCTIONS: Check your answers with the Key to Practice Exercise 23 in Appendix C.

PRACTICE EXERCISE 24: SEMICOLON

INSTRUCTIONS: Insert the missing semicolons, or (if time permits) type the sentences on a separate piece of paper, inserting the missing semicolons where necessary.

1. You cannot live on your past glory, you must strive to improve.

2. There will be four minicourses offered; namely, Introduction to Astronomy, Consumer-Oriented Information, Genealogy, and Growing House Plants.

3. They arrived late nevertheless, our meeting was pleasant and beneficial.

4. I don't know if I can do it however, I'll give it a good try.

5. We agreed that we wanted to rent the cabin for two weeks saving enough money was a problem.

6. For travel in most countries, a passport is required but I know it isn't required in Mexico, Canada, or the Bahamas.

7. I feel a housecleaning spree coming hope I get to my desk drawers before it passes.

8. You decide how to invest your time and energy , what to study, where to go therefore, you determine and control your professional future.

9. Planning, organizing, coordinating, controlling, motivating, evaluating, and directing can all be learned but it takes interest, effort, and time.

10. In some areas of our state, for example, almost 75 percent of the high school graduates go into postsecondary education however, in other states, the percentage is much less.

INSTRUCTIONS: Check your answers with the Key to Practice Exercise 24 in Appendix C.

PRACTICE EXERCISE 25: HYPHEN

INSTRUCTIONS: Insert the missing or delete the unnecessary hyphens, or (if time permits) type the sentence on a separate piece of paper, making the necessary changes.

1. We will attend several company sponsored development programs.

2. The work re-entry seminar will have a session on inter-personal skills.

3. My vacation is always scheduled on July 4 to 17.

4. Take a long range look ahead, and be prepared for your opportunity when it comes.

5. The new employee was thought of as a selfcentered and selfish person.

6. The conference was well designed and executed.

7. Commencement is held each mid-June and mid-winter.

8. The conference has a limited registration figure of approximately thirty five.

9. The terminal pay should be ten twenty-thirds of $1,429.

10. The previously discussed topics will be tested on the next examination.

INSTRUCTIONS: Check your answers with the Key to Practice Exercise 25 in Appendix C.

PRACTICE EXERCISE 26: DASH

INSTRUCTIONS: Insert the missing dashes, or (if time permits) type the sentences on a separate piece of paper, inserting the missing dashes where necessary.

1. Violin, composition, orchestration I wanted to learn everything.

2. John told me to take the River Road he meant the Great River Road to Guttenberg.

3. Susan bought several books all on history at the Union Book Store.

4. Swimming, hiking, boating, and dancing—these are what I'm longing to do on my vacation.

5. Rain, hail, and wind these were the unpleasant things we encountered on our vacation.

6. Many types of problems especially personal can affect your production.

7. A good listener and a good speaker they are signs of a good manager.

8. Some don't know which way to turn they are uncertain.

9. It does mean—I'm happy to say that we'll be remaining here a long time.

10. Testing, final evaluations, and orientation for the school year—the closing activities—will be on Thursday and Friday.

INSTRUCTIONS: Check your answers with the Key to Practice Exercise 26 in Appendix C.

PRACTICE EXERCISE 27: QUOTATION MARKS

INSTRUCTIONS: Insert the missing quotation marks or correct the existing quotation marks. If time permits, type the sentences on a separate piece of paper, inserting the quotation marks where necessary.

1. I never thought about it, he remarked.

2. Frank stepped out of his office at 3 p.m. saying, Let's go home early, and we all laughed.

3. The chapter, Consumer Survival, is your assignment for tomorrow.

4. I asked, Why are you leaving so soon?

5. The highway sign was marked Do Not Enter; however, we observed that several cars ignored it.

6. He screamed, The art of conversation is lost!

7. Your stroking goal is ''speed;'' ''control'' will be next.

8. At this time of year, he frequently says, ''When winter comes, can spring be far behind?''

9. John Hanson remarked, ''You must read the first article, Your Trip to the Moon, when you have time.''

10. The following are parts of the area called ''The Pentacrest:'' Schaeffer Hall, Macbride Hall, MacLean Hall, and Jessup Hall.

INSTRUCTIONS: Check your answers with the Key to Practice Exercise 27 in Appendix C.

APPENDIX C
KEYS TO EXERCISES AND
KEYS TO PRACTICE EXERCISES

KEYS TO EXERCISES

KEY TO EXERCISE I.1:
PHASE I WORKSHEET

1. The transcriptionist is the link between the dictator and the final document produced.
2. More communications need to be processed in business. Many businesses are establishing word processing centers which employ highly skilled transcriptionists.
3. A good communication system builds internal efficiency, provides a good company image, and provides better service to the public.
4. Internal communication: Memos, reports, policy statements.
   External communication: Letters, minutes of meetings, statistical reports, proposals.
5. Listening, utilizing English skills, displaying a professional attitude, proofreading, knowing equipment, typewriting, formatting.
6. The transcriptionist in a traditional secretarial position is concerned with other duties in addition to transcribing—receptionist, filing, mailing, reprographics, etc. The transcriptionist in a word processing center is employed to transcribe from machines and to do straight typing—almost exclusively. Thus the word processing employee becomes more or less a specialist in transcribing.
7. a. Longhand—Advantage:
      Easy for the originator
         Disadvantage:
      Slow; handwriting may be difficult to read
   b. Shorthand—Advantage:
      Convenient for dictator; easy to ask questions and confer; faster than longhand
         Disadvantage:
      Time of both dictator and secretary tied up; secretary may have difficulty transcribing notes

   c. Machine Dictation—Advantage:
      Most efficient in terms of speed of dictation; transcriber has no notes to decipher; time of two persons isn't involved
         Disadvantage:
      Dictator needs to invest in equipment; dislike, on dictator's part, of using equipment
8. Provide information; help sell products; substitute for personal visits; serve as a permanent record; substitute for telephone call; provide service to customer.
9. A system through which information is processed correctly, tactfully, promptly, and with a minimum of effort AT THE LOWEST POSSIBLE COST.
10. Documents can be processed at top speed; accuracy is insured, provided the original document has been carefully proofread; documents can be stored on tapes, discs, or in memory and be recalled and typed back automatically in a matter of minutes or even seconds.
11. The originator may dictate the instructions on the belt, tape, or disc and alert the transcriptionist to these instructions by means of an indicator slip or an electronic cue; the dictator may also give verbal or written instructions.
12. An administrative secretary performs nontyping duties in an office and is responsible for such things as the following: handling telephone calls and receiving callers; research projects; assisting with financial matters; records management; decision making; reprographics; and serving as an assistant to the executive.
    The correspondence secretary performs duties that involve typing and transcribing and is a highly qualified specialist who produces large numbers of documents. The docu-

ments are expected to be of high quality and are expected to be processed in a minimum of time.

KEY TO EXERCISE I.2:
TRANSCRIPTION ORIENTATION

No key provided.

KEY TO EXERCISE II.1:
RECOGNIZING YOUR ATTITUDES

Answers will vary. No key provided.

KEY TO EXERCISE II.2:
DICTATION PRACTICE

Answers will vary. No key provided.

KEY TO EXERCISE II.3:
DECISION MAKING IN JOB SITUATIONS

Note: These answers are guides and are not meant to be the only solutions.
 1. a. Yourself, originator, finished product.
    b. Consult with your supervisor.
 2. a. Originator, finished product.
    b. Type the document as dictated. Once you have gained your originator's confidence, you may wish to suggest alternative wording to update the document.
 3. a. Time, equipment, finished product.
    b. Attempt to repair the tape. If your attempt fails, consult with the originator for completion of the project.
 4. a. Yourself, originator, co-workers.
    b. Thank your boss for the confidence. If appropriate, mention the importance of "teamwork."
 5. a. Originator, finished product.
    b. Check a reference book and make the necessary correction.
 6. a. Equipment, time.
    b. Check the outlet to make sure the plug did not work loose. Check on/off switch. Ask a co-worker or supervisor to look at equipment. Call repairperson. See if another machine is available for you to use to complete your work.
 7. a. Time.
    b. Run a copy on a copy machine if available. If a machine is unavailable, retype the letter with the word "copy" typed across the top of the letter.
 8. a. Yourself, originator, co-worker, time, work area.
    b. Emphasize to the co-worker the need to complete a project. Offer to visit with the co-worker during your break. If the chatter persists, talk with your supervisor about the possibility of a different desk arrangement to discourage unnecessary talking.
 9. a. Time, equipment.
    b. Make an appointment with your supervisor to discuss the need for an equipment change. Be sure to have your reasons documented.
10. a. Originator, finished product.
    b. Listen to the phrase a second or third time. If you have a supervisor, consult with the supervisor. Your goal is to reword the sentence without changing the meaning. Consult with the originator as a last resort.
11. a. Originator, time.
    b. Talk with the originator and explain that time is lost because of the rapid speech.
12. a. Time, finished product.
    b. Ask your supervisor or co-workers for help.
13. a. Originator, finished product.
    b. Type the document as dictated. After gaining the dictator's confidence, you may suggest minor changes.
14. a. Originator, yourself, finished product.
    b. Ask originator if signed duplicate letter needs to be sent.
15. a. Yourself, originator, co-workers, time, work area.
    b. Explain the situation to a co-worker and ask for help. Ask the co-worker to cover the telephone for you. Offer to do the same for the co-worker at another time.

KEY TO EXERCISE II.4:
LISTENING TAPE

SITUATION 1

Part A:
 1. 1:30
 2. Rhonda Little

Part B:
 1. Alice Smith, George Daniel
 2. Two
 3. Mr. Short
 4. Mrs. Miller

Part C:
 1. Wednesday morning
 2. Hudson House
 3. Wednesday or Thursday
 4. Dickens
 5. Within the first 10 rows
 6. A later performance
 7. Late Friday evening

SITUATION 2

Message A

WHILE YOU WERE OUT

To Mrs. Billings
Date XX   Time XX
Name Bill Carney
of
Phone 202-555-3244

☑ telephoned	☑ please call
☐ returned your call	☐ will call again
☐ wants appointment	☐ urgent

Message He is unable to make the committee meeting because of a New York trip.
     Please call him after 10 p.m. at the Hotel Granda in N.Y.

Operator XX   ☐ continued ➤

Message C

WHILE YOU WERE OUT

To James Rose
Date XX   Time XX
Name Mrs. Billings
of
Phone

☑ telephoned	☐ please call
☐ returned your call	☐ will call again
☐ wants appointment	☐ urgent

Message Mrs. Billings called from Chicago. She wants you to approve the attached minutes and return them to me for copying and distribution. You'll need 3 copies for John Weston, Ralph Ford & Betty Redman.

Operator XX   ☐ continued ➤

Message B

WHILE YOU WERE OUT

To Mrs. Billings
Date XX   Time XX
Name Frank Hardin
of
Phone

☑ telephoned	☐ please call
☐ returned your call	☐ will call again
☐ wants appointment	☐ urgent

Message He will meet you at 12:15 (NOT 12:30) in Royal Room of Brown Palace (not Carlton). He'll bring Brookings report. If OK, he'll bring Luci Davis.

Operator XX   ☐ continued ➤

Message D

WHILE YOU WERE OUT

To James Rose
Date XX   Time XX
Name Julio Salazer
of
Phone 712-555-5874

☑ telephoned	☑ please call
☑ returned your call	☐ will call again
☑ wants appointment	☑ urgent

Message
     Still wants to see you this afternoon about project.

Operator XX   ☐ continued ➤

SITUATION 3

Missing words:
1. of
2. Williams
3. Manufacturing
4. was
5. Arizona
6. the or his
7. hopes or plans
8. with

SITUATION 4

Instructions for transcription:

Type the Ellis letter on Power Club letterhead, and date it one week from today. Sign and mail letters to Stevenson, Rider, Baker, and Garrett. Send the other letters to Mrs. Billings for her signature.

Type one carbon of each letter for Mrs. Billings.

SITUATION 5

Equipment Needed	*Supplies Needed*
1. 1 two-drawer file cabinet (with lock)	1. 1 gross No. 2 pencils
2. 1 secretarial chair (flexible back)	2. 10 reams bond paper (20 lb. 25 percent rag)
3. 1 straight chair (green, padded back & seat)	3. 1 dozen ball point pens (black ink)
4. 1 typing table	4. 12 boxes paper clips (regular)
	5. 12 boxes paper clips (jumbo)
	6. 10 boxes rubber bands (No. 33)
	7. 10 bottles correction fluid
	8. 10 reams letterhead

Additional action or information:
1. Check dimensions for the file cabinet.
2. Obtain description of secretarial chair.
3. Check shades of green for straight chair.
4. Check availability of typing table and let supervisor know.

SITUATION 6

Mr. Ross:

Madge is leaving for Miami on the 9 a.m. flight for a meeting with Don Jackson of Robinson, Inc., at the Regency Hyatt.

She will return on the 11 p.m. flight tonight but will not be in the office before 1:30 tomorrow.

KEY TO EXERCISE II.5: INFORMATION SOURCES

1. Word book
2. Secretarial handbook (word division)
3. Secretarial handbook (punctuation)
4. Secretarial handbook (letters)
5. Dictionary
6. Secretarial handbook (capitalization)
7. *National Zip Code and Post Office Directory*, word book, secretarial handbook
8. Secretarial handbook or style manual
9. Dictionary
10. Thesaurus
11. Style manual
12. Telephone directory
13. Secretarial handbook (abbreviations)
14. Secretarial handbook (secretarial tips)
15. Interstate map
16. *National Zip Code and Post Office Directory*
17. Dictionary or secretarial handbook (metric measurements)
18. *National Zip Code and Post Office Directory*
19. Airline schedule or travel agency
20. Dictionary

KEY TO EXERCISE II.6: EFFICIENCY AND INFORMATION SOURCES

Note: Page numbers will vary, depending upon the specific word book you used.

Evaluation	*Total Time*
Superior efficiency	Less than one minute
Efficient	One minute to one and one-half minutes
Adequate	One and one-half minutes to two minutes
Inefficient	Over two minutes

KEY TO EXERCISE II.7: PROOFREADING FOR CONTENT

1. Your new typewriter should arrive in a month or six weeks, according to the representative you sent to my office.
2. When you have the next opportunity, be sure to stay at the downtown location.
3. Let Ms. Perez know as soon as you have finished the travel itinerary.
4. Please introduce my brother, Marv, to Coni when she arrives.
5. Katy was charged too much for the item at the cashier's desk.
6. Our department works very well together.
7. If you complete the form before Tuesday, you'll receive a gift from the bank.
8. I wanted to thank you, Daniel, for helping me last week.
9. Did you hear about the precedent that was set by the unit members?
10. The Southland Corporation on South Yale Boulevard is the best local source for the product.

KEY TO EXERCISE II.8:
PROOFREADING SENTENCES

1. Show enthusiasm for your (job) *each* day.
2. Display good (business) manners as (you) work with colleagues and clients(.)
3. (Form) the habit of looking for the good qualities (in) others.
4. (Decide) today (to) get along with everyone in your (office.)
5. Build your self-(confidence)—it is an (integral) quality of (success.)

KEY TO EXERCISE II.9:
PROOFREADING A PARAGRAPH

Learn to spot your (typing) errors. Proofreading skills (can be) (improved,) but you must want to improve. (Perhaps) if you (recognize) that uncorrected errors can result (in) extra expense, you will (develop) sharper proofreading skills. Just decide today that you want to develop a positive (attitude) toward "finding and correcting" those (errors.) Your improved job (performance) will be noticed() and rewarded!

KEY TO EXERCISE II.10:
PROOFREADING A MEMO

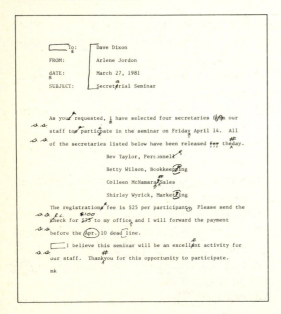

```
TO:      Dave Dixon

FROM:    Arlene Jordon

DATE:    March 27, 1981

SUBJECT: Secretarial Seminar


As you requested, I have selected four secretaries from our
staff to participate in the seminar on Friday, April 14.  All
of the secretaries listed below have been released for the day.

            Bev Taylor, Personnel

            Betty Wilson, Bookkeeping

            Colleen McNamara, Sales

            Shirley Wyrick, Marketing

The registration fee is $25 per participant.  Please send the
check for $100 to my office, and I will forward the payment
before the April 10 deadline.

I believe this seminar will be an excellent activity for
our staff.  Thank you for this opportunity to participate.

mk
```

KEY TO EXERCISE II.11:
PROOFREADING A LETTER

```
February 5, 19--


Miss Mae J. Albers
1455 West Alps Road
Athens, GA 30604

Dear Miss Albers:

CONGRATULATIONS!  We just read in The Alumnus magazine that you

have passed your C.P.S. examination.  You must be very proud of

your accomplishments.


If you can get away from your job, the college would like

to honor you at the annual graduate luncheon on Thursday,

February 16 1 p.m.  The luncheon will be held in the Governor's

Room in Memorial Hall.


Enclosed is a reply card for your convenience in responding.

We really hope you will be able to join us the 12th.

Cordially,


Donna Browning, Chairperson
Graduate Luncheon Committee

tn

Enclosure: Reply Card
```

```
February 5, 19--



Miss Mae J. Albers
1455 West Alps Road
Athens, GA 30604

Dear Miss Albers:

CONGRATULATIONS!  We just read in The Alumnus magazine that you
have passed your C.P.S. examination.  You must be very proud of
your accomplishments.

If you can get away from your job, the college would like
to honor you at the annual graduate luncheon on Thursday,
February 16, 1 p.m.  The luncheon will be held in the Governor's
Room in Memorial Hall.

Enclosed is a reply card for your convenience in responding.
We really hope you will be able to join us the 12th.

Cordially,


Donna Browning, Chairperson
Graduate Luncheon Committee

tn

Enclosure:  Reply Card
```

KEY TO EXERCISE III.5:
SPACING AFTER PUNCTUATION

PART A

1. Please give the information to Mr. S.⦵Q.⦵Ortiz.

2. Did you see a Broadway musical when you were on
   your two⦵week vacation?

3. The policy implies that a $15 deposit is⦵required.

4. Are the members ready?⦵I hope so⦵

5. If possible, try to produce 2,400 parts before March 30,⦵1982.

6. It's important⦵very important.

7. Yesterday, Mr. Avis said, "Jim's contract requires that $50
   (fifty dollars) be deposited by noon on Friday."

PART B

Enclosed is a check for $8,500.65 and
a supply of request-for-payment forms. I want
to remind you of the necessity for quarterly
financial progress⦵reports. Send five (5) copies
of the report to:⦵Archdiocese of Detroit, 305 Michigan
Avenue⦵Detroit, Michigan 48226.⦵Also enclosed is a copy
of the memorandum outlining what should be contained
in the quarterly report ending June⦵1982.

KEY TO EXERCISE III.1:
PAPER AND RIBBON SELECTION

1. Plain bond	Fabric	1
2. Letterhead bond	Carbon	1
3. Sulphite	Fabric	1
4. Plain bond	Carbon	1 (optional)
5. Letterhead bond	Carbon	1
6. Letterhead bond	Carbon	4
7. Sulphite	Carbon	1 (optional)
8. Plain bond	Carbon	4 or 5
9. Plain bond	Carbon	1
10. Sulphite	Fabric	1

KEY TO EXERCISE III.2:
ALIGNMENT

Answers will vary. No key provided.

KEY TO EXERCISE III.3:
PLACEMENT OF TYPING ON A FORM

Answers will vary. No key provided.

KEY TO EXERCISE III.4:
CROWDING AND SPREADING

Answers will vary. No key provided.

KEY TO EXERCISE III.6:
ABBREVIATIONS

1. Bradley is a recent graduate of the University
   of Alabama.
2. On January 5 the Collins Company will merge
   with Rockwell, International.
3. Did Dr. Ben Mahachek give you that advice
   about Model No. 16, or did Professor Erica
   Kane give it to you?
4. New York City has the largest population of
   any city in the United States.
5. The steak weighed 2.2 pounds or 1 kilogram.
6. Our national speed limit is 55 miles per hour
   or 88 kilometers.
7. Will you be working next Saturday, October
   21?
8. She has lived in Los Angeles, California, for
   11 years because she moved there in 1970.
9. C
10. William and Sue's new address is 14537 North
    Girard Boulevard, Columbus, Ohio.

KEY TO EXERCISE III.7:
FOLDING A LETTER

Student will demonstrate the technique to instructor. No key provided.

KEY TO EXERCISE III.8: CONVERTING ADDRESSES

```
MRS ARLENE MIKSCH-BENTON
CLAIMS SERVICE REPRESENTATIVE
GRINNELL REINSURANCE CO
INTERSTATE 94 AT HWY 150
ASHBY MA 01431


DR HERMAN SILLMAN
15211 ASHDALE BLVD S
PORTLAND OR 97223


TURNER CORP
ATTN ROBERT TURNER
4302 ALVIN ST
HOUSTON TX 77051


MS MARJORIE YELLOW CLOUD
APT 418
6233 S RHODES
CHICAGO IL 60637


MR TERRY K THIBEDEAU JR
13975 LA PLAISANCE
CAPTAIN COOK HI 79704
```

KEY TO EXERCISE III.9: VERTICAL AND HORIZONTAL PLACEMENT

1. Letter
   a. The left margin is too narrow.
   b. The right margin is uneven.
   c. The first paragraph should not be indented.
   d. There is too much space between the first and second paragraphs.
   e. The letter is a bit high on the page.
2. Memo
   a. The right and left margins are too narrow.
   b. The guide words are not aligned.
   c. The margins are uneven.
   d. The memo is too low on the page.
3. Envelope
   a. The return address should be closer to the left edge of the envelope.
   b. The address lines are too long and should be aligned at the left.
   c. The notation in the lower left corner should be typed above the address to permit electronic sorting of the envelope.

KEY TO EXERCISE III.10: PARAGRAPHING

The three logical paragraphs begin with the following words:
1. With the spiraling
2. Starting the first week
3. In case you don't live in the

KEY TO EXERCISE III.11: SELECTING A FORMAT

ATTENDANCE AT THE NATIONAL CONFERENCE

City	1980	1981
Chicago	5,490	6,322
Des Moines	1,495	1,940
Detroit	2,367	3,922
Kansas City	2,893	2,066
Minneapolis	4,852	7,364

KEY TO EXERCISE III.12: WORKING WITH "ODD" SIZE PAPER

1.	9	25	30
2.	30	40	48
3.	35	38	45
4.	26	28	33
5.	42	58	69

KEY TO EXERCISE III.13: CREATIVITY

Note: Answers will vary. Listed below are the essentials for a complete flier.
1. Name of company
2. Type of function
3. Date
4. Location
5. Who is invited
6. What to bring and what is furnished
7. Various sporting activities
8. How to sign up for picnic

KEY TO EXERCISE IV.1: SPELLING LIST TAPE

1. acquire
2. agenda
3. a lot
4. accommodate
5. achievement
6. acknowledgment
7. advisable
8. all right
9. among
10. apparent
11. appreciate
12. appropriate
13. assistance
14. attorneys
15. benefited[1]
    benefitted
16. canceled[1]
    cancelled
17. coming
18. controller
    comptroller
19. concede
20. confidential
21. conscientious
22. conscious
23. convenient
24. deductible
25. definitely
26. description
27. eligible
28. embarrassed
29. enthusiasm
30. environment
31. excellent
32. existence
33. expenditure
34. experiences
35. explanation
36. fascinated
37. financial
38. forty
39. grateful
40. immediately

[1]Preferred spelling.

41. incidentally
42. interest
43. its
44. it's
45. judgment[1]
    judgement
46. laboratory
47. maintenance
48. marriage
49. merchandise
50. merely
51. miscellaneous
52. mortgage
53. necessary
54. nevertheless
55. occasion
56. occurred
57. occurrence
58. opinion
59. opportunity
60. pamphlet
61. particularly
62. performance
63. personal
64. personnel
65. possible
66. practical
67. preceded
68. prevalent
69. privilege
70. procedure
71. proceeds
72. profession
73. prominent
74. promissory
75. pursue
76. questionnaire
77. quietly
78. receive
79. recommend
80. referring
81. rhythm
82. right
83. salable
84. secretary
85. sense
86. separate
87. significance
88. studying
89. subscription
90. succeed
91. surprise
92. technique
93. their
94. there
95. thoroughly
96. transferred
97. unanimous
98. unnecessary
99. valuable
100. writing

KEY TO EXERCISE IV.2:
SPELLING LIST

Answers will vary. No key provided.

KEY TO EXERCISE IV.3:
SPELLING RULE 1

disagree	imprudent	noninflationary
disapprove	inconclusive	nontaxable
disqualify	indirectly	preconceive
dissimilar	ineffective	predetermine
illegal	informal	preoccupied
illegible	misfile	prepayment
illegitimacy	mistrial	unequal
illogical	misspell	unnecessary
imbalance	misstate	unqualified
impatient	noncompetitive	unwritten
impractical	noncompliance	

KEY TO EXERCISE IV.4a:
SPELLING RULE 2.a

piece	field	hygiene
retrieve	variety	relieve
yield		

[1]Preferred spelling.

KEY TO EXERCISE IV.4b:
SPELLING RULE 2.b

conceive	deceive	conceit
perceive	receive	deceit
receipt		

KEY TO EXERCISE IV.4c:
SPELLING RULE 2.c

freight	vein	neighed
their	neighbor	sleigh
weigh		

KEY TO EXERCISE IV.5:
SPELLING RULE 3

dropped	witty	clannish
planning	baggage	shipper
jobber	quizzed	sitting
stopping	taxing	

KEY TO EXERCISE IV.6:
SPELLING RULE 4

preferred	beginning	excelled
omitting	forgotten	equipping
controlling	occurrence	transferred
allotted	referred	

KEY TO EXERCISE IV.7:
SPELLING RULE 5

credited	profited	labeled
difference	budgeting	developing
diagraming	visitor	cataloged
traveling	offering	

KEY TO EXERCISE IV.8:
SPELLING RULE 6

arrival	excitable	noticing
coming	excusable	simply
continual	famous	writer
desirability	guidance	

KEY TO EXERCISE IV.9:
SPELLING RULE 7

extremely	absolutely	ninety
careless	completely	resourceful
excitement	likeness	definitely
nineteen	management	

KEY TO EXERCISE IV.10:
SPELLING RULE 8

huskiness	reliability	burying
heaviest	variable	luckily
beautiful	emptiness	reliable
accompaniment	easier	

KEY TO EXERCISE IV.11:
SPELLING RULE 9

technicians	brothers-in-law	newsstands
chambers	accounts	standards
of commerce	shoppers	templates
manufacturers	tourists	typewriters

KEY TO EXERCISE IV.12:
SPELLING RULE 10

addresses	geniuses	lunches
potatoes	heroes	Joneses
speeches	scratches	waitresses
echoes	foxes	

KEY TO EXERCISE IV.13:
HOMONYMS AND WORDS SIMILAR IN SOUND

1. except
2. add
3. edition
4. adopt
5. advice
6. effect; affect
7. illusion
8. assistants
9. attendance
10. Besides
11. biannual
12. capital
13. choose
14. cite
15. Compliment
16. conscience
17. continuous
18. correspondence
19. counsel
20. dissent
21. devise
22. disprove
23. Do; due
24. entrance
25. further
26. fourth
27. forward
28. formerly
29. here; hear
30. elicit
31. It's; its
32. later
33. lay
34. led
35. lessor; lessee
36. loose
37. past; passed
38. patients; patience
39. piece
40. prosecute
41. personal
42. fiscal
43. proceed
44. principal
45. quite
46. respectively
47. stationery
48. then
49. There; their
50. to; two
51. week
52. weather
53. Whose
54. you're; your

KEY TO EXERCISE IV.14:
ONE OR TWO WORDS

1. allot
2. all ready
3. all right
4. altogether
5. all ways
6. Any one
7. Anyway
8. every day
9. Maybe
10. Nobody
11. Someone
12. some time

KEY TO EXERCISE IV.15:
MY SPECIAL SPELLING LIST

Answers will vary. No key provided.

KEY TO EXERCISE IV.16:
WORD DIVISION

1. Divide after prefixes.
2. Divide between double letters when the final consonant is doubled before adding a suffix.
3. Divide before suffixes.
4. Avoid dividing numbers.
5. Don't divide contractions.
6. Avoid dividing dates.
7. Don't divide words pronounced as one syllable.
8. Don't divide abbreviations.
9. Divide compound words only at the hyphen.
10. Avoid dividing parts of a person's name.
11. Don't divide after a beginning one-letter syllable.
12. Divide between double letters when the final consonant is doubled before adding a suffix.
13. Avoid dividing numbers.
14. Don't divide contractions.
15. Divide before suffixes.
16. Divide before suffixes.
17. Avoid dividing between consecutive one-letter syllables.
18. Avoid dividing before a two-letter syllable word ending.
19. Avoid dividing two-syllable word endings.
20. Avoid dividing two-syllable word endings.

KEY TO EXERCISE IV.17: CAPITALIZATION

```
        Current Date



        Ms. Evelyn Mahoney, Office Manager
        Base Manufacturing Company
        4532 Sandalwood Court N(E)
        Grand Rapids, MI 49505

        Dear Ms. Mahoney:

        For the last ten years, Franklin Products (C)ompany of (G)rand (R)apids
        has been proud to serve your document production and reproduction
        needs.  To show our appreciation, we invite you to an open house
        at our Lake Michigan (D)rive office on Highway 11, just north of our
        main office.  We'd be pleased if you would join us for refreshments
        on (S)eptember 8 or 9 from 4 to 6 p.m.

        Our entire staff will be on hand to show you our new (S)ales (D)epartment
        facilities.  On both days, (P)resident Owen will be present to speak
        with you.

        We all look forward to having you visit with us.

        Sincerely,



        Alice G. Walters
        Sales Manager

        xx

        PS:  While at our open house, be sure to pick up copies of our
             latest brochures:  "(H)ow to (G)et (R)esults," "(T)echniques for (E)ffec-
             tive and (E)fficient (U)se of (E)quipment," and "(W)hy (W)e (A)re (N)umber
             (O)ne."
```

KEY TO EXERCISE IV.18: NUMBERS AS FIGURES

```
        Current Date



        Mr. Donald J. Carlston
        Arum Book Store
        467 Fifth Avenue
        Dallas, TX 75203

        Dear Mr. Carlston:

        Please accept our apology for shipping your order of February 12 for
        (67) books (Invoice No. 2545E) to One (51) Street instead of 467 Fifth
        Avenue in Dallas.

        This shipment was only (25) percent of your total order and amounted
        to $729.  Our present plans call for sending the remaining books out
        on March 5 or 6 but certainly no later than the (8th).

        All of our (12) million customers are important to us.  Please keep us
        informed as to how we can better serve you.

        Sincerely,


        Thomas Zajicek
        Shipping Coordinator

        xx
```

KEY TO EXERCISE IV.19: NUMBERS AS WORDS

```
        TO:      Jenny Hansmann

        FROM:    Van Abraham

        DATE:    Current Date

        SUBJECT: Update on Job Applications


        Approximately (ten) persons, or (two-thirds) of the applicants who applied
        for the position of Administrative Assistant, have now been interviewed.
        Of the 14 persons who were interested in the position, 5 have taken
        the (four) 3-hour courses in computer science or data processing.  (Three)
        of the (five) had an exceptionally fine record.

        Miss Susan Lollaton, (one) of the (three) mentioned above, will be returning
        for a second interview on Wednesday, April 5, at 1:30 p.m.

        After the (fifth) candidate has returned for the (second) interview, I'll
        bring you up to date on the selection process.

        xx
```

KEY TO EXERCISE IV.20: SERIES COMMA

```
        TO:      Department Heads

        FROM:    Purchasing

        DATE:    Current Date

        SUBJECT: Service Agreements


        Any department may request service agreements to maintain company-
        owned typewriters and calculators.  The department wanting a service
        agreement should submit a written request.  The request should list
        the items of equipment with their correct names(,) model numbers(,) and
        serial numbers.

        The Purchasing Department will contact the dealers(,) negotiate the
        charges to be made(,) and sign the agreements.

        xx
```

KEY TO EXERCISE IV.21:
INTRODUCTORY COMMA

Current Date

Mrs. Betty February
Route 3
Morgantown, IN 46160

Dear Mrs. February:

Welcome to the Indiana State Personnel Managers Association (ISPMA)!
It was with pleasure that I learned of your decision to join us. I
hope you will become actively involved in our program. Through your
participation in ISPMA, you will gain the satisfaction of seeing an
idea mature. Also, you will broaden your professional skills and
associations.

As a member of ISPMA, you will be receiving our newsletter periodically.
If you have any topics to suggest for inclusion in the newsletter,
please write me.

Once again, welcome! I look forward to meeting and working with you
in the coming year.

Sincerely,

Roger J. Catalog
President

xx

KEY TO EXERCISE IV.22:
EXPLANATORY COMMA

TO: Vehicle Users

FROM   Motor Pool

DATE: Current Date

SUBJECT: Company Vehicle Use--Speed Limit and Fuel Purchase

The Motor Pool has received a number of reports about speeding by
drivers of company-owned vehicles. All users of company vehicles
are reminded that the highway speed limit, 55 miles per hour, is
federal law. Our attorney, Frank Dallas, has recommended that a
conviction for speeding be followed by a suspension of driving
privileges.

We would like to remind drivers that self-service gasoline pumps
are to be used when gas is purchased on a company credit card.
Saving a few cents a gallon should result in a reduction of our
fuel costs by thousands of dollars over the year.

xx

KEY TO EXERCISE IV.23:
PARENTHETICAL COMMA

Current Date

Mrs. Joleen Standeven
1004 Gladlane Drive
Montgomery, AL 36111

Dear Mrs. Standeven:

It's hard to believe that a whole year has passed since you ordered
your Christmas gift subscription. Although it may seem early in
the season to be thinking again of Christmas and of gift-giving, we
urge you to send us your gift instructions right away so that your
special person can keep on receiving ACME for another happy year.

We must, of course, remind you that in order to insure prompt
continuation of your gift subscription your order must reach us no
later than December 10. Complete instructions and an order form
are enclosed.

Sincerely,

Betty L. Birmingham
Circulation Director

xx

Enclosures: Instructions
             Order Form

KEY TO EXERCISE IV.24:
DIRECT ADDRESS COMMA

```
        Current Date



        Miss Sarah Goldberg
        100 Indiana Avenue
        Monaca, PA 15061

        Dear Miss Goldberg:

        Thank you so much, Miss Goldberg, for your patronage.  You have our
        assurance that we shall make every effort to maintain the friendly
        type of relationship so necessary for your continued confidence and
        good will.

        All of us are eager to serve you at all times and in every way possible.

        Thanks again, Miss Goldberg.

        Sincerely,



        Harry L. Steinwell
        Salesperson

        xx
```

KEY TO EXERCISE IV.26:
NONRESTRICTIVE COMMA

```
        Current Date



        The Reverend E. E. Raymond
        Chaplain
        The Episcopal Chaplaincy
        Trinity Episcopal Church
        1500 Gordon Avenue
        Charlottesville, VA 22903

        Dear Chaplain Raymond:

        I want to express my appreciation for your help in moving Frances
        Newman to her new apartment last week.  The use of the truck, which
        was a pleasant surprise, proved to be a real time-saver.

        We have always been appreciative of our relationship with the
        Episcopal Chaplaincy and look forward to its continuation.

        Sincerely,



        Stella Samuels
        Social Worker

        xx
```

KEY TO EXERCISE IV.25:
MODIFIER COMMA

```
        Current Date



        Dr. Jose Negrete
        College of Education
        University of Wisconsin
        Madison, WI 53706

        Dear Dr. Negrete:

        It is a pleasure to write a letter of recommendation for Roberto
        Segura.  I feel that I can give a fair, honest evaluation of his
        work and of his potential for a graduate fellowship in bilingual
        education.

        Roberto is a very conscientious worker and has demonstrated excellent
        organizational capabilities.  He is always willing to put forth
        extra time and effort to get things done.  His initiative in all
        aspects of his work is highly commendable.  He is a most pleasant,
        cooperative worker.

        It has been delightful working with him professionally and knowing
        him socially.

        Sincerely,



        Becky Baker
        Administrative Associate

        xx
```

KEY TO EXERCISE IV.27:
INDEPENDENT CLAUSES COMMA

```
        Current Date



        Mr. Hugh Gibson
        One Sparkleberry Lane
        Columbia, SC 29206

        Dear Mr. Gibson:

        I am very pleased to confirm our telephone conversation of this
        morning regarding your appointment to the position of Personnel
        Job Analyst.  We feel that you can make a great contribution to
        our staff, and we look forward to working with you.

        Staff benefits are outlined in the enclosed booklets, and a full
        description of all other benefits will be provided shortly after
        you begin employment with us.  Please sign the enclosed employment
        contract, and return it to us within ten days.

        We look forward to welcoming you to our staff in the near future.

        Sincerely,



        Della Phillips
        Personnel Director

        xx

        Enclosures:  Staff Benefits Booklets
                     Employment Contract
```

KEY TO EXERCISE IV.28:
DATES AND STATES COMMAS

```
TO:       All Employees

FROM:     Personnel Department

DATE:     Current Date

SUBJECT:  Retirement Seminar

A free course for staff members who are making plans for retirement
will be offered on February 28⊙19--⊙ in the auditorium of our Omaha⊙
Nebraska⊙office.  Husbands and wives are encouraged to attend.

The next retirement seminars have been scheduled for July 25 and
December 28.  These will be held at our office in Moline⊙ Illinois.

You are encouraged to attend one of these sessions if you plan to
retire soon.

xx
```

KEY TO EXERCISE IV.29:
SINGULAR NOUN POSSESSIVES

1. lawyer's
2. clerk's
3. witness's
4. father's
5. physician's

KEY TO EXERCISE IV.30:
COMPOUND NOUN POSSESSIVES

1. brother-in-law's
2. attorney's
3. secretary-treasurer's
4. State's
5. stockholder's

KEY TO EXERCISE IV.31:
PROPER NAME POSSESSIVES

1. Sam's; Ella's
2. Bill's
3. Smith's
4. Sanchezes'
5. Walterina's

KEY TO EXERCISE IV.32:
INANIMATE OBJECT POSSESSIVES

1. The design of the newsletter was outstanding.
2. The elevators in our building are always dark.
3. The key to the cabinet is lost.
4. The cover of the folder was ripped.
5. The wording of my will is confusing.

KEY TO EXERCISE IV.33:
PLURAL NOUN POSSESSIVES

1. policyholders'
2. women's
3. boys'
4. senators'
5. Motorists'

KEY TO EXERCISE IV.34:
NOUN UNDERSTOOD POSSESSIVES

1. month's; month's
2. Today's; yesterday's
3. Victor's; Todd's
4. Dara's; Kristen's
5. children's; adults'

KEY TO EXERCISE IV.35:
PERSONAL PRONOUN AND
INDEFINITE PRONOUN POSSESSIVES

1. everybody's
2. Correct
3. Correct
4. Everyone's
5. Correct

KEY TO EXERCISE IV.36:
TIME AND MEASUREMENT POSSESSIVES

1. gallons'
2. months'
3. week's
4. day's
5. dollar's

KEY TO EXERCISE IV.37:
COLON

1. Correct
2. They will visit the following countries on their tour⊙Germany, Switzerland, and Italy.
3. Three courses are required for students in the advanced secretarial program⊙Office Management, Written Communications, and Records Management.
4. Correct
5. In view of the low attendance so far, we have decided to adopt the following new policy on meetings⊙Instead of starting at eight o'clock, we will begin at seven; and we will adjourn promptly at nine.
6. Correct

KEY TO EXERCISE IV.38:
SEMICOLON

1. Correct
2. Correct
3. All work in our word processing center is logged in when it arrives⊙ that is, the supervisor records the type of document and the name of the person to whom it is assigned.

4. Correct
5. I plan to visit the Hughes Insurance Agency, Denver; the First National Bank, Omaha; and the Clemson Real Estate Office, Atlanta.
6. Yvonne Pederson is interested in the position of Correspondence Secretary in our office; Lisa Lowenberg is not.
7. Your training period in our word processing center will extend over a three-month period; namely, June, July, and August.
8. The Administrative Secretary dictated the memo; the Correspondence Secretary typed it.

KEY TO EXERCISE IV.39:
HYPHEN WITH NUMBERS

1. His office is somewhere between rooms 400 and 412.
2. Thirty-five employees will be promoted in July.
3. I was surprised to hear that one-third of our staff do not carry health insurance.
4. We'll be in Nashville from September 13 to 19.
5. Correct

KEY TO EXERCISE IV.40:
HYPHEN WITH PREFIXES AND SUFFIXES

1. Marjorie will take her midsummer vacation in July.
2. Any employer is interested in hiring people who are self-starters.
3. Correct
4. I will have two weeks off beginning in mid-August.
5. I need to check the antifreeze before winter comes.

KEY TO EXERCISE IV.41:
HYPHEN WITH COMPOUND ADJECTIVES PRECEDING AND FOLLOWING NOUNS

1. Correct
2. It is a well-known fact that businesses that implement word processing often cut their costs by 25 percent after the first year.
3. The day-by-day routine in an office can be challenging and interesting.
4. Correct
5. There was a friendly-sounding knock at the door.

6. Correct
7. The sculpture was very lifelike.
8. John and George are enjoying their air-cooled office.

KEY TO EXERCISE IV.42:
DASH

TO: Sales Department Staff

FROM: Pat Dixon, Administrative Assistant

DATE: Current Date

SUBJECT: Our Move to Fourth Floor

Boxes, boxes, and more boxes--I'm sure you're tired of seeing them and shoving them around. I do have good news for you! The latest word is that we will move on Thursday--next Thursday, that is--for sure.

You've all worked hard to prepare for this move--I knew you would--and you'll be happy to be settled in our new quarters. After my tour of them yesterday--it was a short one--I'm convinced that it's all been worth it. Colorful dividers, soft brown carpeting, and the newest in beautiful modular furniture--these are some of the things you have to look forward to.

xx

KEY TO EXERCISE IV.43:
QUOTATION MARKS

Current Date

Miss Julie Scott
4578 Kings Cove
Cincinnati, OH 45230

Dear Julie:

Congratulations on your new job! I first found out about it when I read "People and Places," one of the regular columns in the Press-Citizen. You'll enjoy working for Louise Stroud. She's a real "go-getter," and I'm sure she is an excellent word processing manager.

We had some good laughs during the Word Processing National Convention--especially when she said, "I hear you're moving to my town." "Not a chance," I said, "but have you ever thought about moving to New York?" You have to know Louise better to get the idea of that conversation.

Louise asked me if I'd read your article, "How We Started Word Processing." She thinks it's a real "zinger," and I agree.

One more thing. She told me that she's writing an article entitled "What Is New in Word Processing"; it's scheduled to be out next month. Are you helping with it?

Best of luck, Julie. See you one of these days.

Sincerely,

Tedi J. Ames
Manager

xx

KEYS TO PRACTICE EXERCISES

KEY TO PRACTICE EXERCISE 1:
HOMONYMS AND WORDS SIMILAR IN SOUND

1. two
2. accept
3. choose
4. ad
5. addition
6. attendants
7. council
8. illicit
9. There
10. continuous
11. assistance
12. lead
13. personnel
14. physical
15. adopt
16. affects
17. proceed
18. capital
19. here
20. lie
21. lesser
22. beside
23. decent
24. correspondents
25. advice
26. farther
27. It's
28. Your
29. principal
30. lose
31. formally
32. forward
33. do
34. week's
35. quit
36. disapproved
37. forth
38. later
39. passed
40. stationary
41. allusion
42. biannual
43. conscious
44. patients
45. site
46. device
47. entrants
48. peace
49. compliments
50. prosecuted
51. Whether
52. Respectfully
53. Who's
54. than

KEY TO PRACTICE EXERCISE 2:
ONE OR TWO WORDS

1. always
2. everyday
3. No body
4. A lot
5. sometime
6. Some one
7. all ready
8. may be
9. all right
10. any way
11. all together
12. Any one

KEY TO PRACTICE EXERCISE 3:
WORD DIVISION

1. (can't)   can'-t   ca-n't
2. (patio)   pat-io   pa-tio
3. (Elizabeth)   Eliz-abeth   Eliza-beth
4. similar   sim-ilar   (simi-lar)
5. creative   (cre-ative)   crea-tive
6. (December, 1982) (December,- 1982) Decem-ber, 1982
7. resignation   (resig-nation) (resigna-tion)
8. (passed)   pass-ed   pas-sed
9. (o'clock)   o'-clock   o'clo-ck
10. (Peterson)   Peter-son   Pe-terson
11. separate   sep-arate   (sepa-rate)
12. prescription (pre-scription) (prescrip-tion)
13. accommodate   (accom-modate) ac-commodate
14. (S. L. Schneider) (S. L.- Schneider) S. L. Sch-neider
15. retroactive   re-troactive   (retro-active)
16. (245,652)   245,-652   245,6-52
17. (briefly)   brief-ly   br-iefly
18. (solved)   solv-ed   sol-ved
19. (along)   a-long   alon-g
20. (ass't.)   ass'-t.   as-s't.

KEY TO PRACTICE EXERCISE 4:
CAPITALIZATION

1. The hearing is scheduled for (T)hursday, (M)arch 29, and (F)riday, (M)arch 30, at the Federal (B)uilding in (P)rovo, (U)tah.
2. "(L)anguage," she sighed, "is hard to define."
3. Kansu is (C)hina's northwest corridor to western regions.
4. It was described in the (J)ournal of the (A)merican (M)edical (A)ssociation.
5. Correct
6. We'll send you a copy of the article, "(P)lan for the (F)uture," free of charge.
7. In any venture, the lack of a plan can be serious: (I)t can mean failure.
8. Wellman (C)ompany headquarters will be moving to the (N)orthwest.
9. The (P)ayroll (D)epartment has the lowest staff turnover.
10. Please check the applicants' credentials to identify those who have taken eight quarters of (S)panish.
11. When will (P)rofessor Buchwald submit her travel vouchers?

12. We will interview some journalists from the (N)orth.
13. I attended Columbia (U)niversity for graduate studies.
14. Correct
15. Correct

KEY TO PRACTICE EXERCISE 5: EXPRESSING NUMBERS

1. He published his first piano composition at age (12).
2. Correct
3. Correct
4. The custodian used (3) gallons of liquid wax on the lobby floor.
5. A full-size sheet of paper measures (8 1/2) by (11) inches.
6. Our factory is located at 15 (First) Avenue; our outlet store, at (One) West (59) Street.
7. We hope to have it competitively priced at about $(8).
8. It will be released on the (15th) of March.
9. Bring (4) sandwiches, (8) apples, and (12) drinks.
10. Correct
11. Correct
12. Over (20 million) persons participated in the recent poll.
13. (Two hundred seventy-five) musicians attended the concert.
14. The company plans to purchase (5) typewriters, 14 desks, 3 (four)-drawer files, and 20 calculators.
15. Mr. Sandcastle plans to order 6 (two)-drawer files and 12 (four)-drawer files.
16. She estimated that (two-thirds) of the office staff would vote for flexible hours.
17. Bob's (second) color choice was brown.
18. Correct
19. Do you plan to resign by the (5th) of June?
20. (Twenty-five) percent of our staff members are out of work today with the flu.

KEY TO PRACTICE EXERCISE 6: SERIES COMMA

1. We will discuss human relations in the office(,) different problem-solving and decision-making techniques(,) and building team skills.

2. The following persons have been awarded 20-year service pins: Harold Frank(,) Charlotte Healey(,) Joseph Sebastian(,) and Heidi Gruber.
3. All faculty(,) staff(,) students(,) and area residents will be able to donate blood on January 29 and 30 during the annual blood drive.
4. The basketball teams for the charity game will be made up of city officials(,) candidates for public office(,) and several disc jockeys and television personalities.
5. Current unclaimed lost-and-found items include a watch(,) a camera(,) and a woman's winter coat.
6. An examination of policies relating to land(,) water(,) and energy in Montana's future will be the focus of the one-day meeting on July 24.
7. The service is intended to provide a liaison person for patients and their families in time of confusion(,) doubt(,) or worry.
8. The registration fee covers a conference packet(,) attendance at all sessions(,) and a Friday evening banquet.
9. Nominations shall include a brief description of the candidate's qualifications(,) past and present service to the organization(,) consent to serve(,) and the candidate's reason for seeking election.
10. He comes to our department with an impressive background in scholarship(,) teaching(,) academic administration(,) and government.

KEY TO PRACTICE EXERCISE 7: INTRODUCTORY COMMA

1. Over the next few years(,) solar energy will make a significant contribution to our energy supply.
2. However(,) let me point out the fallacies in these statistics.
3. By including more data in the record-keeping book(,) reconciling the monthly financial statements has become much easier.
4. When I have a lot of work to do(,) I have some trouble prioritizing the assignments.
5. If you wish to place names in nomination for national offices(,) you should submit them on the enclosed form by May 29.
6. For more information concerning eligibility requirements(,) call the Donor Bank at 555-6710.

7. If you wish to enroll for the payroll deduction plan for Savings Bonds, please contact Nancy Barnes.

8. If it is necessary to make a personal call from a company phone, it must be operator-assisted and charged to a home phone number.

9. While at the Department of Labor, she was on leave from Tulane University.

10. As of the last of the year, there has been no judicial interpretation of the new law.

KEY TO PRACTICE EXERCISE 8:
EXPLANATORY COMMA

1. The Alumni Service Awards will be presented during Alumni Weekend, February 27 and 28.

2. The book will be available at a reduced price, $5 per copy, if you buy ten or more.

3. Marion Scott, coordinator for staff development and training, will speak at our council meeting.

4. Our summer hours, 7:30 a.m. to 4 p.m., will be effective June 15 through August 15.

5. The United Way began its campaign on September 15 with a goal of $85,000, 15 percent more than was given last year.

6. Craft, an outdoor festival, is intended to encourage interest in the arts.

7. A travel guide for the handicapped, Access to the World, is now available in the Bookmobile.

8. Costs for increased staff fringe benefits, approximately 15 percent above last year's, were factors in the budget increases.

9. The four charter members, Roy Kern, Marilee Sloan, Peter Kraus, and Davis Flynn, will be honored at the banquet.

10. Mr. Jones, president, will address the convention.

KEY TO PRACTICE EXERCISE 9:
PARENTHETICAL COMMA

1. Congress, frankly, has occasionally done a less than admirable job.

2. Higher education, historically, has functioned as a chief means of social mobility.

3. Actually, we know that the tests only have value as diagnostic instruments.

4. You should, if possible, begin inquiring about housing prior to your arrival.

5. Obviously, such factors were used in the evaluation of the secretarial candidate.

6. Anyone interested in these issues, especially professionals in programs for handicapped persons, should attend the conference.

7. This program, funded by the Department of Education, has been approved for three years.

8. Therefore, I find it extremely difficult to understand your resistance.

9. Your projected costs, if negotiations are successful, can be adjusted downward.

10. There was no increase in departmental allocations for this fiscal year, as you are well aware.

KEY TO PRACTICE EXERCISE 10:
DIRECT ADDRESS COMMA

1. There is no charge, Mr. Stein, for this office call.

2. Read this report, Steve, and take some notes on it for me.

3. Carol, did you know that it is most important to brush your teeth at night?

4. Stop it, Francis!

5. Sir, come on in.

6. Katie, will you please finish typing that report before you go out for lunch.

7. You're getting too old to still dress alike, Leonard and Lenard.

8. Correct

9. Helen, please come into my office when you have a minute.

10. Guess who is here, Brenda.

KEY TO PRACTICE EXERCISE 11:
MODIFIER COMMA

1. Estella Meeks is a dependable, efficient secretary.

2. Many customers return again and again because of our courteous, complete service.

3. His rude, surly office behavior makes everyone uneasy.

4. The older, deeper roots of a reseeded lawn need more watering than the roots of a newly planted lawn.

5. A sign of heat stroke in a dog is dry(,)hot skin.
6. Ozone is a tasteless(,)pungent gas used in purifying water.
7. An adequately sized(,)architecturally barrier-free facility is needed for senior citizens.
8. I'm acquainted with several knowledgeable(,)responsible people who would be willing to serve on the committee.
9. It is a low-interest(,)federally insured loan.
10. The hand-framed(,)cabled vest is reasonably priced.

KEY TO PRACTICE EXERCISE 12: NONRESTRICTIVE COMMA

1. This jewelry(,)which comes from Spain(,)is inexpensive and sells well.
2. Mrs. Price(,)whose job takes her out of town frequently(,)is now in Minneapolis.
3. Your lawn fertilizer should contain nitrogen(,)which gives grass its deep green color and thickness.
4. Joe Abramson(,)who is a well-known and well-liked employee(,)will retire next month.
5. The statement from the Food and Drug Administration(,)which wrote and will enforce the rules(,)said that it was designed to protect consumers.
6. Ballots(,)with self-addressed envelopes(,)will be mailed from the national office.
7. Nasal decongestants(,)which provide immediate relief to people with clogged noses(,)can cause tissues to swell once the initial effect wears off.
8. We feel that Santa(,)with his rosy red cheeks and laugh(,)will make a perfect public relations person.
9. This form(,)which is available from your counselor(,)must be completed and returned to the guidance office by the date specified on the form.
10. More students than ever are participating in foreign study(,)which offers unique laboratory conditions.

KEY TO PRACTICE EXERCISE 13: INDEPENDENT CLAUSES COMMA

1. Tax cuts are a good method of stimulating the U.S. economy(,)and some people feel that we need them at the present time.

2. Correct
3. These changes are very evident(,)and they are changing the character of our industry.
4. The slate of candidates will be mailed to the membership in July(,)and a written reminder of voting procedures will be sent to all voting members in August.
5. I have deadlines to meet(,)and I would appreciate your cooperation in meeting your deadlines so that I will be able to meet mine.
6. The merchandise delivered is not the quality we use(,)nor is it the quantity requested.
7. It was our first trip to the Grand Canyon(,)but it won't be our last to Arizona.
8. You are permitted to sell your contract for services(,)but this may prove to be very difficult to do.
9. Take a look at the schedule(,)and we think you will find a topic that whets your curiosity.
10. A senior center does exist(,)but it is located in a deteriorated structure.

KEY TO PRACTICE EXERCISE 14: DATES AND STATES COMMAS

1. President Thompson announced that the Recognition Reception held on July 5(,)1981(,)had the highest attendance.
2. My resignation will be effective July 31, and I will be moving to Eugene(,)Oregon.
3. All full- or part-time permanent employees who have been employed for one year prior to June 15(,)1980(,)are eligible to apply.
4. This will verify that Patricia Rowell was employed by our office beginning August 1, 1979(,)through December 12 of this year.
5. All employees having accumulated compensatory time due for the period from July 1(,)1981(,)through June 10(,)1982(,)should report their total unpaid compensatory hours on their June 13 time cards.
6. Dallas(,)Texas(,)is a popular convention location.
7. She moved from Morrison(,)Iowa(,)to Morrison(,)Illinois.
8. I attended the Midwestern Energy Conference at the Pick-Congress Hotel in Chicago on November 19–21(,)1980.
9. There was an earthquake in the Santa Barbara(,)California(,)area on August 13(,)1978.

10. The General Assembly enacted legislation on July 1, 1980, relating to smoking in public buildings.

KEY TO PRACTICE EXERCISE 15: SINGULAR NOUN POSSESSIVES

1. I am my brother's keeper.
2. The doctor's office is open on Saturday mornings.
3. The client's name was misspelled.
4. My mother's parents are naturalized U.S. citizens.
5. The child's toys were left out in the rain.
6. The lawyer's advice was sound.
7. The eyewitness's report was filed with the police.
8. The student's paper was turned in on time.
9. That lady's luggage was put on the plane to Tampa.
10. My secretary's work piled up during her illness.

KEY TO PRACTICE EXERCISE 16: COMPOUND NOUN POSSESSIVES

1. My mother-in-law's flower garden never has a weed in it.
2. The editor-in-chief's article was controversial.
3. The attorney general's opinion will be published next week.
4. The district attorney's office is in the courthouse.
5. The Vice President's report is attached to the meeting minutes.
6. His brother-in-law's will named his wife as executor.
7. A businesswoman's portfolio was left on the bus.
8. That salesman's salary is considered too high by the other sales personnel.
9. My sister-in-law's name is the same as mine, and it is sometimes confusing.
10. That stockholder's comments were misunderstood by the other stockholders.

KEY TO PRACTICE EXERCISE 17: PROPER NAME POSSESSIVES

1. Nevelson's work will be displayed at the Museum of Art.
2. Andy and Sid's complaint will be considered.
3. Do you know Stephen Smith's phone number?
4. Ruth's and Letitia's cars are identical.
5. Miss Alexander's and Mr. Boyd's employment papers are ready for review.
6. The Walter Hoffbergs' home is on the left side of Elm Drive.
7. Do you screen Mr. Joseph's and Mr. Baskerville's calls?
8. Lisa and Larry Trenches' restaurant opens tomorrow.
9. Susie and Ron's apartment is nicely decorated.
10. Phillip and Ray's report was concise.

KEY TO PRACTICE EXERCISE 18: INANIMATE OBJECT POSSESSIVES

1. The terms of the lease were unclear.
2. The left side of the car was extensively damaged in the accident.
3. The closure of the street caused traffic congestion on First Avenue.
4. Correct
5. The format of the résumé is outstanding.
6. The complimentary closing of the letter is out of date.
7. The weight of the paper is not correct for this machine.
8. The door of the building is locked at 5 p.m. daily.
9. The pages of the dictionary are falling out.
10. The pages of the calendar measure 3 1/2 by 6 inches.

KEY TO PRACTICE EXERCISE 19: PLURAL NOUN POSSESSIVES

1. Correct
2. It was considered a gentlemen's agreement.
3. The three postal carriers' routes are posted monthly.
4. Contributors' gifts are acknowledged the same day they are received.
5. Doctors' prescriptions are nontransferable.

6. The secretaries' recommendations will be considered.
7. We are the largest manufacturer of ladies' shoes.
8. Police officers' uniforms are usually blue.
9. Several customers' accounts are past due.
10. All infants' apparel is half price.

KEY TO PRACTICE EXERCISE 20:
NOUN UNDERSTOOD POSSESSIVES

1. Sharon's was the best report handed in.
2. Today's weather is just like yesterday's.
3. Correct
4. I'm Mary Lou's friend but not Katie's.
5. Lloyd's grades are better than Eddie's.
6. Marjorie's paper was typed; Lula's was handwritten.
7. The women's tennis team challenged the men's.
8. Whitebrook's sales are better than Clancey's.
9. This month's expenditures are less than last month's.
10. Marian's typewriter is cleaned weekly and covered nightly; Terry's is not.

KEY TO PRACTICE EXERCISE 21:
PERSONAL PRONOUN AND INDEFINITE PRONOUN POSSESSIVES

1. Correct
2. Correct
3. Sports are frequently activities engaged in during one's leisure time.
4. The accident was nobody's fault.
5. Correct
6. Correct
7. Correct
8. Anyone's receipts will be in the file cabinet.
9. Correct
10. Everyone's happiness is important.

KEY TO PRACTICE EXERCISE 22:
TIME AND MEASUREMENT POSSESSIVES

1. He will be docked a day's pay.
2. Give me a dollar's worth.
3. Correct
4. This year's festival will be held from January 29 through February 4.

5. This gives you an idea of a typical day's work.
6. I expect an hour's work for an hour's pay.
7. I need four yards' worth.
8. You must give us two weeks' notice to assure delivery.
9. Yesterday's sunset was beautiful.
10. It will appear in next month's issue of our newsletter.

KEY TO PRACTICE EXERCISE 23:
COLON

1. Three important skills we look for in a worker are: speed, accuracy, and neatness.
2. The following items are also carried in our lumberyard: building hardware, hand tools, electrical supplies, plumbing supplies, and cabinet hardware.
3. Correct
4. These holiday hours will be maintained by the library: December 23, 10 a.m. to 5 p.m.; December 24, 10 a.m. to noon; and it will remain closed through December 26.
5. Correct
6. They drove to the northeast part of town via this route: Kirkwood Street to Gilbert Street, Gilbert to Church Street, and Church to Johnson Street.
7. Most often a letter consists of the date line, an inside address, a salutation, the body, a complimentary closing, the writer's name and title, and reference initials.
8. Correct
9. Unfortunately, rather than ability and experience, the following combination frequently determines promotions: vacancies, the type of business, and timing.
10. Correct

KEY TO PRACTICE EXERCISE 24: SEMICOLON

1. You cannot live on your past glory; you must strive to improve.
2. Correct
3. They arrived late; nevertheless, our meeting was pleasant and beneficial.
4. I don't know if I can do it; however, I'll give it a good try.
5. We agreed that we wanted to rent the cabin for two weeks; saving enough money was a problem.
6. For travel in most countries, a passport is required; but I know it isn't required in Mexico, Canada, or the Bahamas.
7. I feel a housecleaning spree coming; hope I get to my desk drawers before it passes.
8. You decide how to invest your time and energy, what to study, where to go; therefore, you determine and control your professional future.
9. Planning, organizing, coordinating, controlling, motivating, evaluating, and directing can all be learned; but it takes interest, effort, and time.
10. In some areas of our state, for example, almost 75 percent of the high school graduates go into postsecondary education; however, in other states, the percentage is much less.

KEY TO PRACTICE EXERCISE 25: HYPHEN

1. We will attend several company-sponsored development programs.
2. The work-reentry seminar will have a session on interpersonal skills.
3. My vacation is always scheduled on July 4-17.
4. Take a long-range look ahead, and be prepared for your opportunity when it comes.
5. The new employee was thought of as a self-centered and selfish person.
6. Correct
7. Commencement is held each mid-June and midwinter.
8. The conference has a limited registration figure of approximately thirty-five.
9. Correct
10. Correct

KEY TO PRACTICE EXERCISE 26: DASH

1. Violin, composition, orchestration—I wanted to learn everything.
2. John told me to take the River Road—he meant the Great River Road—to Guttenberg.
3. Susan bought several books—all on history—at the Union Book Store.
4. Correct
5. Rain, hail, and wind—these were the unpleasant things we encountered on our vacation.
6. Many types of problems—especially personal—can affect your production.
7. A good listener and a good speaker—they are signs of a good manager.
8. Some don't know which way to turn—they are uncertain.
9. It does mean—I'm happy to say—that we'll be remaining here a long time.
10. Correct

KEY TO PRACTICE EXERCISE 27: QUOTATION MARKS

1. "I never thought about it," he remarked.
2. Frank stepped out of his office at 3 p.m. saying, "Let's go home early," and we all laughed.
3. The chapter, "Consumer Survival," is your assignment for tomorrow.
4. I asked, "Why are you leaving so soon?"
5. The highway sign was marked "Do Not Enter"; however, we observed that several cars ignored it.
6. He screamed, "The art of conversation is lost!"
7. Your stroking goal is "speed"; "control" will be next.
8. Correct
9. John Hanson remarked, "You must read the first article, 'Your Trip to the Moon,' when you have time."
10. The following are parts of the area called "The Pentacrest": Schaeffer Hall, Macbride Hall, MacLean Hall, and Jessup Hall.

APPENDIX D
GLOSSARY

administrative secretary A specialist who handles primarily the nontyping functions within a word processing system—managing records, receiving callers, assisting with financial matters, providing help on miscellaneous projects.

automatic typewriter A typewriter with a capability of storing typed material in a memory (disc or other medium) and of printing out copy automatically.

career path A planned, systematic progression through a series of job positions.

cassette A small cartridge containing magnetic recording tape, often used in dictating and transcribing equipment found in word processing installations.

central dictating unit Equipment that permits an originator to dictate by telephone or other equipment specially linked to a transcribing unit at a central location.

centralized word processing center A word processing center that processes communications for an entire company or a large department.

correspondence secretary A secretary specially trained to process written communications, usually on automated equipment. Also referred to as a *typing specialist* or *transcription specialist*.

cost efficiency The production of accurate work with a minimum of waste, effort, time, and cost.

dictating unit A machine into which an originator dictates—by means of an attached or built-in microphone—a message recorded on a cassette, belt, or disc. Some dictating units are portable.

discrete media The cassettes, discs, or belts that must be physically moved from the dictating unit to the transcribing unit.

electronic cue A sound or light on a dictating/transcribing unit enabling the originator to alert a transcriptionist to revisions and special instructions or that an item is ending. (See also *indicator slip*.)

endless loop system A dictation/transcription system using a magnetic loop housed in a unit to which both the dictator and transcriptionist have access.

external communication Communication sent outside the company.

indicator slip A small visual device inserted in the dictating/transcribing unit that enables the originator to transmit to the transcriptionist special instructions and corrections or to indicate the end of an item. (See also *electronic cue*.)

input Any type of material to be processed into typewritten form, including dictation on a cassette, disc, or belt; handwritten copy; verbal instructions; or typewritten rough draft.

internal communication   Communication transmitted within a company.

job instruction sheet   A printed form used by the originator to give instructions for work to be produced.

keyboarding   Operating a typewriter.

line count   A tally of the number of typed lines produced during a specific time.

machine shorthand   A method of recording dictation on a machine equipped with a special keyboard and paper tape from which the transcript is prepared.

magnetic belt   Discrete media in a form of a belt on which dictation can be recorded, erased, revised, stored, or transcribed.

magnetic disc   Discrete media in the form of a disc on which dictation can be recorded, erased, revised, stored, or transcribed.

mailability   Acceptability of a document for dissemination in terms of the accuracy of its grammar, spelling, punctuation, format, and content.

NCR paper (**N**o **C**arbon **R**equired)   Paper with a coating on the back that enables the typist to make copies without using carbon paper.

originator   A person who dictates or drafts, in handwritten or typed form, a document to be transcribed.

production records   Statistics detailing the volume of communications produced.

text-editing typewriter   An electronic typewriter that enables the operator to keyboard instructions to insert, delete, move, and format text material before the final document is printed at high rates of speed.

transcribing unit   A machine that contains a cassette, belt, or disc from which the transcription specialist transcribes dictated material.

transcription specialist   A person who transcribes a message in proper typewritten form.

turnaround time   The elapsed time (in minutes, hours, or days) between the submission of a document for processing by the transcriptionist and delivery of the finished copy to the originator.

visual display screen   The part of a text-editing typewriter on which copy appears as it is typed or revised.

word processing   The system of processing communications on automated equipment by trained personnel using standardized procedures.

word processing center   Any location within an organization where communications are processed on automated equipment by trained personnel.

work flow   The channels through which production tasks are routed.